The Natural Way

2ND EDITION

Julie Hill

Copyright © 2003, 2014 Julie Hill

First edition published by WSN in 2003

This edition published by Julie Hill in 2014
Carcant Farm, Heriot, Midlothian,
Scotland EH38 5YE.
Website: www.NethHillBorderCollies.co.uk
sheepdogjulie@btinternet.com

ISBN: 978-0-9929022-0-9

A catalogue record of this book is available from the British Library.

Art direction of photographs and illustrations by Julie Hill
Copywriting and copy-editing by Pen Rashbass (www.PeakPawPrint.com)
Cover design, book layout and illustrations by Pen Rashbass
Photographs: Marianne Berga – p 192; Carol Campion – p 189 (F,G,H); Lola Chaffin – p 189 (D,E);
Angie Driscoll – p 194; Janet and Paul Henning – p 174; Julie Hill – p 171, 174 (A,B) 189 (A,B,C) 191 (A –H);
Hill Family archive – 168, 169, 170, 172 (A), 173 (B), 179 (A,B,C) 180 (A), 181, 184, 186;
Rich Kane – p38; Ray Kennedy – p 172 (B); Keith Morris – p173 (A), 175;
Peterborough Evening Telegraph Photo Department – p167, 180 (B); Gwen Wallace – p157;
Mark Williamson – p 183; Pen Rashbass – All other photographs.
Typeset in Baskerville (main body, text boxes) and Minion Pro (titles, headings, picture captions) by Pen Rashbass

Printed and bound by Airdrie Print Services Ltd, Scotland.

CONTENTS

In loving memory of my father,

Ronald Hill

who shared my passion with the dogs

and supported my life choices.

PREFACE

It is now over ten years since I (writing as Julie Simpson) wrote the first edition of *The Natural Way* (published in 2003 by WSN press, ISBN 185829058-9). This has been out of print for several years and I decided that rather than just reprinting the original version, I wanted to update it. Specifically, I wanted to bring out more about canine communication, sheep-sense and the body language that I use to interact with my dogs as these three aspects enable me to build the respect, trust and loyalty that underpin my training method.

This new edition has been divided into three sections. Part one discusses how dogs (and sheep) communicate with each other and how you can harness this language to interact effectively with your own dog and stock. The second part describes how I train a dog to work sheep, from the basic introduction right through to taking an experienced dog out onto the hill. The final section contains my life story combined with brief notes about some of my dogs and what each has taught me. In addition to the new photos, I have updated the diagrams and included inset boxes containing Anecdotes, From the Clinic stories, Fact Boxes and Julie's Tips to further illustrate the points and provide additional information. I have also added a glossary of sheepdog and shepherding terms and some readers may find it useful to refer to this as they read the book.

The whole process of updating the book and producing its companion DVD has taken two years (one more than I had originally envisaged) as I had to fit writing it around my other daily chores.

I hope you find both the book and DVD enjoyable as well as informative and that they help you see things from the dog's point of view and that this gives you a better understanding of how to develop a wonderful partnership.

J.H. February 2014.

ACKNOWLEDGEMENTS

This book would never have been written without my being privileged to work with dogs who have educated me along the way and given me a sense of purpose and pride.

A big thank you to Pen Rashbass who has worked closely with me throughout this project, re-structuring and re-editing the text as well as providing layout and design services and taking many of the illustrative photographs to bring key points to life. Her times living and working closely with us, has enabled Pen to help me convey in this book, my passion and devotion to my dogs, sheep, the nature around me and my journey to Carcant.

I would particularly like to acknowledge the contribution of my close friend of many years' standing from the East Anglia Sheepdog society (from the 1980s) Sarah Jenkins with whom I have intensely debated sheepdog behaviours and instincts over the decades. Sarah and I have co-taught at many clinics in the UK and together run Groveshill Dog Whisperers (www.groveshilldogwhisperers.co.uk). Sarah and I share a similar approach to canine communication and developed comparable techniques of pressure / release. However, in certain situations when I would use a long line, Sarah adapted a 'horse whisperer' technique of a round pen in which human and animal (whether dog or horse) may more easily begin to communicate on the same wave-length. I have now adopted this technique myself and use a round pen (without any sheep involved) in training and re-training canine communication.

I would like to acknowledge the help given by members of the East Anglia Sheep dog Society, Norman Seamark, and a very special and close friend Bill James whose input and encouragement kept me focused on improving myself and my dogs. Thanks to my mentors, John Thomas, in my early years. Johnny Wilson and Bobby Henderson, who inspired me in my later years, and influenced my shepherding ethics.

My friends Ria Vrolijk and Els Wippo were crucial to my development as a teacher, and gave me the confidence to hold the workshops, clinics and demonstrations that I now enjoy. Ria and Els were good enough to read and comment on early drafts of the book. On the editorial side I should also acknowledge the contribution of Jacquie L'Etang who helped with proof reading and Bobby Henderson for verifying and endorsing factual content.

Many family members and friends volunteered their photographs and these are acknowledged individually. However, in particular I'd like to thank: Carol Campion; Janet and Paul Henning; Rich Kane; and Marianne Berga. I especially want to thank Lola Chaffin for agreeing to let me use her late husband's photos of the winter at Braegrudie. Lola and Jim helped me through tough times, welcoming me in to their home in the States.

Since the first edition of this book I have moved to Carcant Farm, by Heriot and would like to thank the Somerville family for their generous permission to allow me to run clinics and demonstrations and to use many photographs of the estate. (Likewise the accompanying DVD includes many shots of the stunning location). My time at Carcant has been very happy and I hope it continues to be so. A special thank-you to Rosie Somerville for her support and encouragement and also to Harry Somerville for all his help.

On a more personal note I'd like to thank my Mum for her support in the path I have taken, even though she definitely does not like muddy dogs, and also my sister and her husband who help me settle in at Carcant when I moved here. They gave me my much-loved cat Fluffy and her brother as a house warming present. Wild and untouched, they brought much fun, amusement and companionship in those early years. Fluffy continues to be my feline comrade and protector.

Last, but not least, Bobby, who has given support and has put up with the constant disruption in our everyday lives in order to update the book.

FOREWORD BY GUS DERMODY

In September 2013, I attended the International Sheepdog Society's Supreme Championship at Stoneleigh in Warwickshire. It took place over three days and incorporated both single and brace competitions. The handlers had previously qualified at their respective National Trials, so it was the best meeting the best.

On looking at the course there was plenty of room in the outfield, but it narrowed at the handler's end like an inverted triangle with grandstands and viewing areas on either side making it appear very restricted for the flighty North Country mule ewes as they approached the handler. Many sheep needed to be pushed hard at this point and once turned at the post, some shot off like a cork out of a bottle as they raced for freedom. The pens and shedding ring were also in the narrow area, so handlers and dogs had to exhibit all their skills to complete the last part of the trial.

On the final day, I watched Julie Hill walk to the post with her two dogs, Mac and Ban. There was a slight delay in getting the fresh sheep to the lift post and I remember wondering if this would upset the dogs as they waited for 'the off'.

Once away, it was a trial to remember – Julie made it look easy where many struggled – they sailed through – it was as if they had better sheep than everyone else. The two final pens made for a great finish. Only one more brace run was to follow, but I was certain Julie had gone to the top and couldn't be beaten. I was right – she was the brace winner by a considerable margin. It was a fantastic display of her knowledge of dogs and sheep after years of study, practical experience and her unique method of training sheepdogs which she calls 'The Natural Way'.

We used to say a person would 'break' a dog – or a horse for that matter and some of the old fashioned methods must have been unpleasant and boring to say the least. I know of one man who would teach his dogs their flanks (to run clockwise or anti-clockwise round the sheep) by using a six foot long wooden 'bull bar' clipped onto the dog's collar. He would walk round an enclosed yard keeping the dog up to the outer wall with the bull bar so they went round in circles to the shouts of *come-bye* and *away* depending on which direction that they were going and not

even a single sheep in sight. Another was one of the most miserable men I've ever met – never a word of praise or encouragement, but his dogs put up with this because they had their release from tension when they were allowed to work stock.

We don't now 'break' an animal but rather we train it. This doesn't mean we let it do it's own thing. Julie gives her dogs three options when she gives an instruction – firstly to 'ask', then to 'tell' and finally to 'insist'. The dog has to trust and respect its handler as its true leader and a correct balance needs to be struck.

My wife trains, instructs and judges Western Riding and we often discuss the similarities in training horses and dogs. On the horse side, she has the books by brothers Bill and Tom Dorrance, Ray Hunt, Buck Brannaman and others – the original 'horse whisperers' who changed the way these American horses were trained – not broken. I never thought some of their principles could be applied to a dog as it is a predatory animal as opposed to a prey animal, but Julie shows how this can be done using pressure / release techniques.

I've watched many times how a horse can be trained to 'Join Up' to its handler, but I've never seen it done with a dog prior to reading this book.

At some dog trials, the sheep can be particularly difficult, with many handlers failing to even get their sheep around the course. But then along would come a top handler who puts up a good run. Several disgruntled competitors would moan that the top handler had better sheep. What they failed to appreciate was that he made the sheep better by his skilful observation of how they reacted to the dogs, the course and the best way to keep them calm and compliant.

At the Supreme Brace trial in 2013, I shouldn't have worried about Julie's dogs 'winding up' as they waited to start their competitive run because she even trains them to be patient. Her sheep seemed better than others because she 'read them' correctly and knew how they would react. Both she and her dogs worked as a team – each respecting the other, with the dogs working without command at times.

A great book to read and refer back to – covering every aspect of training. There are many roads that lead to Rome, but this is one of the best.

INTRODUCTION

The start of another day and the air feels fresh as the late summer sun tries to push its way through the high cloud. The truck rumbles over the wooden bridge as my partner, Bobby, sets off with his dogs to check the sheep at my field which is thirteen miles away near Innerleithen. Overhead, the last few swallows swirl and soar as they dance through the air before landing on the telephone wire in preparation for their migration south. Meanwhile, Fluffy, the cat, sits in the porch watching two young pups play in the run as Mac and Ban stand alert on the path in anticipation of me firing up the quad.

A cock pheasant, startled by the sudden roar of the exhaust, gives his distinctive 'kor-kawk' and takes off on a low trajectory over the fence. With a short bark and friendly jostle, the dogs turn and start cantering alongside as I head up onto the hill. Just passed the trees behind the main house, a few ewes with their lambs are grazing by the lochan. Some raise their heads with their ears twitching forward, others continue to graze knowing that their pals will give a warning snort if they consider us a threat. I give them a glance to check that all looks well and, leaving the group alone, we continue out onto the moor.

As we go round the corner and over the brow of the hill, I can see my flock dotted around in small groups spread out over the estate. We turn off the path towards a larger group that have loosely congregated at the area where I fed them earlier in the year. Asking Mac to remain by my side, I quietly send Ban to gather them together. As the sheep reach me, I ask both dogs to lie-down. They stare intently at the flock, flicking an ear towards me, wondering which, if any, I require to be shed off from the rest. The energy they portray is one of solid, stable authority and in response, the ewes and lambs remain relaxed and calm in their presence. This group of sheep look well and with a *that'll do*, I restart the bike.

The rutted ground and long undulating tufts of grass browned by the hot summer camouflages many of the sheep and I meander over the terrain checking the stock as I go. On reaching the perimeter wall, I again stop the bike. Beyond the farm, the Pentland Hills and Edinburgh's Arthur's Seat rise up at the edge of the lower flat plain and, on a clear day like today, the Kingdom of Fife is clearly visible beyond the slate blue Firth of Forth.

Carcant estate
Wind turbines stretch out behind the big house. The farm buildings are those on the right.

I turn my back on this view and survey the farm: the three wind turbines turn steadily in the light breeze and a pair of buzzards circle and glide on the thermals above the woods. Thirty ewes and lambs are grazing about four hundred metres away on the other side of a patch of boggy marsh and after driving back to the path, I send Mac to the left and Ban to the right to fetch them to me.

Their sleek, athletic bodies power effortlessly through the undergrowth. A hare darts out from under Mac's feet but he ignores it as he focuses on the task in hand. The two dogs drop out of sight as they cross a ditch and although they can no longer see me or the stock, they know the terrain and I am not surprised when Mac lifts the sheep in an assured, but careful, manner and then starts fetching them towards me. Ban arrives shortly after and Mac acknowledges his presence by repositioning himself slightly so that the two of them work as a team, gracefully moving the sheep forward.

Initially they need few commands from me, but as they approach the treacherous bog, I whistle so that they alter their route and navigate safely around the hazard. Just then, I see a couple of ewes poke their heads over a dry stone wall. Asking Mac to stop and hold the flock, I redirect Ban and he willingly takes my command to head back and gather the strays.

As I watch my dogs work together in perfect harmony, I think of the chances and life choices that brought me here. Growing up in a small English North Midlands town in a house with wonderful parents and a sister, but no pets allowed. Feeling trapped during the year that I worked in a factory after leaving school.

Then at seventeen, leaving everyone I knew and taking a leap of faith to follow my dream of working with horses at a stud farm in Cambridgeshire. Getting my first pup, Meg, the result of an unplanned litter from the farm's collie. My fascination with her instinctive need to work leading me to become a full-time shepherd. My move to North Scotland: first Elgin and then Aberdeen, before spending almost eighteen months as the sole shepherd on the remote and desolate ten thousand acre Braegrudie Estate.

Then back in 2005, I heard on the grapevine that the farm tenancy at Carcant might become available and once again I made the difficult decision to leave almost everyone I knew to start over one more time.

And the dogs, always the dogs. When I began working with them, I thought it was all about obedience: *lie-down, come-bye, walk-on*. But the dogs knew otherwise. Fiery Cath, mischievous Gwen, powerful, protective Don, Bess who taught me patience, gentle powered Nell, Moss, who was so attuned with me that he seemed to be able to read my mind and, of course, my soul-mate Tess who saw me through some very tough times. These and all the others taught me there was so much more.

Another way, a different way and, for me, a infinitely better way. I remember spending nights awake analysing what had happened the previous day. Why would the same ewe confront one dog, be panicked by another, but then be content to be directed in a calm fashion by a third? What were the subtle cues that one dog gave to another in order to maintain harmony in the pack?

Gradually, I began to understand what my dogs and the sheep were really saying to each other and also what they were trying to tell me. Once I truly appreciated this, I then worked on adapting my own methods so that I could communicate back to them using their own language. Rather than forcing a dog to bend to my will, I learnt to adapt my approach to suit his temperament, sensitivity and talent. Using this method, I have forged strong bonds with my dogs built on mutual trust and respect.

They have given me everything and it is thanks to them that I have found the contentment I now feel as I watch my healthy stock respond to my wonderful dogs.

Gathering stock

Walking with Ban and Mac

Anecdote. International Competition 2013

It's September 2013 and I'm at Stoneleigh Park near Coventry representing Scotland in the International Brace competition. Watching the different runs before my turn I can tell that the course itself is good, but that the English mule sheep are proving tough: they tend to pull to the left, and even worse they won't let the dogs get near to them. A single wrong move is making them flee and when it comes to the final close-up work, many handlers are having significant problems during the shed and at the pen. I feel the adrenaline surge in anticipation. However, once I starting walking out to the post with Mac and Ban on either side I suddenly feel calm and focused.

Knowing that my dogs have already spotted the sheep, I send them in a similar manner as I would work them on the hill at home: Mac to the left and then Ban to the right. Although it may lose me a couple of points, Mac arrives at the balance point first and although he lifts the ten sheep just before Ban arrives, his presence blocks them from veering off the fetch line just as I intended. My own stock at Carcant are used to my dogs, so Mac and Ban usually work close to them, but today I notice they are holding themselves well back. They have obviously sensed that the mules are not used to dogs and they have naturally adapted their own working style to keep the ewes as calm as possible.

As they near the end of the fetch, the close proximity of the fence and spectators make the sheep increasingly nervous. It's a delicate moment and takes fine judgement: we can't take the pressure off, but at the same time we can't put too much on. Fortunately, the sheep go smoothly around the post and start on the drive. The ewes' body language tells both me and my dogs that they are still highly agitated. Personally, I would prefer my dogs to run nearer to their stock as it makes it easier for me to decide where to position them, but I trust them, so I let them choose the best distance to be from the ewes as they guide them around the course.

Once in the shedding ring, the sheep are still uneasy and mill around looking for a way to escape. With Ban lying outside the ring, Mac and I watch and wait for the ewes to settle. A gap appears and I call Mac through and he immediately sheds off the required five. However, before Ban has a chance to come in and take control of the second group, they try to rejoin the first set. I ask Mac to turn and hold the two groups apart until Ban can get into position. While Ban holds the second group, Mac and I start to pen. Like many of the previous runs, the ewes do not want to go in. Mac's ability to work naturally without command stands me in good stead. He knows the sheep feel anxious about him so he holds the pressure in exactly the right place. Although he hardly moves at all, his body language convinces the sheep that he is an authority to be reckoned with. In contrast, the sheep are obviously not concerned about humans and I have to move around, first this way and then that in order to encourage them to turn and look at the pen. However they will still not go in. Using all of our sheep sense, Mac and I gradually close in on the ewes and eventually they agree with us that the pen is the best place to be.

With relief, I ask Mac to *lie-down* and guard the entrance. Worrying about how much time remains, I ask Ban to push his group of ewes towards the second pen slightly more forcibly than I would really like as I jog over to open the gate. Ban brings the sheep to the pen mouth and instinctively moves into the appropriate place to encourage the sheep into the pen. A couple of ewes make a sudden move to escape and before I had a chance to say anything, Ban instantly responds with a quick jiggle that turns them back towards the pen. On my request, Ban stands his ground and after a short while the sheep walk into the pen.

We've done it. I feel elated. I am so proud of my dogs: the whole run, but especially the end, showed how well we communicate with each other and how much knowledge and natural feel my dogs have for sheep.

PART 1
Communicating
The Natural Way

Listen, your dog is talking to you. Take the time to understand what he is saying and learn how to communicate back to him in a calm, consistent manner, using a language he understands. This will enable you to build a strong partnership based on mutual respect, trust and loyalty.

CHAPTER 1
CANINE COMMUNICATION

Dogs communicate all the time both with each other and with every other animal that they meet. However, the language that they use is often very subtle and humans may miss what the dog is saying. Dogs will almost inevitably signal their intent before they act. Because most handlers do not take the time to study their dog's behaviour closely, they are usually unaware that any message is being relayed. This lack of understanding means that an inexperienced handler is surprised when the dog reacts to a situation in an 'unexpected' fashion. In contrast, if the handler can appreciate what the dog is telling him and so understand his dog's intent and mindset then he can pre-empt the dog and quickly stop him from acting in an unwanted manner.

I base my Natural Way training method on having watched and worked with packs of working border collies for 30 years. I regularly have ten to twenty un-neutered dogs and bitches exercising together in harmony. I keep my dogs in individual kennels, and every time that they are let out together, they use their different senses to identify each other and reassess their status. They also reaffirm the bonds that tie them together through touch, scent and taste.

My own experience has taught me that the key to communicating effectively with any modern dog is to appreciate his evolutionary past and to nurture his innate pack instincts. To me, it is obvious that the pack always has a hierarchy. However, my pack is stable and so the subtle interactions that maintain this hierarchy are often missed by other people who are less adapt at understanding canine communication. I call the most dominant dog and bitch within my group the **Alpha male** and **Alpha female** respectively.

Dominance / submission

A Dominant Tig (dog in front) is cocking his leg on Elle (young bitch submitting on floor) to inform Skid (male dog behind) that she is his property. Skid has his tail raised stating his masculinity. However his tail is not tightly positioned and his gaze is away from Tig indicating he is not threatening Tig's dominant status. **B** As Skid goes in to sniff Elle, Tig warns him off with a hard stare as he stands over submissive Elle.

Fact Box. The leader of the pack

Over the years, I have come to realise that different dominant dogs actually have very different natures and ways of leading the pack. So when Bill was the dominant Alpha, he projected a calm, firm, quiet, dignified, assertive manner. In contrast, when Tig took over he was more obviously a dictator: he had a very short fuse and would tolerate less from the lower ranking members.

He would often growl his displeasure and if not checked by Bobby or me, would discipline lower ranking members much more severely. Despite this manner and attitude towards lower ranking adults, he would still happily nurture and play with pups, letting them climb over him to build their confidence. He took an active role in teaching them how to fit into the pack and was always fair and tolerant with them. He also accepted the position of Kim, the Alpha female, who would sometimes show her annoyance with him and check his overbearing ways (just like a marriage!). Similar to the opposite natures of Bill and Tig, Tess when she was the Alpha female controlled the pack in a different way from stubborn Kim. I think the pack runs smoother with the calmer, fairer leadership of Bill and Tess and so I also rule in this manner.

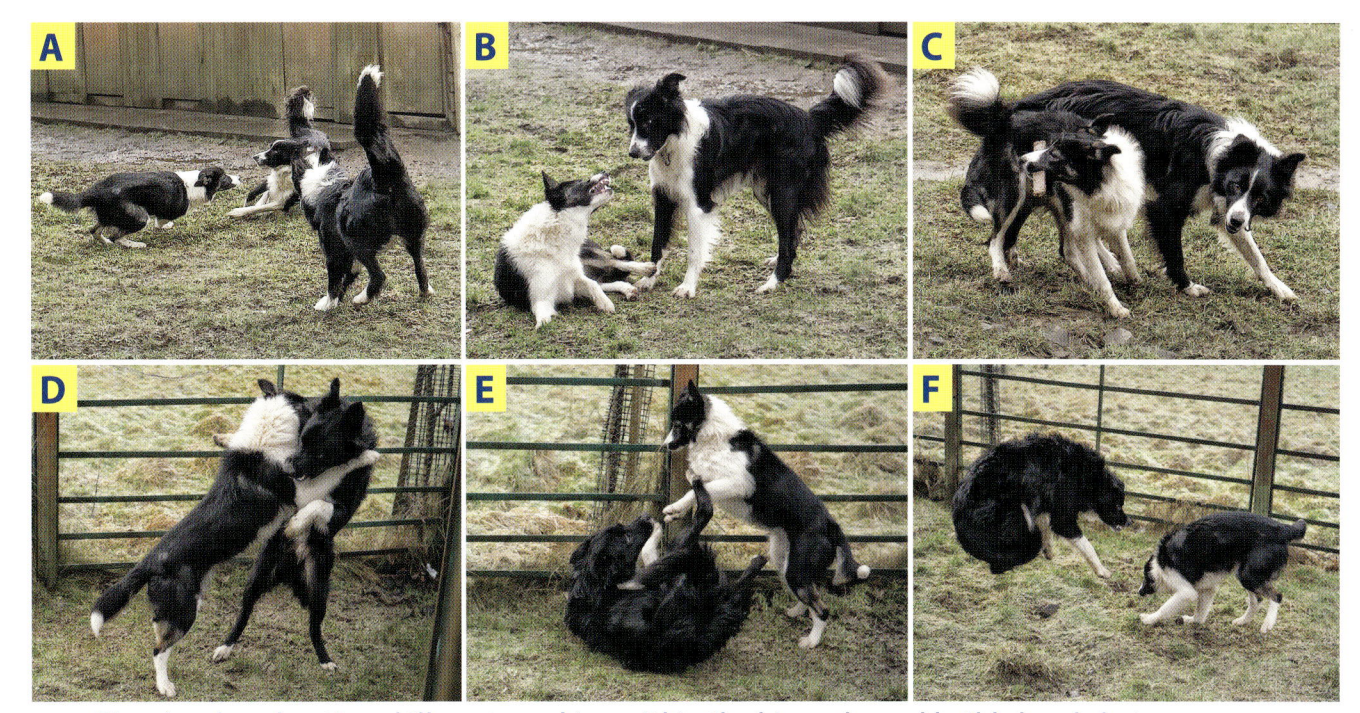

Play develops hunting skills, sets ranking within the hierarchy and builds bonds between different pack members

A Gyp (bitch at back right) the slightly higher ranking and older bitch encourages Elle (bitch at back left) to chase her. Pip (bitch in front) is uncertain whether she is allowed to join in. All 3 bitches are showing 'play mode' and excitement with tails raised and front legs lowered. **B** Elle is lying down but not submitting as she snaps back at Gyp who is standing back but still indicating her higher status with her curled raised tail. **C** Elle is keeping ownership of a stick and on this occasion, Gyp lets her. If she overstepped her boundaries, Gyp would instantly reprimand Elle to remind her that she (Gyp) has a higher rank in the pack hierarchy. **D, E** and **F** Play fighting between two similarly ranked adolescents can look very violent as they tussle to develop their hunting skills. The two dogs suss each others' strengths and weaknesses which eventually will determine their rank within the pack. Dogs read the energy and intention behind the actions and so both are aware that this is play rather than an aggressive situation.

Unrelated, but similarly aged pups show many dominant / submissive gestures as they play together

During this period they build bonds and determine each other's strengths and weaknesses. These early interactions will determine their relative status as adults in the pack.

Below the Alpha pair, the other dogs sort out their pecking order based on their strength, skill, agility and confidence. Teamwork and harmony within the pack depends on respect to the leader and each dog not only knowing, but also keeping to, its place within the social order. Within my stable pack, the more dominant dogs only need show subtle signs and gestures to indicate their high status and they rarely consider physically attacking another pack member: **dominance is certainly not the same as aggression.**

I believe that all dog breeds wherever they live in the world have an innate understanding of this hierarchy and even young pups will use dominant and submissive stances and gestures as they play with each other. In addition, the mother will teach and guide her pup to behave appropriately. She will never allow disrespect and, when necessary, she will discipline her offspring by using a graduated scale of authority as she asks, tells and then finally insists that the pup modify his unacceptable behaviour.

Once the pup is weaned, the other members will also help to teach him the pack rules. One way that dogs bond the group together and teach younger members is through play.

It can appear to humans that dogs playing together are very rough with each other as they subconsciously test each other's relative strengths and weaknesses. However, the playmates are both aware that there is no aggressive intent behind their actions as they realise that 'the bark is worse than the bite.'

If an argument does break out, these usually end very quickly without any significant physical damage to either party. Often an older dog will let the pup guard items and stalk or chase him. Sometimes it may even appear that the young dog is allowed to dominate the higher ranking animal. All this will encourage the youngster to build up his confidence and to develop his hunting skills. However, if the young dog crosses a line and behaves inappropriately, the older one will swiftly and appropriately reprimand the pup to remind him to mind his manners.

This ongoing tuition ensures that the pup grows into an adult that possesses a **well-balanced mind** and is fully able to participate in pack life.

Dogs communicate through a complex combination of touch, smell, sound, visual signals, body language and gestures. A subtle alteration in any of these can significantly change the meaning. Dogs will signal their intent and status to each other from a distance and a flash of the eyes is often enough to show another dog what he is thinking. Moreover the degree of intent behind the look is often sufficient to indicate his rank and mindset.

Dominant dogs will assert their position on more submissive dogs by using pressure / release. Through both play and real confrontations, a dominant dog will clench his muscles so that he appears stronger and taller than the other. He will often lean slightly forward, invading the other dog's 'personal space' as he holds his tail high and stiff.

If a dog is challenging another, he will also raise his hackles along his back and neck while at the same time curling his lips back to show his front teeth. His eyes will be wide and staring. These physical signs may be accompanied by a low growl and the overall intent is to exert pressure on the other dog to submit and give to these dominant gestures.

In response, a lower ranking dog will drop his head and shoulders or just turn his head away to indicate that he does not want to confront the other dog's dominant position. A more submissive dog will crouch down with his tail between its legs and he will pull back his ears and draw back his lips into a submissive 'smile' whilst keeping his eyes narrow, soft and blinking. He may also lick his lips to show that he is uncertain about the other dog's intent or sniff the ground to indicate that he wants to defuse or avoid the situation.

In complete submission, the dog will roll over to expose the vulnerable parts of his body. In turn, the dominant dog will accept these submissive postures by relaxing his own stance and sniffing the other dog. By doing this, he will release the pressure he has exerted on the other.

Tig, Gyp and Pip

Tig (dog top left) is a dominant male who was reintroduced into the pack after an absence of several months. Gyp (dog top right) and Pip (dog at bottom) were both young bitches who had not previously met him. **A** Tig shows a dominant stance with raised tail, ears pricked and stiff body. He is moving into Gyp's space and putting pressure on her whilst also 'strutting his stuff' as he determines whether she is receptive to his sexual advances. Gyp is not completely submitting as she has her tail raised slightly. However, she shows her uncertainty about his intentions by licking her lips and averting her gaze. In **B, C** and **D** Gyp gradually submits to Tig's higher status. However, by keeping her tail slightly raised, she indicates that she does not accept his sexual intent. In response, Tig relaxes his dominant strutting stance. Throughout the sequence, Pip is focused on Tig and intentionally moves forward to position herself between the two other dogs. She lies down in a very submissive position to act as pacifier to defuse any aggressive intent. As Tig relaxes (in **D**), Pip raises her head to determine whether he accepts her submission.

Fact Box. The five main forms of canine communication

- **Touch**: This is very important and starts straight after birth when the bitch licks her pup to promote bonding between them. As the pup grows, the mother will use different kinds of touch depending on the situation. For example, she will use a gentle reassuring touch to calm him when he is anxious compared with a firmer grip to reprimand him when he becomes overexcited and unruly. Adult dogs will only let other dogs that they consider trustworthy touch sensitive areas such as the belly.

- **Visual signals:** Dogs use their eyes and the strength of their gaze to provide cues as to their intention. A direct and intensely held stare will signal dominant intent, whilst soft, blinking shows passive non-aggression. In contrast, averting the eyes or turning the head away either indicates submission or else it is a way of decreasing pressure.

- **Body language / gestures**: The mother and other adult dogs will teach the pups about social behaviour, and how hierarchy works within the pack. The pup also uses play to learn about social order, dominance and submission. Moving into another dog's space and signalling dominant gestures through standing tall, tail up, ears forward and alert is telling the other dog 'Give to pressure. Respect me and move out of my space.'

- **Sound:** Different barks and sounds indicate different things: to initiate play, provide an alert of nearby danger, or give a warning signal to others. Howling may bond the pack or call to absent members whilst at the same time communicating to others that the pack is strong.

- **Smell:** Every member of the pack has his own distinct smell that allows other dogs to recognize him. Marking territory produces a strong odour that each dog uses to gain information. Smell enables dogs to recognize the Alpha Male right down to the lower ranking members of the pack and a higher ranking dog or bitch will often urinate over the scent mark left by a lower ranking animal. Similarly males will use smell to identify a bitch coming into season well before she is ready to mate. Scent also plays an important part in the bonding process between bitch and pup.

As well as conveying their rank within the pack, dogs will also communicate with each other to show affection, friendship, distrust or aggression – or even just to pass the time of day. Their body stance and behaviour not only demonstrate their rank but also indicate their mindset – that is, whether they are relaxed, excited or anxious about a situation.

Dogs within a pack will have on-going 'conversations' that can continue over long periods of time. For example, a mid-ranking dog that is challenging the Alpha will not confront his leader on every occasion, but gradually over time, he will test his boundaries. The Alpha will often just need to signal his higher rank for the younger dog to back down and move away from the pressure that the higher ranking dog has subtly exerted. However, if the young dog continues to push himself forward on several different occasions then eventually there will come a time when the Alpha will act quickly and more assertively to demonstrate his right to be the leader.

At this point, if the lower ranking dog does not back down and submit completely, he may be forced from the pack rather than be allowed to continue to disrupt the group's dynamics and social order. The dog's innate instinct to be part of a pack is strong probably because his wild ancestor would have had little chance of surviving on his own. Therefore, rather than be pushed out from the pack, the dog will try to negotiate his way back by demonstrating his respect to his leader.

Furthermore, within my own pack, my dominant bitch Kim will support my role as overall leader and she will reprimand another dog who is behaving inappropriately either towards me or another dog in the pack. Her body stance indicates her annoyance and often the mid-ranking dogs will come up, lick her face and give other submissive gestures to acknowledge her status. This will pacify her and diffuse any further aggression. To me, this indicates that all the dogs in the pack play a role in maintaining the social order and harmony within the group.

Moving on

In order to gain respect from his dogs, the human handler needs to be the leader of his pack. In the next chapter, I will show you how to use similar pressure / release techniques that the canine Alpha employs, to develop your dog's trust and respect. These underpin my Natural Way training method and will enable you and your dog to work in harmony together around stock.

Anecdote. Gem acting as nanny

Every dog within the pack has a specific job and even young dogs take on various roles and responsibilities within the pack. When Gem was less than a year old she took over the role as nanny. Gem was a submissive, caring, quiet dog and so the job of nurse maid probably came naturally to her. Her worthiness to the pack became apparent to me when we were crossing a shallow stream. A 12 week old pup was struggling to follow the rest of the pack over the water. Yapping furiously, to alert the others of his concern about the situation, he ran up and down whilst continually whining in case the pack would leave without him. At this point Gem crossed back over the stream to reassure the pup that everything was fine. She then re-entered the water and looked behind to see if the pup was following. When he didn't, she went back towards him and barked at the pup to follow. The pup tentatively stood by the water and sniffed at the lapping movement. At this point Gem went back to the pup and prodded him in the shoulder before moving back into the stream. She waited here until the pup plucked up the courage to start feeling his way into the water. Once he had started to tentatively enter the water, Gem quickly moved out of the stream onto our side and again looked back over her shoulder at the pup. This time, her gestures were sufficient to encourage the pup to keep splashing across the stream to join the rest of the pack on the other side. This interaction between the two dogs went on while the rest of the pack went about their own business. It was not their job to intervene, it was the job of the nanny.

Pack dynamics
A Mac (dog behind) is eyeing dominant Tig in an attempt to trigger a reaction as he starts to test his boundaries and challenge Tig's Alpha status. **B** Mac being amorous towards Gail who ignores his advances. **C** Dominant Tig playing with pups to teach them social manners. **D** When a pup oversteps a boundary, Tig reprimands him by gently squeezing the pups muzzle. By combining play with appropriate discipline, Tig teaches the pups how to become responsible pack members.

Anecdote. Kim disciplining her unruly pup

One day, when my pack was exercising in the field, I noticed Zac, a 4 month old male pup, roughly pulling at one of the more submissive adult dogs. His mother, Kim, who is my current Alpha female, gave him a sidewards look. Zac who had a tendency to be quite thuggish, gave a fleeting glance back at his mother before continuing to torment the other dog. Normally I would have stepped in and handled the situation, but this time I wanted to see how Kim would deal with it. A few minutes later, Kim cut in, stalked her pup and gave him a warning stare. Zac acknowledged her by lowering his body stance, putting his ears back whilst licking and chewing. Kim released the pressure by moving away. Despite this, it was not long before the young pup was back picking on his victim. I could instantly tell that Kim was now really annoyed: she held her body stiffly and glared angrily at him. She quickly moved and turned Zac upside down. Her mouth was around his neck and although she held him there was no indication that she was hurting him. He appeared to have submitted totally: lying completely still on his back with his tail tucked in, belly exposed and head to the side. However, I noticed though that Zac's eyes were looking elsewhere and though he was showing all the appropriate signals to his mother that he was sorry, I got the impression that he really was thinking about something else. I thought 'This pup is still not convinced that Kim means it' and shortly after she released her hold, he again returned to pester the other dog. Before Zac knew what had hit him, Kim bolted in like a bullet and tipped the youngster off his feet and turned him upside-down. She gripped him around the throat and this time tightened her grip and growled. When she loosened her hold, she still straddled him and held her body stiffly with her head held high to further assert her authority. Her whole posture indicated that he had better listen because she was not to be disobeyed again. This time, Zac remained lying down on his side with his eyes closed whilst taking very slow breaths as if to play dead. After he was allowed up, he started to act like a responsible pack member. While Kim confronted her pup, it appeared that the other dogs ignored what she was doing. When she walked away, her body language indicated that she was still annoyed with the situation. At this point, the other pack members approached her one after the other and gave her a submissive lick in an attempt to pacify her.

The episode demonstrates three things. Firstly, it is natural for dogs to test members of the pack including their mother. Secondly, if the Alpha female is not obeyed when she asks her pup or any lower ranking dog to modify his behaviour, then she will gradually escalate the pressure on the troublemaker until he submits to her wishes. Thirdly, when the Alpha is annoyed, the other members will reaffirm the bonds in the pack by showing submissive gestures towards her even though she has not directly disciplined them.

Fact Box. Body language* and sounds indicating a dog's mindset

	Well balanced and receptive	Dominance	Submissive	Anxiety	Excitement
Tail	Relaxed, low and soft.	Held rigidly and stiffly arched over back.	Slightly tucked beneath body.	Tightly tucked beneath body.	Raised and often flicks up.
Body stance	Relaxed and soft. Confident. Facial features relaxed.	Stiff, standing on toes and puffing out chest.	Lowered body posture, may roll over to expose belly.	Held stiffly often with a hunched back.	Variable. May be held slightly tight or bouncy. May shake with excess energy.
Eyes	Soft and round.	Wide, fixed and staring.	Softened eyes which are narrowed and blinking.	Wide open, large pupils. Glaring and bulging eyes. Often shows whites of eye.	Slightly wide and staring.
Mouth	Relaxed, and quiet.	Lips curled up to show front teeth.	Lips curl up into a submissive smile. Licking lips and chomping.	Lips drawn back and tight.	Slightly taught or open.
Hair	Down and soft.	Hackles may be up along back and tail.	Flat.	Slightly raised.	Slightly raised.
Ears	Relaxed.	Pointed forward, set high and stiff on the head.	Pulled back.	Held back tightly against top of the neck.	Flicking or pointed forward.
Vocalisation**	None required, but they may give friendly noises.	Low, deep grumbles or growls.	None or soft whines.	High pitch and makes sudden sharp yaps.	High pitch sounds and barks.

* Some breeds have been genetically selected to hold a particular stance and this may influence how they hold their ears, tail etc. This should be taken into consideration when reading a dog's body language.

** Often the dog does not need to vocalise to indicate his mindset.

CHAPTER 2
HOW TO SPEAK THE DOG'S OWN LANGUAGE

I believe that a working dog instinctively sees the handler and himself as the predatory pack, with the sheep as the prey. If you intend to work your dog on stock, then to ensure good animal welfare, it is imperative that you have gained your dog's respect and trust and that he considers you his leader. If you have allowed your dog to become the Alpha, he will take charge both on and off the field, leading the hunt and chasing after sheep if he so wishes. So a crucial part of training The Natural Way is to establish the correct balance in your relationship. This ensures that your dog respects you and will want to listen and respond appropriately to your wishes.

I find that many people do not understand the difference between respect and obedience. **Respect is a dog's proper mental attitude towards the handler** whilst obedience is the dog's response to a command. If a dog respects his owner then he will want to please his handler and will happily choose to respond promptly to his human's requests.

In contrast to this, I often have inexperienced handlers say to me 'My dog is obedient when he is near, but he does not listen when he is at a distance'. This is usually because the dog does not respect his owner and therefore does not have the correct attitude towards him.

In order to develop respect from your dog using my Natural Way training method, you need to remember several key points.

1. An Alpha dog will usually only allow a subordinate dog into his personal space when the subordinate displays a proper respectful attitude. Similarly, you need to decide what is appropriate behaviour and be consistent in your response when he crosses the boundaries you have set. Play is slightly different and as I discussed in the previous chapter, the Alpha will often roll over and let a youngster climb over him. However, even in a play situation, if the pup crosses the line and acts inappropriately or too aggressively, then the Alpha will instantly and appropriately reprimand the young dog. This way the pup learns which actions are allowed and which are not.

2. You cannot expect your dog automatically to be perfect: you have to teach him what you want and give him time to understand and learn. Your dog will inevitably make mistakes. Not all mistakes are of the same magnitude. You need to use a graduated scale of response, so that the amount of correction you use is appropriate to the situation. I call this scale '**ask, tell, insist**'. Moreover, the intensity of your 'tell' or 'insist' should vary with different dogs and you need to adapt your approach depending on your dog's natural temperament. If your dog is sensitive, you need to build his confidence, not crush it. When your dog acts appropriately, it is important that you release the pressure so that he associates doing the right thing with feeling comfortable. At the end of a session or when you want to praise your dog, you should release all pressure and also use soft gentle strokes along his cheeks and under his mouth that mimic his mother's nurturing licks. This touch is a potent and fulfilling reward for your dog and so you should only use it when he is calm and has an appropriate respectful attitude.

Fact Box. The graded scale of 'ask, tell, insist'

Ask: Physically, take one step forward and lean your body slightly forward towards the dog, then release by stepping back. Vocally, use a quiet voice.

Tell: Physically, step forward and hold pressure for longer until the dog shows submissive gestures. Vocally, add a soft growl.

Insist: Physically, stalk the dog and dart forward as if to strike so that the dog perceives that you will attack if necessary. Vocally, add a deep, brusque, firmer growl.

3. Within a pack, a young dog learns what is acceptable behaviour by testing his mother and other more senior pack members repeatedly over a period of time. The higher ranking dogs will not ignore this inappropriate attitude, instead they will use the same graded scale of 'ask, tell, insist' to make the youngster alter his mindset and behaviour so that he becomes a stable, integrated and useful member of the pack.

4. Dogs use sound, touch, body language, gestures and smell to indicate and reinforce their position in the pack's hierarchy. Your dog is continually using these same signals with you as he lets you know his intent and mindset. The way he looks at you, his attitude towards you, how his ears move and how he carries his tail will indicate whether he is anxious, excited, submissive or dominant. Usually,

rather than just a single gesture, the dog will use a combination of signs to indicate his intent. Some people find it very difficult to understand what their dog is really saying, but in order to bring out the best in your dog, you need to interpret these signals correctly and then respond using appropriate pressure / release. This is explained in detail on page 16.

5. Whenever you interact with your dog, he is always reading your body language, mindset and energy levels. He will instinctively decide whether you really mean what you say. No doubt, you feel the difference when a person in authority tells you to do something compared to someone who just casually asks you to do the same thing. Your dog is also sensing this difference and he is much better at interpreting the energy behind our actions than other humans are!

We communicate with our dogs all of the time

A and **B** Exercising the pack near a stream. Even in this informal situation my relaxed, yet confident manner, still shows I am the leader. The dogs acknowledge this through their gestures and behaviour towards me. **C** As I groom Elle, we mirror each other's soft facial expressions. She has a submissive pose as I gently touch her side. **D** I share a moment with Fluffy my cat and Tess who had come to visit. (She had retired from work and was living with a good friend).

The way you touch your dog is important

A I put pressure on Ban by giving short gentle squeezes on the muzzle until he gives and starts to submit. Once Ban starts to give to pressure, I stop squeezing but still keep my hand loosely around the muzzle until he has submitted as far as I wish him to. It is the release from pressure that shows him that he has responded correctly. In this example, Ban would move to position shown in **B** Ban is showing total submission, he is relaxed but not worried as he is looking at me with passive blinking eyes that demonstrate his trust. In return my face is soft and passive whilst I touch his belly with gentle rubs to reassure him. This is a similar touch to one used by a bitch as she soothes and bonds with her pup. **C** Ban is well used

to pressure / release techniques and here he is showing how easily he gives to minimal gentle pressure: in this case just the touch of a finger. It takes time for a dog to learn how to give to gentle pressure, I would not expect a youngster to respond as readily as this. **D** Gentle touch (without stroking) on the side of Ban's nose reassures him. This could be considered similar to holding a hand or gently touching another human's shoulder. **E** Gently stroking under the chin and along Ban's cheeks rewards him and lets him know that I am satisfied. If used at an inappropriate time, this could reward bad behaviour. In contrast, fast, heavy, stroking on different parts of the head and body can either stimulate unwanted excitement or else be perceived as threat.

Fact Box. Signals and what they really mean

Individual gestures from your dog can mean several things. **It is important that you look at the whole dog to interpret his intent.** For humans, this is similar to individual words having several definitions and you need to look at the whole context to understand what is really meant.

- **Tail flick:** I am either excited or unsure and feeling uncertain. This attitude often pre-empts a sudden movement, gripping or backing off.

- **Tail up high:** I do not know what to do. This sign may also be a playful gesture if his tail is presented high and loose, waving like a flag in the wind.

- **Tail held up tight over body, body stance tall and stiff:** I am dominant.

- **Tail curled slightly under the body:** I am submissive.

- **Tail tucked up tight up against his belly:** I an worried and feeling intimidated.

- **Tail down, slightly curled and relaxed:** I have a balanced mind.

- **Ears back and rigid, eyes wide and staring**: Be wary of me.

- **Body slightly lowered, ears slightly back, eyes blinking, tail under, licking and chewing:** I'm listening plus I am submissive to you and wish to negotiate.

- **Sniffing the ground, eating dirt, peeing, tail down/fleeing from pressure:** I'm uncertain and avoiding the situation.

- **Continue sniffing the ground, cocking leg with tail held straight or high** (e.g. when called by handler): I am showing dominance and disrespect.

- **Excited, bouncy stance, smiling, with head high, eyes bright and tail raised:** I am not taking you seriously. I think you may be giving signals that you want to play with me.

- **Yawning is a submissive gesture:** A large yawn means I don't want a fight and I really need the pressure released. With a young dog, it can also mean that they are getting mentally tired (and the handler should consider giving a break in the training session).

- **Tongue flick/quick lick of the lips:** I acknowledge you, I do not want a confrontation.

What is pressure / release?

When I talk about **pressure**, I mean the assertive positive energy that the dog picks up from his handler's demeanour. You can either soothe or intimidate your dog depending on your body stance and gestures; how close you stand; the way you look at him and the tone of voice that you use. So it is vitally important that you realise what you are really saying in his language.

In order to indicate that you hold Alpha status, you need to take up an assured, authoritative, dominant stance. This is when you stand tall, with a stiff posture, square shouldered, leaning slightly towards your dog, with your eyes locked onto him. By breathing slowly, calmly and deeply, you will indicate that you are in control of the situation. This will calm your dog and give him time to think.

Do not forget that dogs can read our body language, gestures and state of mind much quicker than we can read theirs. Your dog is not just picking up and reacting to your positive energy, he will also respond to any negative signals that you are unintentionally providing about your energy, emotion and mood. If you do not want to give mixed messages when you are training and working with your dogs then you need to control your energy. Anger and aggression are not the same as dominance. A quiet, calm, confident individual will often portray dominance in a much more effective way, than a red-faced, shouting, irate handler.

Some handlers always shout and harass their dog. In these cases, the dog cannot escape from the pressure and they often stop thinking clearly. Your dog may also become tense and uncertain if your own body language indicates that you are anxious or stressed. Dogs with either of these mindsets often rush into the sheep and may grip out of frustration and uncertainty.

I also find that some dogs interpret an inexperienced handler's gestures in a different fashion than the one intended. For example, the handler may run at the dog, shouting and waving his arm about. The dog's response will depend on his innate character. He may respond by becoming overexcited and stimulated into a play response. Alternatively, other dogs can become worried by these loud shouts and over-exaggerated gestures.

You need to be fully aware of how your dog may perceive your actions

A As I move into Ban's space, I indicate that I wish him to move away from me by extending my right arm to the side and clicking my fingers as I step forward. My body stance is assertive, upright with squared shoulders. My body language applies pressure on him. In return, Ban shows me respect and moves away from me. His tail is down and his body relaxed, indicating that he has a calm, submissive mindset. He looks back towards me to work out my intention. If your dog does not have enough respect for you, his response to your forward assertive movement may be aggressive or excited rather than submissive. **B** I have stepped out of Ban's space to acknowledge his submission. My body stance is relaxed, leaning slightly backwards and I have gentle soft eyes as I smile at him. In response, Ban is relaxed, his head is raised and he too shows gentle soft facial features. This release from pressure is important if you wish to build a willing partnership built on trust and respect.

Many inexperienced handlers find it hard to act in a dominant fashion and these individuals usually lack conviction or show uncertainty when they try to reprimand their dog. For example they may smile whilst they try to tell their dog off. Your dog is reading your energy levels: if your body language portrays your uncertainty, then your dog will know that he does not have to take you seriously. However, if you alter the intent behind your command by becoming more authoritative and assertive (which often equates to becoming quieter and firmer), then your dog will start to realise that you are a force to be reckoned with and he will start listening to you.

When your dog makes the wrong decision, you need to apply appropriate pressure to show him that he has made a mistake. You need to learn how to vary the degree of pressure you give and move up and down the intensity scale as required for different situations. By this, I mean that you need to be able to communicate the difference between asking him to reconsider his attitude to the other extreme where you demand that he alters his behaviour. As I have mentioned previously, I call this pressure scale 'ask, tell, insist'. It would not have been fair to illustrate this using photos of me with a dog, so I had pictures taken of myself with a friend to show how our body language and physical proximity alters as our intent and attitude changes.

As well as exerting appropriate pressure, an equally important part of training The Natural Way is **release from pressure**. When you release pressure you show your dog that he has acted correctly. Release of pressure will also help him relax and release any tension that he may have developed through any inappropriate pressure being applied.

There are several gestures that you can use to indicate to your dog that you have released the pressure on him. These include dropping the tone and level of your voice, relaxing your body (including lowering your arm if it is raised). You should stop your forward movement and allow him some more personal space. You can lean back and if necessary, also turn slightly to the side, whilst dropping your shoulders and lowering your eyes. This release should be done in a controlled, calm manner so that your dog does not think that you are starting to submit to him and that he has now taken control of the situation. If you release when the dog is not acting appropriately, then he will pick up mixed messages of what is right and what is wrong. For example, if you release pressure while the dog is resistant and pushing into your space then you are saying 'Yes, this behaviour is acceptable, come into my space with this inappropriate attitude whenever you choose'.

Body language between two humans to demonstrate 'ask, tell, insist'

A Ask: I am facing my friend with a relaxed but direct gaze, I step forward but my body is leaning back slightly and my shoulders are relaxed. My friend is slightly leaning back, but her facial features show slight anxiety. **B Tell:** I am moving forward, my shoulders are slightly raised. I am making eye contact with a sterner gaze. My friend's body language is questioning my intent as her shoulders are slightly raised while she stands her ground. **C Insist:** I have moved into my friend's personal space and my stern eyes and tense body indicate that I may attack. My friend is reading my dominant energy. She is still making eye contact while she weighs her options. However, she has taken a step away from me indicating she does not want a confrontation.

When putting pressure onto your dog, the amount you need to use will depend on how your dog responds. In addition, if he resists, you need to work out why he is doing this. In the section at the end of this chapter, I go through some common problems that people have when working with pressure / release techniques.

It is also important to remember that too much pressure will create a **fight-or-flight** response. When two dogs are sussing each other out, they each will use posturing techniques and dominant gestures. This body language will indicate to each other which is the stronger and higher ranking. Therefore most confrontations are resolved without resorting to actual physical aggression. A fight will only occur if neither dog backs down or when submissive signals from the weaker one are not acknowledged by the stronger. If your dog responds by looking aggressively at you, for example with wide menacing eyes and hackles raised, then you need to be certain that you know how to deal with the situation before you continue with this training exercise. This type of dog may consider itself the Alpha. However, because he has not previously been challenged by you, he may not have needed to demonstrate his dominant position in the pack. If not handled properly, a dog in this mindset could decide to attack if it is provoked further. If you are in any doubt, you should consult an experienced dog trainer on how to alter a very dominant dog's attitude.

Other dogs who receive too much pressure will go into flight or else may try to diffuse the situation by sniffing the ground or eating muck. If a dog is fleeing, he needs time to calm down. Once you have removed the pressure, give your dog time to relax. When he is calm and in this mindset, he will show submissive gestures and be willing to negotiate.

A common behaviour that I often see is when the dog does not respect the handler. This type of dog will use avoidance to indicate that he does not take you seriously. He may move further away from you, but this is not out of worry. Instead, he will continue with his cocksure, assertive behaviour and perhaps sniff the ground and cocking his leg as he carries on doing what he likes. You could consider this to be similar to a child who is being rude to an adult and is taunting him from a distance ('Ha, I can do whatever I want and you can't get me'). A dog with this attitude may also come into your space or jump up at you in a disrespectful or playful attitude, while ignoring any pressure gestures you attempt to keep him at a distance.

Unfortunately, you cannot just look for any one single gesture to indicate a particular mindset. An inexperienced handler may find that it is difficult to detect the subtle differences in body language. For example a dog sniffing the ground could either be trying to diffuse the situation or else could be showing

The energy and intent behind your actions are important

A My energy is calm and my posture is relaxed. Both of us are standing within our own personal space. This allows my friend to relax. **B** My friend attempts to move into my personal space. However, her energy is not sufficient to support her body language. I respond by not giving as I maintain my gaze. I also unintentionally remove my hands from my pockets and raise my shoulders as I subconsciously prepare to defend my position and not give ground to her.

arrogant disrespect. In the former, the dog will have a lowered stance, tail tucked between its legs, soft eyes and will often lick his lips. All these signs indicate he wants to negotiate with you. In contrast, when the dog is in avoidance mode, although he is sniffing the ground, he will maintain his strutting, arrogant posture because he is really saying 'I can do what I like and I will only listen to you when it suits me.'

It is important that you can interpret your dog's body language correctly, because your subsequent actions will be different. If your dog is willing to negotiate with you, then you should release pressure to indicate he has made the correct decision. In contrast, a dog that avoids you so that he can continue 'to do his own thing' will require additional pressure applied before he will start to pay attention.

When learning The Natural Way, most dogs will often go through resistance and avoidance stages before they are willing to negotiate with their hander. An inexperienced person may find this confusing until he learns how to read the subtle differences in a dog's body language that indicate that he has developed the appropriate attitude towards his owner.

I cannot emphasize enough how important it is to study canine communication to understand what your dog is really saying to you.

Using The Natural Way

As I have already discussed, a dog is a pack animal and, as such, he is evolutionarily hard-wired to know that he needs the pack in order to survive. In the hierarchy, the lower ranking dog will move out of the Alpha dog's space to show respect. The Alpha female in a pack will drive a disrespectful adolescent away and will not let him return until he indicates that he wants to negotiate by displaying submissive gestures.

My Natural Way training method uses the same strategies to tell your dog that you are his Alpha. Remember, the leader in the pack makes the decisions. If you want your dog to come into your personal space, you need to use the correct body language and gestures to say that you are happy for him to approach you in a respectful manner.

When I started using The Natural Way, I used a long line to keep in close contact with my dog. However, my good friend, Sarah Jenkins, began to use a round pen similar to that used by horse whisperers as they 'join up' with horses. I have also adopted this method and have a ten metre diameter pen specifically for dog training. Obviously, you can use any small enclosed area. If your dog is not used to giving to pressure and you try to do these exercises in a large open area, it gives him more scope to evade you.

Fact Box. Signs of respect / disrespect

It is important that the dog understands where he fits in the pack so that he can be settled and confident within the relationship. It is the handler's job to earn respect through understanding, guidance, nurturing and by setting boundaries. I respect my dogs, and in return, I expect them to respect me.

The dog shows respect if:	The dog shows disrespect if:
He moves out of the handler's space as the handler moves forward into his.	He may barge into the handler's space when uninvited and refuses to move away when the owner attempts to push him out.
His posture is submissive by lowering his body and head and he gives passive, relaxed, blinking eye signals.	He may present a dominant stance with tail held stiffly over his back. He may stare directly at the handler with hard eyes. He may growl or raise his hackles.
When invited, he should come in slowly and often from behind or to the side of the handler.	He may jump up onto the handler when uninvited.
He will willingly want to follow the handler.	He pulls on a lead.
He responds appropriately to the handler's body language, gestures, and voice.	He does not come when called (or will delay coming by obviously sniffing the ground and / or cocking his leg).
	He marks his territory by frequently urinating. This may include peeing on the handler's leg.

By avoiding you, he will be able to continue to please himself. If this is your only option, then I would recommend that you use a long line with the same body language and gestures that I will describe when working in a round pen.

As I have already said, a dog will often move through a stage of resistance followed by one where he attempts to avoid you. This will happen no matter whether you are using a round pen or a long line. Both methods are used to prevent him from moving too far away. In other words, he may try to avoid your pressure but he cannot ignore you. In addition, when you use a long line, you also need to be careful that you do not unintentionally pull on it (exert pressure) when you actually should have released pressure and let it be slack. If you make this error, your dog will receive mixed messages. This will confuse him and he will not understand what you are asking from him.

The aim is to **teach your dog to give to pressure**. This is where all your skills are required as you need to interpret your dog's signals to understand what he is saying and then respond appropriately. You first need to tell your dog that you are dominant to him. You do this by putting sufficient pressure on him so that he moves out of your space. This should arouse his instinctive need to be part of the pack and make him want to negotiate with his Alpha (you) so that he is allowed back. A dog that has the correct attitude will want to negotiate. In contrast, a dog that is resistant to pressure will refuse to be pushed into flight and may just ignore you. Alternatively, if your dog considers himself Alpha or is naturally very dominant, then he might consider that you are challenging his position in the hierarchy and turn to confront you. As I have said before, if you have any doubt about working with a dominant dog seek professional help from an experienced trainer.

When your dog has moved away from your pressure, you should only let him back into your space when he shows signs that he wants to negotiate. These include lowering his head and neck, putting his ears back, licking his lips and chewing, giving soft passive eye signals, as well as holding his tail low and between the legs. These gestures are not indicating that he is worried, instead your dog is showing submission and demonstrating that he wants to be accepted back into his pack.

It is important, especially when you start using my training method, that as soon as your dog's attitude is correct and he indicates that he wants to negotiate, you immediately respond by releasing pressure. This acts as a reward and tells him that he has made the correct choice.

To release pressure, you should relax your gaze and your shoulders, turn slightly to the side with your head down and your eyes soft and passive. Do not look directly at your dog. Your dog should relax and give you passive non-aggressive signals in return. Now, if you want to invite him into your space, you need to maintain a non-threatening posture and not look directly at him. Instead drop you head, soften your eye and turn away slightly from your dog. Use a quiet and encouraging voice to ask him to come forward. You may also gently tap your thigh to indicate that you wish him to come to be by your leg. In addition, you may need to crouch down (still turned slightly to the side) to make yourself appear less threatening. When your dog comes in with an appropriate submissive attitude, you need to reward him by soft strokes along his cheeks.

Julie's Tip. Use the here command when you call your dog to you. This will help you later on when you start to teach both the inside flank and shedding.

Now stand up and walk away. Your dog should **follow up**. By this I mean that he should follow behind you with the appropriate respectful attitude. If he does not, use pressure to push him away again until he displays submissive gestures indicating that he wishes to renegotiate. Repeat the rest of the exercise. Be patient and do not get annoyed or frustrated with your dog: calm, assertive persistence pays dividends. As you continue with these exercises, your dog will learn to respond to lighter pressure and, with time, the signals you need to use will become more subtle.

Once your dog is happy to give to pressure, then you can also block or stimulate more movement in him as you desire.

Call in and follow up

A I have turned to the side. My lowered shoulders and head indicate to Ban that I am relaxed. I have dropped my gaze down and am blinking to show passive (but not submissive) gestures. Lowering my arm towards my side invites Ban into my space. Ban starts to approach me in a polite, calm fashion using submissive and passive gestures (blinking eyes, lowered ears and body carriage). Once by my side, I would touch his cheek in a calm, gentle reassuring fashion. **B** and **C** I calmly walk with a relaxed, quiet posture (slightly lowered shoulders and head) and my arms are loose by my side. Ban wants to follow me. He closely watches me so that he can gauge what I require from him. This desire to follow up is a direct result of my dog accepting me as his leader. **D** Ban has come forward, whilst maintaining his submissive posture. He is trying to make eye contact with me and is attempting to touch my hand for reassurance. He is also licking his lips. He has read a very subtle change in my energy as I have inadvertently quickened my pace and tensed my body slightly (as indicated by my raised hand and slightly raised shoulders). As soon as I realised that Ban's slight anxiety, I stopped and reassured him by gently touching his nose.

From the Clinic

Handler: Why does my dog not give to me when I move into his space?

I observed that the handler moved forward, but instead of using the correct stern facial expressions (that give substance and underpin her body's movement), her facial expression was relaxed and smiling. Furthermore, her energy levels were low and there was no intent behind her movement.

My opinion: The dog was willing and was not fighting his owner. However, he did not yield to his owner because she had given him mixed messages: her body language attempted to say 'Give to me', but her facial expression and energy said 'I'm no threat'. The lack of clear guidance made the dog uncertain and he therefore appeared to resist her. I also noted that he gave some intermittent tail flicks to indicate his uncertainty. As his owner continued to give mixed messages, the dog's uncertainty increased. He would then move suddenly and push forward ignoring his owner's request for space. This provoked a stronger command (a 'tell') from the owner, because she felt she had no choice but to respond with increased pressure.

My advice: The owner should use correct, consistent 'ask' gestures. This willing dog would then respond appropriately. However, the initial mixed signal meant that the handler needed to exert more pressure than was really necessary to get a response. This escalation of pressure had caused the dog to mistrust his owner.

People often think they are being kind to their dogs by showing soft expressions. However, I believe that you should only do this when it is appropriate. Mixed messages build confusion and mistrust in a dog. Many people find it difficult to direct their energy appropriately so that it reinforces their gestures. This lack of intent is perceived as weakness by the dog. In response, he feels he has no choice but take over and lead the pack.

The block

The **block** position teaches a dog to stop. It is a neutral position. To block your dog, you need to position yourself so that you mirror your dog's movements. If he tries to move to the left, you move across to block his direction. If he then moves back to the right, you mirror this to again block his movement. You continue to block the dog in a calm, focused fashion until your dog has stopped. It is important that you constantly read your dog's reactions and alter the level of pressure / release as appropriate. For example, when you move to a block position, do not also move forward and put pressure on your dog (unless your dog shows resistance in which case he may require more pressure in order to listen to you).

Once your dog has stopped in response to your block, it is important that you release pressure to show him that he has made the correct choice. This is a fundamental part of training The Natural Way because he must always associate making the right decision with feeling comfortable. As explained previously, you release pressure by relaxing your gaze and dropping your eyes to stop making contact. You should also soften your stance, by relaxing your shoulders and turning your body slightly away from him. However there is often only a subtle difference in your posture between releasing pressure and asking your dog to come into your space. In this case, you only want to release pressure, so be certain that you do not turn your body too much or you will ask him to come in to you.

The block position

The way you stand, your eye contact and intent plus how you hold your hand can significantly effect the amount of pressure you exert on your dog. **A** Standing straight, with a passive gaze and lowered hands is a neutral block position. **B** Leaning backwards slightly will release pressure. **C** and **D** Raising your hand will increase the pressure on your dog and leaning forward will increase this further. **E** If you lean to the side you will encourage your dog to stop moving to that side. **F** Raising your hand will further increase the pressure and encourage your dog to move in the opposite direction.

Directing movement

Once you have blocked all movement, you should then use light pressure to ask the dog to move forward (away from you) around the pen. This flight response from the dog is actually a normal reaction as part of the fight-or-flight instinct that all animals (including ourselves) have. By positioning and applying the correct pressure in the correct place, you will teach the dog to move in the direction required.

When I want my dog to move to the left or right, I encourage him to move along an arc rather than a straight line. This is because, I know my dog will need to move this way later on when he is flanking around sheep. In order to teach my dog that he needs to move in an arc, I move into my dog's space and position myself so that he moves away from me in the direction and manner in which I want him to go. For example, to move my dog in anti-clockwise (right) direction, I put my right hand out and direct it to his rear end. This drives him away from my pressure and so he moves forward.

If my dog starts to come in on his turn, he will drop his inner shoulder down slightly just before he moves inward. When I see him starting to do this, I point towards this dropped shoulder to encourage him to lift it up. As he lifts his shoulder, outward, he will shift his weight onto his outside leg. This will encourage him to take the correct arc-like movement that I require.

When you try this exercise, the amount of pressure / release you use will depend on how much your dog 'gives' to you. If your dog shows resistance to your request then you need to slightly increase the pressure sooner and initially point towards his shoulder to push his head and shoulder out. You should then put your hand out to direct his rear end forward. However as soon as he responds, you need to reward him by releasing the pressure. If the dog indicates that he is worried then you have to take off the pressure. Encourage and reassure him before starting again but adjust the amount of pressure you use.

In order to make sure that your dog does not become 'one-sided', you should use the same technique for the clockwise (left) turn, but this time your gestures should be in the opposite direction.

To teach your dog to move towards you (the *walk-on / get up* command), you need to face him, but this time encourage him to walk steadily towards you. You do this by moving backwards and giving passive, calming signals by dropping your head slightly and giving him a soft eye with a quiet and encouraging voice. If necessarily, to control the speed of approach, you can raise your hand slightly to block any rapid forward movement. Your hand is acting as a half-halt to check the pace rather than force him out.

When you want to teach the *out* command, you need to be able to move your dog back out to the edge of the round pen. Again you should do this using your body language and gestures. In this case, you need to stand tall and confident and look at your dog with more intent. Move slowly towards your dog and if necessary give a low growl until he gives to this pressure.

Remember it is vital that you read your dog's body language correctly so that you can accurately determine whether he is showing appropriate respect, disrespect, excitement or uncertainty. I advise that you look carefully at the pictures and their captions throughout this book to get an insight into how a dog's body language indicates his mindset and attitude.

You are aiming for your training sessions to be quiet and focused. Your dog needs time to absorb the information. When you start teaching your dog to give to pressure, you should initially be satisfied with a little (a small try). In addition, you should give him the opportunity both to work out what you are asking and also to consider what is the appropriate solution. These thought processes obviously take time. Therefore if your dog hesitates, you should not instantly assume that this delay is because he is not listening to you and you should not rush your commands nor move quickly to the next level of intensity (tell or insist) in the 'ask, tell, insist' graded scale. In contrast, if you attempt to push your dog through these early stages too hard or too quickly, he will become anxious or confused and then he may make unintentional mistakes.

Creating movement that is balanced between handler and dog

A I lean slightly to the right with my right arm outstretched. This puts pressure on Ban's rear. Because Ban's head is turned slightly inward, I have also lifted my left hand slightly so that it points towards his shoulder. This puts pressure on his shoulder and encourages Ban to shift his weight onto his outside leg, thus keeping him out of my space. My combined actions encourage Ban to move in a semicircle around me. **B** I move forward with some intensity whilst looking at Ban, my right hand is still slightly raised pointing at a spot just behind his tail. This drives Ban into a flight response and he speeds up as he moves away from me. The amount of pressure I put on him will dictate how fast and far he moves. Ban not only responds to the speed of my movement, he also reads my energy and intent. It is important that you do not put too much pressure on your dog or he will flee. However, if you move quickly but with little intent behind your action, then your dog may see your approach as play. **C** I stand still and straight whilst directly facing Ban. My right hand is raised and is directly mirroring the position of his head. This creates the block that tells him he needs to stop moving forward. **D** and **E** show how subtle this language can be. In **D** my body leans slightly to my left and my stick points slightly towards Ban's tail. This asks him to move to his left and he responds appropriately. However, I see he is slightly anxious, so in **E**, I have modified the pressure. Now my upper body is asking him to move to the right, but my hips and legs are turning out and away from him to reduce the pressure and his anxiety. He mirrors my body position as he turns to the right. **F** At the end of a session I always reward my dog by calling him to my side to praise him. I do this by giving him rewarding soft strokes along the side of his cheek and body. As I stroke him, my own body and face are relaxed. All this makes Ban feel comfortable sitting by my side and tells him that I am pleased and satisfied with him.

Finishing a training session

At the end of each session, I will give a command of *that'll do* and invite my dog into my space using the appropriate body language. If your dog comes towards you with the correct attitude, then you need to reward him by totally releasing the pressure. Gently touch and softly stroke the sides his cheeks and under his chin, while using a quiet soothing voice. These actions indicate that you are happy with him and, because they mimic his mother's nurturing licks and soothing vocalizations, they are rich, rewarding and sufficient praise. By doing this, you will teach him that the *that'll do* command represents the end of the working session. You want to encourage your dog to have a calm, steady attitude around both humans and stock, so do not overexcite him when you give praise.

Over time, your dog's understanding will grow and he will start to respond more promptly. You can then gradually ask him to give more. As your dog progresses, remember that you should always release pressure when he has done the right thing. He must always associate being correct with feeling comfortable.

A dog will learn very quickly if you are using his language correctly and it will not take long before you can gain full control of his movement, speed and attitude. However, not all dogs learn at the same speed and some will take longer than others. This certainly does not mean that the fast learner will inevitably be the better work dog in the longer term. Similarly, some dogs will need more encouragement and stimulation to respond than others. This is something that you will need to assess along with your dog's innate level of dominance.

Finally, I cannot emphasise enough how necessary it is for you to portray confidence in a relaxed way as you work with your dog. If you are anxious or angry, your dog will pick up on this and your attitude will make him either worry or else take advantage of the situation. Importantly, always remember that no two dogs are the same. I cannot state often enough how vital it is to read your dog correctly in order to make the right decision at the right time.

Problems

There are several different ways that you may create problems by using pressure / release inappropriately. Often the issue is not just 'too much' or 'too little' pressure, but rather wrongly timed or wrongly placed pressure / release. Your dog does not realise that you do not understand his language as well as he does. If you respond too slowly, then your dog will interpret this as 'Yes, you can do what you like'. In these situations, your dog does not take advantage because he is innately badly behaved. Instead, he thinks that as you do not use his language to say 'Hey, don't do that', then he is allowed to decide what is acceptable behaviour. When your dog feels that he is making the decisions, it reinforces his belief that his rank within the pack is being raised. By the same reasoning, he considers that your status is being lowered. It is not until you take over control and assume a clear leadership role that your dog will allow you to dictate what he does. Why should a dog follow a leader that he does not believe in?

Fact Box. Why a dog may misunderstand his handler's real intention

• **Handler has a worried expression:** The dog reads that there is a problem and a reason to be concerned.

• **Handler moves erratically:** The dog interprets this to mean that handler wants him to make a sudden movement.

• **Handler moves towards his dog waving his arms attempting to make the dog back off:** The dog either becomes irritated by such a gesture or alternatively reads it as a playful gesture with no substance. Either way, he ignores the handler's attempt of applying pressure and continues forward.

• **Handler shows anger through body stiffness and facial tightness:** The dog may feel insecure and react suddenly. His own instinct for survival is aroused and he may be put into flight to avoid conflict. If a handler puts too much pressure on him with no obvious escape route then the dog may think he is about to be attacked and feel his only option is to fight back. Remember fight creates fight.

The dog 'comes to pressure' rather than 'gives to pressure'

This is something I see very often and usually my clients are not aware that the way they give their commands is actually confusing the dog.

As I have discussed in the previous chapter, a submissive dog will give ground to the Alpha. One of the most common problems I encounter is dogs who have been forced to either come towards pressure or not move when they have pressure put on them. In either case, the dog is forced to endure a higher intensity of pressure at a closer proximity than he actually feels comfortable with. For example, if you move in towards the dog in an aggressive, dominant forward movement whilst shouting *lie-down*, your dog is actually receiving mixed messages as your body language is saying 'Move out my space', but your vocal command is enforcing a 'Don't move' command. This inevitably creates confusion in your dog's mind and makes him feel uncertain how to respond. He will either cower, avoid or resist you. Think about it, would you lie-down if someone was intimidating you and coming in to your space or would you choose to move?

If your dog is confused in this way, you need to use the blocking technique I described previously. It may take several minutes, but as you do this, you will see your dog change his attitude and become less agitated and more settled. Once he is responding and thinking about what you require, ask for a *lie-down* in a calm, quiet voice. Your dog will feel more comfortable because he is receiving a clear, consistent message that he understands. He will therefore be more willingly to accept your vocal command.

The handler uses inappropriate pressure

Another common problem is when the handler reprimands every misdemeanor no matter how minor with excessive pressure. Furthermore, the handler always maintains a dominant stance throughout the training session. In this scenario, the dog never knows when he is doing the right thing. In response, the dog may rush in and grip the sheep. Then, in anticipation of the handler's response, the dog either moves swiftly out of contact or else starts sniffing the ground indicating avoidance and uncertainty. The problem has arisen because the dog is uncertain when he is correct and also because the handler has never given the dog the opportunity to <u>choose</u> to do the right thing.

If your dog behaves this way, you need to stand by the sheep and watch him carefully. When he starts to drop his shoulder or his facial expression alters indicating that he intends to rush towards his sheep, you need to ask him to consider his actions and to release some of the pressure he is exerting on the sheep. You do this by moving into the block position and, if necessary, raise your hand. Say your dog's name in a low voice. By quietly and assertively blocking your dog, you are really saying 'These are my sheep, consider your options'. If your dog either stops or shifts his weight back onto his hocks, then he is indicating that he is thinking and responding appropriately. In response, you should move backwards and encourage him to walk forward onto his sheep with a steady pace. This release of pressure will make him feel more comfortable and lets him know he has made the correct decision. Even small attempts to do the right thing (small tries) should be rewarded. However, you should not move backwards (release the blocking pressure) unless your dog has attempted to behave correctly.

Julie's Tip. Always remember that pressure tells your dog he is wrong while release tells him that he is correct. It is important to make your dog feel comfortable (remove pressure) when he does the right thing and this, in turn, will encourage him to want to try to please you.

If your dog continues to ignore your block and starts to come forward onto the sheep without your permission, then you have to maintain the block. If necessary you may need to lean forward slightly with your hand slightly more raised. This time growl his name with a low voice. These actions are <u>telling</u> your dog to consider his actions. This problem can take patience to sort. Do not be surprised if initially, your dog starts to push forward too heavily when you start to move backwards. If your dog does this, you need to remind him to give to your pressure before blocking his movement again.

It may seem that much of the training session is spent with you hardly moving at all. However, this calm approach of using repeated, authoritative blocks with appropriate pressure / release gives your dog time to consider his options. Gradually, he will begin to wait until the blocking pressure is released before coming forward. This exercise will also make him think about what you are asking of him and he will develop a more respectful attitude towards both you and the sheep.

The dog becomes dull to pressure

If you do not use the 'ask, tell, insist' technique, but rather always insist and then do not release pressure appropriately, your dog will become desensitised to the continual high intensity. This can become a vicious circle because you think you need to use even more pressure to achieve the same response. What you are really doing to your dog is similar to someone nagging at you all the time: eventually you will just switch off, and stop listening, ignoring the wishes of the other person.

In human-dog interactions, this often happens when a dog pulls on the lead and does not respond to repeated tugs from his owner who is attempting to get his dog to walk by his side. The owner responds by then holding his dog continually on a short, tight chain. This keeps maintained pressure on the dog and, because there is no release, the dog never feels comfortable. He therefore does not know what his owner wants. Instead he just learns to ignore the reprimand and just carries on pulling. To sort this problem out, the handler needs to maintain a calm, relaxed attitude plus ensure that there is no tension on the lead when his dog is walking correctly. This shows the dog that walking by his owner's side is more rewarding than pulling forward. When the dog starts to move forward, he needs to be asked in a calm voice to return to the handler's side. This gives the dog the option not to pull. If the dog chooses to ignore this request, then the owner should exert pressure (a short tug with a low growl). As soon as the dog returns to his side, it is important that the handler relaxes and again walks with a loose lead to release

pressure on the dog. This way the dog feels comfortable when he is walking correctly by his owner's side.

In some cases of lead pulling, the desensitisation is so extreme, that the only way to overcome this problem is to alter the pressure point so that the lead attaches to another part of the body. However, this solution will only be temporary if the owner does not combine this new position with correct pressure / release training. Otherwise the only result will be that the dog becomes desensitised to this new position.

The dog may also become dull to pressure when the handler rushes towards him while shouting *lie-down*. In canine communication, body language takes priority over a vocal command and therefore the dog has to react to the handler's actions rather than his words. If the handler continues using this mixed message, eventually the dog will become desensitised to the *lie-down* command and the dog will either ignore the command or else it will make him leave the field. The solution to this problem is described in the section above.

The dog gets anxious from too much pressure

Anxiety is not the same as submission. When the dog is submissive, he has a calm mindset. In contrast, when a dog is anxious, his adrenaline levels rise and he is unable to think clearly.

If your dog starts to get anxious and signals his concern (e.g. by sniffing the ground), you need to release all pressure, coax him back to his work and reassure him that all is well. If needed, his concern maybe soothed by being called into your space (by you turning to the side, crouching down and lowering your eyes) and given a reassuring touch by stroking his cheek. This will settle your dog's mind and lower his adrenaline levels and prevent him from becoming increasingly worried and anxious.

There are differences between a dog starting to show concern and a 'full-blown' anxiety attack. It is important to read the difference. If the dog is showing some concern, then a touch or quiet voice will help steady his mind and calm him down i.e. you are attempting to nip a potential flare-up in the bud. However, once the dog is over-stimulated he may panic and his anxiety will cause him either to flee or to act in an overexcited manner. You do not want to reward a full-blown anxiety attach by stroking him. Instead, once he is in this state, he will need sufficient, appropriately-timed pressure to quickly steady his mind back to a calm, focused state.

If your dog tends to gets anxious, you need to watch his body language and soothe him when he shows the early signs of concern. When you correct your dog, you need to use appropriate pressure. You also need to release the pressure when you see him submit to your wishes. This is important because it allows the dog to realise that a steady, calm submissive attitude is rewarded. As long as you remain calm, confident and encouraging, your dog will be reassured that all is well.

Moving on

Every dog is different and the dog's natural temperament combined with the way he is brought up will determine how he responds to you and to the different situations that he encounters during his working life. However, if you listen to your dog and communicate using the language he instinctively understands, then he will quickly learn to trust and respect you as his pack leader. Despite this, I find that there are some common problems that many inexperienced handlers face when they train a sheepdog and I will discuss these in the next chapter.

Anecdote. Fluffy: my feline protector

I train many different handlers and dogs at Carcant and I can usually assess the energy and mindset of the dog from the moment it arrives. However, I still take new dogs into the round pen without sheep so I can further assess and establish any ground rules in a safe and controlled environment. During these initial sessions, I often see my cat Fluffy sitting on the pen's perimeter fence watching events unfold. Sometimes, she moves off shortly after the start, but there are other times when I cannot get rid of her and in a few instances she has been a complete nuisance as she tries to distract the dog away from me.

On one of these initial assessment sessions, I was working with a client who needed guidance on how to manage her excitable pet border collie. She felt that he was becoming completely unpredictable and unmanageable. Being fully aware that my cat was not going to be safe near such a dog, I tried to insist that Fluffy went into the house. However, she completely refused and all I could do was shoo her in the direction of the barn. As my session started, I quickly realised that the collie was not just over excitable but that he also had a dominant temperament. At the same time, I heard Fluffy making a high pitched screeching sound behind me. Simultaneously, the dog's body language started to change as he took up a more dominant stance. In response, I took up a blocking position. I could feel and see the dog's energy and aggression increase even though I was not actively confronting him. I knew that whatever happened, he must not believe that I would submit to him. If he thought this then he would probably have bitten me. I therefore demonstrated my inner control by displaying a calm, confident authority that made the dog start to consider to give to my authority.

Throughout my encounter with the dog, Fluffy continued to grumble and spit at him Out of the corner of my eye, I could see my cat sitting on the gate staring wide-eyed and angrily at him with her hair standing on end as she screamed and hissed like a demented banshee. In a moment of dread, I thought that the dog was definitely going to attack my cat and my body pumped with adrenaline as I realised that I had no choice but

to increase the pressure on him. My eyes became wide with intent as I stared directly at him, my body became rigid and tense to display my dominant position. I even growled as the adrenaline surge gave me an extra boost of energy. After a short stand-off, the dog stepped back and showed submissive gestures before sitting well away from my cat and me.

In hindsight, I realise that Fluffy had read the dog's intentions from the moment the client and collie entered the yard. My cat considered that she was there to protect and support me: she would not leave me alone in what she perceived was a dangerous situation. Ever since, when a new dog and owner come onto the farm for training, I look at my cat to gauge her reaction. Fluffy tells me what I need to know.

Chapter 3
Insight and Enlightenment

When I started working with sheepdogs over thirty years ago, I had little stock sense and my understanding of the predator/prey interaction between sheep and dog was limited. My lack of knowledge often resulted in me getting into difficult situations. For example, my dog would rush in to grip the sheep or else the stock would try to escape and consequently flee into a river or break through a fence. I knew that the fault was either mine or my dogs, but in those distant days, I did not know what to do to solve the problem. Looking back I realise that my inexperience and inability to read the situation properly meant that I missed the cues that my dog and sheep were sending me. In addition, I would then often make the situation worse by putting pressure on my dog and sheep at the wrong time and in the wrong place.

I have now spent many years learning the subtle communication signals that dogs and sheep continually relay between each other and also use as they talk to me. This insight and enlightenment has enabled me to develop The Natural Way training technique that in turn promotes a strong partnership between my dog and myself that is founded on mutual trust, loyalty and respect. Moreover, this approach has meant that all types of dog from dominant to submissive, and sensitive to tough are content to work with me.

In addition, my own past experiences mean that I also appreciate the issues that new handlers often face. Many of these are based on a few common underlying problems that if understood and addressed can dramatically improve all aspects of how the novice handler interacts with his or her dog.

Understand your dog

Learning to understand what your dog is telling you and developing a **feel** for your dog are both fundamental if you want to appreciate why your dog behaves the way he does. Your dog will signal his intent through his body language just before he acts. If you respond appropriately to these signs then you will find that you communicate much more effectively with him and, in return, your dog will start behaving as you would like him to. You will not develop this insight overnight. You need to be prepared to take time, both during and after your training sessions, to analyse yourself,

your dog, the stock and the situation. To help you on this path, I recommend that you look carefully at the body language of the dogs, handlers and sheep in the different pictures throughout this book and read the captions to see my interpretation of what is happening in each illustration. Also consider videoing yourself working with your dog. Do not use too many close-up shots, instead try to capture the whole picture. Watch the playback carefully and focus on what you, your dog and the sheep are doing. If your sheep flee or your dog grips, look what happens before the event. What were you doing? When did the sheep start to get unsettled? What signals did your dog give before he acted? What could you have done differently to help your dog?

Julie's Tip. Your dog can teach you a great deal if you are willing to open your eyes and your mind.

Remember, no matter how domesticated humans have made our canine companions, your dog retains his evolutionary instinct to be a member of a hunting pack that needs to kill prey in order to survive. If you want your dog to be work stock effectively then you need to control these predatory instincts. Furthermore, if you wish to gain your dog's respect, it is imperative that you are the Alpha of the pack. If your dog considers that you are his leader then he will want to work in partnership with you and be willing to take your commands.

Gaining respect is very different from traditional obedience training. In obedience training, the indoctrination is often 'black and white'. By this I mean that the dog is either right or wrong. Training a sheepdog using these methods tends to create a so-called **mechanical** dog that waits for commands and is not allowed to think on his own.

I need my dog to be able to work his stock safely when he is out of my sight and also be willing to make a split second decision to stop a sheep from breaking away from the flock. Therefore I need my dog to use his own initiative. If you want this from your dog too, then you will find that there are grey areas where you, as the handler, have to give or take. I firmly believe that both you and your dog will benefit if you do this.

'But,' I hear you cry, 'If I allow my dog to do what he considers is okay, then how can I be the Alpha of the pack?' Well, personally, I believe a handler has control of the situation when his dog is capable of making his own decision that helps you manage your flock. As part of this partnership, he should automatically adapt his energy levels to manage the sheep in a stress-free manner.

It is important that we keep this talent in the shepherd's dog and it is one of the reasons why I feel so passionately that we must breed from dogs that can work on the hill and not just from **man-made** dogs that have been trained only to compete on a trial field.

In addition, I find that The Natural Way teaches a dog how to control his emotions, energy and instinct. The pressure / release techniques described throughout this book will let you show your dog how to balance and feel his sheep so that the flock are managed in a stress-free manner.

Teaching a dog to use his initiative

Remember, giving commands for guidance is different from controlling all movement. If you act as a dictator towards your dog and insist that nothing is done without command, then he will not respond to sheep unless he is told it is okay to do so. Eventually, your dog will lose the ability to act on his own initiative. Do you really want your dog to let sheep escape because you told him to *lie-down* and he is too worried to move to stop them without your command?

I use pressure / release techniques to show the dog where he needs to be and how to feel his sheep. I use my eyes, my facial expression, the way I carry myself and how I move to indicate to him when he is right and also when he is wrong. These subtle cues encourage him to balance and move the sheep in a relaxed manner.

Combined with natural work, this method allows the dog to become confident and feel his sheep properly. Together, these also encourage my dog to use his initiative and to make the appropriate decision to suit the situation and the type of stock he is working.

This is very different from obedience training when the handler strives for precision and insists that the dog mindlessly reacts, no matter what the sheep are doing. This obedience-based approach often puts pressure on the dog and produces one that believes it is wrong to think for himself. I believe that you can achieve better results for both farm work and on the trial field, if you help your dog learn how to make the right choice for himself.

In order for this technique to work, it is vital that you also have a good understanding of sheep so that you can help your dog make the correct decision.

Julie's Tip. Do not expect an instantaneous improvement. Look for signs of that your dog is attempting to respond appropriately (that your dog is trying for you). Then gradually and steadily build on this.

Repeating exercises often helps a dog absorb information. However if you control and demand precision all of the time then the pressure will increase on your dog and there will come a time when he either stops listening to you or else explodes (for example, rushes in and grips) in order to release it. If your dog lacks confidence, then forcing perfection may make him not want to work with you.

Anecdote. Pack Dynamics 1. Flash: a dog with no pack social manners

Dogs who grow up within a pack are taught by their elders how to live together in a stable environment without resorting to unnecessary physical fights. The pack cannot survive without maintaining harmony and so when a dog enters the pack that does not respect the usual rules it can unsettle the group and may lead to aggressive conflict. In the past, I often have taken other people's dogs in my kennels to train. I always let the dog settle with me before introducing him to the rest of the pack. Flash, a self assured, quiet and confident two year old entire male, had good manners around humans. However, when he was introduced to the pack, it was quickly apparent that he had poor social skills when interacting with other canines. Rather than posturing his status as a dog with a balanced mind would do, he went straight into an aggressive physical attack. This caused significant disruption as my more dominant pack members wanted to retaliate in a similar fashion. I quickly had to assert significant pressure towards Flash to enforce my position as Alpha and demand he back off and get out of all my dogs' spaces. I did this by using a dominant posture with a powerful determined intimidatory stare. At the same time, I used my body language to quietly insist that my own dogs moved behind me so that I was completely in control of the situation. I maintained a sufficient physical presence targeted towards Flash until he showed some submissive gestures and started to indicate that he wished to negotiate with me. This took about 5 - 10 minutes. Once Flash's mindset had calmed, I let him approach the pack, but I ensured that he was close to me and directly under my influence. My overt assertive stance combined with a hard stare were sufficient to control the situation. I did not need to put any dog on a lead, nor lock any away, nor use any other physical means to control the situation: the dogs, including Flash, knew from my energy that I was a force to be reckoned with. However, for several weeks after this event, whenever Flash's body language indicated that he could potentially become aggressive, I would pre-empt any escalation by stepping into his space. This reminded him to mind his manners and respect his place in the pack.

Anecdote. Pack Dynamics 2. Joe: an insubordinate youngster

Joe was a 10 month old, friendly exuberant pet collie who had grown up in a family home. Because of his age and nature, I did not think there would be any significant issue when he joined the pack. Indeed, at a superficial level, initially everything seemed to be going smoothly. However, because his previous owners had not set strict enough boundaries to teach him how to behave, Joe was disrespectful and insubordinate to the other dogs. In response to this altered dynamic within the pack, Ban, one of my older, more intuitive males became anxious and tried to gain my attention by persistently getting under my feet. By doing this, Ban was acting as a pacifier. He was trying to divert my attention away from the other dogs and diffuse any potential aggression that I, as the Alpha in the pack, might show towards to the disrespectful Joe. This behaviour was similar to that shown in the pictures on page 9 where submissive Pip places herself as a pacifier in front of dominant Tig. The moral of this tale is that our dogs are very sensitive to energy and from experience they can predict what may happen and will act to try to pre-empt an unwanted event.

Anecdote. Pack Dynamics 3. Interaction with two different packs

Although individual members of my pack are not all related, they act as a tightly knit family. Outsiders will only be accepted if they respect the pack rules and hierarchy. Introducing an individual dog has its own issues depending on the attitude and nature of the dog. In contrast, when two packs meet, it brings a whole new dynamic to both groups. The first couple of times that my friend Pen came to Carcant, we kept our two packs separate and exercised them apart so that although they could see and smell each other they could not physically interact. However, as Pen started to stay for longer periods we gradually introduced both packs to each other so that they could be exercised together. Obviously, for harmony to be maintained, the dogs have to accept the new hierarchy of the larger pack and so we ensured these initial meetings occurred under close supervision and we each took responsibility for our own dogs' behaviour, pre-empting events and checking any inappropriate manners before anything could escalate. Now, because the two packs are familiar with each other, the transition period is very short and it only takes a greeting for the two sets to recognise each other before they are content to exercise together. However, any new member of either pack has to also accept the hierarchy of the larger group. One day, Kim who is my Alpha bitch, approached Pen when she had her new young bitch Pip by her side. Although Pip is a submissive member of Pen's pack, she decided she should try to protect her owner from Kim. In response, Kim signalled her annoyance because she considered that Pip was not respecting her senior status in the larger joint pack. Even though she clearly was not comfortable with the more dominant dog, Pip believed that her leader (Pen) would support her (Pip's) stance so she stood her ground and postured to Kim to move out of her pack's space. To stop any escalation, Pen checked Pip's behaviour and I told Kim to move away. A short while later, Kim approached Pip when she was not by Pen's side. Pip immediately submitted and rolled onto her back whilst Kim stood dominant over her. Later that day as Kim and I returned from checking the flock on the moor, we met Pen and Pip who had been checking the sheep in the fields. As we approached, Pip started sniffing the ground to demonstrate that she was not a threat and Kim ignored her, content that the correct hierarchy had once again been established.

You must remember that dogs automatically consider that the humans they live with are their pack and they will often try to protect the group no matter what their status within in. If two packs meet (e.g. on a walk), it is important that the humans read the situation properly and control their own dog's behaviour if harmony is to be maintained.

Do not worry if your dog is not always perfect. When he makes an error, for example flanks tightly then you should just give a slight corrective nudge (either vocally or via body language) that shows him that although his movement was not perfect, it still was not so wrong that it required firmer pressure. By modulating your own response and altering the amount of pressure you put onto your dog, he will learn that there is a scale of mistakes and some misdemeanors are not as bad as others. This approach allows your dog to develop an understanding about his work and enables him to enjoy his training.

Learning to think like a sheep

As well as communicating with your dog, you also need to develop sheep sense. Understanding why sheep behave a certain way will help you predict events before they happen and allow you to control the situation rather than just reacting to it. For example, if you focus too much on your dog and the sheep move away, then the inexperienced dog may end up chasing the sheep rather than gathering them. Sheep will tend to pull towards certain areas, such as gates or sheep in neighbouring fields and, if they are allowed, they will tend to run in that direction. This also will inevitably encourage an inexperienced dog to give chase. So, when you are starting with a young dog try work away from these and instead keep your sheep in an area where they will settle.

Similarly, understanding what sheep are thinking will help you shepherd your flock effectively and also should make your trial runs less stressful for all concerned. Take penning as an example. Here, the sheep will see you and your dog as a predatory pack and the pen as a trap. They want to find a safe haven. However, because they are being trapped between the 'predators' and a small confined space, they will feel tense, and uncertain. You need to convince the sheep that the safest place is inside the pen. However, if the sheep are at the mouth of the pen and you push too hard before the sheep are ready, then, in their stressed state, they will break out past you and your dog. Instead, you need to read your sheep, give them time to settle and then block their movement to indicate to them that there is no escape in either your or your dog's direction. Similar to the block position described in the previous chapter, this block should be in a neutral position that neither exerts pressure nor gives way to pressure.

Once you give the sheep time to consider their options, they will realise that the safest place is the pen and often they will then turn and walk in quietly.

Both dogs and sheep will learn by association and repetition. Because my sheep have learnt that a whistle will mean that a dog will appear shortly to gather them, my sheep will start to flock together as soon they hear one. In fact, when I am out checking them on the farm and I see a group of sheep in the distance, I sometimes use a particular whistle command just to encourage them to flock together. This enables me to see if any are lagging behind and may be in trouble. Similarly, when you are training you will find that sheep that are moved around a field in the same direction, or fed in the same place, or repeatedly penned, will learn what you want. This does not mean that they are guaranteed to do what you want, but sheep that are used to dogs will be much easier to manage than those that only rarely see a dog.

Working naturally
Ban steadily brings sheep behind me.

Working naturally

As my dog progresses through his training, I intermingle formal sessions with the opportunity to work naturally. For example during a training session, I may walk around the field and allow my dog to bring the sheep behind me. Alternatively, I may take a young dog with me to do an easy shepherding chore. When letting an inexperienced dog work naturally, I always keep an eye on both him and the sheep. Even when I am walking with the sheep and dog behind me, I will continually monitor the situation out of the corner of my eye to ensure that my dog is feeling his sheep properly. If he stops thinking, he will either push onto the sheep or else run off contact. If he pushes, I would nudge him with appropriate body language and some vocal correction to remind him to use the right attitude. If he loses contact, I would stop moving and encourage him to walk onto his sheep and back into contact with them.

All dogs are different, and you need to decide with each one how much you can let him learn through work and how much you need to show him what is required. My Moss dog loved to work, and would put every ounce of effort he could into it. In contrast, he did not like me schooling him in training exercises. Moss taught me that I had to give and take more; thank goodness I saw the light, or else he would not have gone on to win the International Supreme title. I used to compete with Moss straight off his work: the only preparation was to ensure that his responses were in tune with what I asked for. Moss and I were a powerfully, closely bonded team as I am now with my current dogs. If you wish to achieve this harmony with your dog, you need to take the time to understand each other perfectly.

There is a fine line between the dog pleasing himself and working naturally. For example when a sheep bolts, you want your dog to turn her and bring her back, even if you have not commanded him. This requires quick thinking from your dog. So in this scenario, it would not matter if you have asked your dog to *lie-down* and he still runs to turn the escaping ewe: his actions demonstrate that he is thinking. You do not want to take this ability out of him, you just need to be able to control it when necessary.

On occasions when I did not want an escaping sheep to be turned, I would respond quickly to the event and use more authority in my command. The tone of my voice and my body language would clearly tell my dog that I really did not want the ewe stopped.

How much pressure is the right amount?

I find that novice handlers often find it difficult to know when they should insist on a command being obeyed. I have already spoken of the three step graded approach to using pressure: **ask** then **tell** and only finally **insist** if it really necessary. Do not forget that each dog is different, so you need to study your dog's body language carefully to determine his mentality and how he copes with pressure. Some dogs need gentle correction followed by encouragement whilst others need stronger correction and firm handling. Similarly, the scale of the problem will also be different. I consider things like a tight flank, not taking a flank, or not completely stopping when asked to be small problems. In contrast, others, like harming a sheep, are big issues. Chasing a sheep with no intention to injure the stock is not as bad as chasing with intent to harm – but both still need correcting. If you have a dog who chases sheep in order to harm them, then you must change his mindset if you are ever going to be able to trust him. Similarly, if your dog starts to take advantage and pushes more than is acceptable then you need to remind him of your relative status in the hierarchy and reassert your authority before retesting his willingness to work sensibly. You may well find that your attempts do not work first time. This does not mean that you are never going to succeed. Analyse the way that you dealt with the situation, look at your dog's response and then alter how you use pressure / release and try again.

When a dog is listening to you, his ear is turned slightly so that it is focused towards you. In addition, a dog which hesitates is often thinking and one that gives submissive signs such as turning his head away when you increase pressure is also indicating that he is listening to you.

Some dogs will look towards you to work out what you want. However, you do not want to encourage this too much as it will take his concentration away from his sheep. To help overcome this issue, position yourself where the dog can see you. This will enable him to keep his eyes on both the sheep and you at the same time. As he becomes more confident and begins to understand the task you require, the less he will need to look at you for confirmation.

In contrast a defiant dog will often show signs of disrespect towards you both when he is away from stock as well as when he is working. During work, your dog may show insubordination by becoming so fully engrossed in the sheep that he does not acknowledge or listen to you. In fact you may just seem to be 'in his way'. Similarly, tightening his flanks or giving very fast and erratic movements can often indicate that the dog does not consider you to be his leader. I find that when a dog has this attitude it has often been created by the handler using pressure / release incorrectly.

Remember, fight creates fight! If you are always putting pressure on your dog, demanding through voice and body language, then he has no choice but either to fight back by resisting you or else move out of contact to avoid any confrontation with you.

One way of putting incorrect pressure on your dog is by shouting at him too much. This can make him frustrated and can often have the opposite effect to the one you intend. In addition, over time he will become immune to the high volume, so this is another reason why continually shouting will also have no effect. You need to vary the volume and pitch of your voice to achieve a good response from your dog. Work mainly with a quiet, calm settled voice. When you need to reprimand your dog, increase your tone and volume gradually: do not start too loud, or else you will have nowhere to go. Use an authoritative, sharper manner and louder volume only when you really need it.

Every dog will need a different level of authority to control his behaviour. If your dog has become immune to you, then 'ask' gently. However, when he does not give immediately to this, move directly to an 'insist' until he learns to respond to the 'ask' again. In contrast, if your dog is very sensitive then you may find that an 'ask'... 'ask'...gentle 'tell' may be sufficient to get the proper response. If you have desensitized your dog to pressure by using excessive body language or over-loud vocal commands then you need to re-establish a proper pressure / release framework. By this I mean that when you exert pressure of any kind and the dog responds with even just a small try, then you must reward (release pressure) immediately. It is important that your dog feels comfortable when he is correct. Releasing pressure tells him he has made the correct decision. Your dog needs to know this and he will begin to understand that you are now going to listen to him. In return, your dog will start to relax. Pressure after pressure only tells your dog that he is always wrong.

Similarly, waving your arms about can also have unwanted affect. Your dog can see very small gestures of movement, you do not need to exaggerate these in order for your dog to pick up your cues. In fact, often exaggerated movements stimulate and overexcite your dog so that he thinks you are encouraging him to play rather than focus on his work. Try to use subtle signals to achieve the desired effect from your dog.

Mixed messages

There are a number of ways that you can confuse your dog. One common way is when your intention and your body language do not match. A dog responds primarily to your body language and will react in a certain way to a given body stance or gesture. For example, if you use body movement to teach the flank, then your dog will learn to move in response to this movement. So far, so good. The problem starts when you actually want your dog to *lie-down* and stay put, but then you turn and move. Your dog interprets your movement to mean 'Oh, my Alpha is asking me to move again' and so he moves. It is not surprising, if he gets confused when you then turn and shout at him for moving – because from his perspective, he did exactly what your body language asked him to!

Your dog is not a mind reader, you need to tell him what you want in a language he understands. If your require your dog to stay while you move, you need to raise your hand to block his movement and give the *lie-down* command at the same time as you slowly move away. This will teach your dog that when you do not want him to react to one particular aspect of your body language (e.g. moving away), you will give him an additional command (hand signal to block and vocal command to lie-down) to tell him what you want.

Although dogs cannot read your mind, they are much better than humans at understanding body language and feeling the energy that all animals portray. If you feel worried and uncertain when you go to train your dog, then he will pick up on this. It will depend on your dog's nature how he responds to your anxiety. He may become tense and anxious himself which could then make him do silly things such as rush in and grip sheep. Alternatively, he could take advantage of the situation and try to take over. In order to improve the situation, you need to relax and portray that you are an assured, confident handler who is worthy to be your dog's pack leader. Similarly, if you go to train your dog when you are in a bad mood, your dog will pick up on your aggressive attitude and again may behave out of character.

I do not recommend that you train your dog when you are in this frame of mind and never take your anger out on your dog. It can be very counterproductive.

Confusion from the handler may also confuse the dog. If you mix up your commands, then you cannot be surprised when your dog flanks in any direction that suits him – how does he know that you are correct this time? A typical problem for the inexperienced handler is to think that *away* is 'right' and *come-bye* is 'left'. Okay, that is fine when the dog is sent out to gather sheep, but once the gather is accomplished, the dog is now facing the handler, so the dog's left is now the handler's right and vice versa so now what is the correct command? When I started, I also struggled with this problem and I, too, felt like pulling my hair out many a time. What I eventually found worked for me was forgetting about my own left and right, and concentrating on the dog's left and right instead. In this way, it did not matter whether the dog was facing me or driving away. Another simple method which works for a lot of people is to remember that **C**ome-bye begins with **C**, when the dog is going **C**lockwise, and *Away* begins with **A**, when the dog is going Anti-clockwise. You need to identify a method that works for you and then be consistent when you ask your dog to do something.

Anecdote. We all make mistakes: we should try to learn from them

One of my earlier dogs, Bess, was quite headstrong when she was young and though she wanted to please me, she also had a stubborn side when pushed. Back then my nature was similar to hers. And so when it came to teaching the flank command, we had a clash of personalities.

In those days, although I believed that I had a lot of patience to teach something, it frayed very quickly if I thought the dog was not trying or was fighting me. Bess and I clashed over her left (*come-bye*) flank. She did not always give me an arced flank, instead she used to test me and try to cut the flank. One day she completely refused this flank and I could not understand why - I just considered that she was defying me.

So we stayed out in the field for a long time arguing over it. It was clear we both were determined that each of us was correct. I became frustrated and angry and she would just stare at me and stick in her heels whilst refusing to flank freely. Eventually I had to accept that Bess would only grudgingly flank to the left.

Later while I was lying there in bed assessing my bad day and feeling guilty about arguing with my dog, I suddenly felt sick because I realised that I was the stupid one. My dog was not fighting me, she was trying to tell me that I had been giving her mixed messages. My voice was saying *come-bye* but my body was saying *away*. All she had been trying to do was tell me that I was not making sense. It was my fault.

I rushed out to her kennel and spent the next hour squatting down and cuddling her as I asked for forgiveness. She must of thought 'This women is crazy.' Next time, I promised myself, I will listen to my dog – it's a lesson I've tried never to forget.

Your dog reads your energy and intent

A A client lifts her stick and darts forward to try to push her dog out. However, the lowered shoulders and chasing actions act to excite the dog. **B** The dog responds by diving in closer to the sheep trying to nip them. **C** As I walk to assist the client, the dog has already responded by moving a short distance from the sheep. She has laid down and turned her head away indicating that she does not want to confront me. **D** As I quietly and assertively put pressure on the dog through my body posture and direct, stern gaze, the dog gives appropriately and moves even further out of my space. Notice how my square body stance and direct stern gaze compares with the clients relaxed posture and smile.

Avoiding the issue

When I teach new handlers, it sometimes feels as if that the words '*lie-down, lie-down, lie-down*' echo repeatedly in my ears. If the *lie-down* command is given in an insistent manner, the dog will believe that he is doing something wrong and he will probably think it is because he is not stopping fast enough. This tone can worry certain types of dogs and they start to feel uncomfortable when asked to lie-down.

In addition, control with the *lie-down* command is often the inexperienced handler's attempt to deal with a problem. In reality, this approach means that the handler is avoiding the issue rather than confronting it. For example, if your dog is pushing hard on the lift and you growl *lie-down* before your dog makes contact with the sheep or after he has startled them into flight then is the *lie-down* command really telling your dog he is pushing too hard and needs to change this behaviour? Or are you telling him just to lie-down?

Similarly, I often find that many handlers will not confront a dog that repeatedly grips sheep. Instead he tries to avoid the problem by holding the dog back off the stock. If you train your dog in this fashion, then it's not surprising if he does not understand that he needs to think about his sheep and make adjustments to hold them together so he can fetch them all in an appropriate manner.

Remember that your dog will inevitably need to work close to his sheep at some point. If your dog has never been told that gripping is unwanted behaviour, you will find that he will still tend to grip when he gets excited as he nears the sheep.

Just as some people will avoid confronting issues, so too will some types of dog try to steer clear of certain situations rather than face up to them. For example, if the dog is worried about working close to his handler, he will tend to go **into orbit**. By this I mean that he runs very wide and often refuses to look at the stock. The result is that the dog loses contact with his sheep who can then do as they please. In these cases, the handler has to soften his body language and reactions in order to give the dog confidence that it is safe to work closer in contact with the stock.

Julie's Tip. When a dog shows inappropriate behaviour, it is important to confront it. You need to use pressure / release properly to show him that this is unacceptable. If you do not do this then your dog will think his actions are acceptable. Your dog will not learn if you either ignore the problem or else use distraction tactics to divert his attention.

Moving on

There are so many things to think about when training a shepherd's dog that it can be daunting to a new handler. Similarly, the mental exercise will also cause your dog to fatigue much more quickly than he would do otherwise. Do not overdo the training sessions. Continuous repetition, without time to stop, may make your dog refuse to work or may make him act like an automaton who can only do what he is told (as he believes that thinking for himself is wrong). Your dog needs time to absorb what he is being taught, so short sessions are better. Training a sheepdog will take time. Sometimes, when you analyse the situation, you may come to the conclusion that it is best to take a step back, let the dog relax and give him time to mature before requesting too much.

I have found that The Natural Way is a successful training method for all types of dog, no matter what their temperament is. However, as a hill farmer and sheepdog triallist, I prefer to work with Border Collies. In the next chapter I will describe the different characteristics and traits that I look for in this unique and exceptional breed.

Fact Box. Some examples of how you can confuse your dog

Inappropriate pressure: These include:

- Putting pressure on the dog when he is doing the right thing.
- Not releasing pressure from your dog when he is starting to respond to your request. If you do not release the pressure when you see him starting to respond, he will become confused or worried. Do not expect him to be perfect straight away, he will need to learn and build up to the response that you require.
- If you over correct every time your dog commits a minor offence. Do not be surprised if he refuses to work for you. Would you respect a handler who did this and be happy to obey? Or would you learn to flinch from doing the task?

Giving an emphasized flank command when a small flank was required, and then over correcting the dog for (correctly) giving a large flank. Try to keep your commands consistent and pitched at an appropriate level for what you wish your dog to do.

Mixed messages: These include:

- Mixing up flank commands.
- Teaching your dog to move to balance sheep to you when you move but then subsequently moving while expecting him to stay without telling him to hold his lie-down.
- Giving an inappropriate fast voice or whistle command causing the dog to either dart at the sheep or grip.
- If you do not show your dog the difference between a stop and a steady, then sooner or later he will not respond differently to these commands and may just ignore both.
- Shouting *lie-down* whilst moving towards him (this pressure is actually telling him to get out of your space).

Others: These include:

If you do not wean your dog off body language, he will become reliant and require that you always use it. For instance, if you block your dog with body language to stop him and do not wean to voice, then he will only stop when he is physically blocked. However, keep body language in reserve in case you need to reinforce a vocal command.

- If the body language you use when training your dog on sheep is exactly the same as you would use in playing a game with him then you cannot be surprised when your dog treats training as a game. You have to help your dog distinguish between 'Now is play time' from 'Now you need a focused attitude for work.'
- If you spoil your dog too much, you cannot be surprised when he acts as though he is more important than you.

Anecdote. We never stop learning if we open our eyes to see

I thought I had seen most things when it comes to dog behaviour around sheep, but Lucy gave me something else to consider. Lucy is a confident, balanced and emotionally stable bitch who lives in Chicago with her owner, Rich, and one other dog. They obviously mean the world to each other and are completely inseparable. When I met them recently at a clinic, I felt that harmony in the pack was usually maintained because Lucy was such a benevolent and calm leader!

The problem had arisen when Lucy and Rich started a new hobby of working sheep together. This new interest had awakened a whole set of instincts in Lucy. However, Rich, being a city dweller, was much slower to comprehend what drove Lucy and the result was that neither could understand the other.

I observed the pair of them work at the clinic. Similar to most novice handlers, Rich used pressure incorrectly. Lucy, in response, tried to deal with the situation by either rushing directly at the sheep or else she tried to avoid the pressure by eating sheep manure. Rich sent Lucy on an outrun and to my amazement, I suddenly saw Lucy pick up a tennis ball that she found lying in the grass. She then completed her run and continued to gather the small group of ewes still with the ball in her mouth. As the session progressed, I could see her chomp slightly on the ball every time she became anxious about Rich's demands. She seemed to be using it to control her stress levels. The overall effect was that chewing the ball kept Lucy calm, which in turn placated Rich. At the end of the session they both walked off the field with broad smiles across their faces.

Rich said afterwards that she had never done anything like this before. In addition, experienced sheepdog triallists who I have spoken to afterwards have not fully believed the story. However, I think Lucy knew she was stressed because she could not get Rich to listen and she had been fortunate to find her own way to deal with the difficult situation. Obviously, the option Lucy chose is not going to work for the majority of dogs. However, episodes like this remind me just how versatile the border collie is when it comes to finding a solution to a problem and that I too can continue to learn from them.

From the Clinic

Handler: My dog is strong headed, dominant and always wants to fight me. I want my dog to *lie-down* when I tell him to.

I observed that as the handler walked her dog towards the sheep she kept on lying him down, forbidding any freedom. She applied pressure on her dog each time he was asked to *lie-down* and the dog started sniffing the ground indicating he was concerned. As the dog was asked to walk forward again, the dog's tail was tightly tucked up to his belly his ears was flat back, his eyes were wide and his demeanour was stiff. In addition, the handler had tension and worry written all over her face. Her body stance was dominant and also showed signs of aggression, but at the same time, her uncertainty was evident. Her walk was ridged and jerky. When her dog was finally able to work the sheep, he rushed around to relieve his pent up energy. This resulted in the handler chasing her dog with a pipe shouting at him to lie-down. This body language put even more pressure on the dog forcing him to run wider away from the sheep. Her behaviour meant he had no choice but to ignore the spoken *lie-down* command.

After I had worked with the dog for a few minutes, it became apparent to me that not only did he avoid pressure, but he had also become dull to pressure. I think this was probably because his owner had previously forced him to come back to her when she was angry. I found that when I put sufficient appropriate pressure onto him, he submitted. However, as I moved into his space and asked him to give to the pressure, he responded inappropriately. Instead of yielding an appropriate distance, he ran wide, lost contact with the sheep and no longer listened to me. All this indicated to me that the dog was panicking and had run away as part of the flight response.

My opinion: Both owner and dog were highly anxious. In addition, both were feeding off the other's emotions. The owner obviously was worried that she would lose control. This had caused her to put pressure on her dog and when he resisted or avoided this pressure, she became more uptight, panicky and the anger grew as her adrenaline levels surged. This made her apply pressure inappropriately and she had never released that pressure even when her dog had made the right decision. The result was that the dog was easily put into either a fight-or-flight mode. He was never given an opportunity to feel comfortable which in turn had meant he never was able to relax and focus on his work. Furthermore, her dog had sensed her heightened adrenaline levels which then stimulated his own to rise and resulted in him acting irrationally.

My advice: The owner should try to time all her gestures so that they were in response to the dog's <u>actual</u> behaviour and not to what she thought her dog may do. By relaxing and giving the appropriate pressure / release gestures, her dog had time to think about the situation. This gave him time to consider his options and he now was able to make the correct decision. As the owner saw her dog improve, so she also relaxed, which in turn gave her dog more confidence. Over time, this change in how the owner communicated with her dog, gave him the opportunity to understand, relax, trust and, most of all, respect his leader.

Anecdote. Working with a 'dyslexic' dog

Gail* was a recent case that once again reminded me to listen to my dogs. Training the flank commands to Gail was no easy task. If I said go one way, she would go the other. She did not seem to think, she just ran. I became increasingly frustrated with her as I spent weeks and weeks working with her and gained very little improvement. The problem worsened, and to top it all, she was becoming increasingly anxious about training with me and this just exacerbated the issue.

I suddenly remembered Bess (see anecdote on opposite page). I was certain she was looking down at me saying 'Hey you! Remember me and what I taught you.' I did do a lot of thinking to try and work out what was at the back of the problem. I started to think that Gail suffered from the dog equivalent of human dyslexia and she was just unable to understand what I was trying to teach her. If this were the case, then how should I continue to train her? What can I learn from this? What would I advise another handler to do?

Fighting with my own nature, I started to wonder whether I should just take a step back. I decided to take the pressure off completely: no formal training, just relaxed work and when I did ask for a flank then I would allow Gail plenty of time to think before she had to respond. So I let her do plenty of natural work and only threw in a command when I could see she was relaxed, thinking and settled. Of course, I did not expect that by taking this approach she would miraculously understand her flank commands, but after several months, it was obvious we were making progress.

I competed successfully with Gail throughout the nursery season and she came in 2nd in the local league. Not bad for a 'dyslexic' dog!

*This is a different dog from the Gail described in Chapter 18 'My Teachers.'

Be prepared for the unexpected

My dogs and I were moving a group of ewes along a track near to a stream with the intention of crossing another ford further upstream. **A** The dogs and I positioned ourselves to ease the sheep over the stream. **B** I sent Ban to turn the sheep away from the edge and so direct them along the path. **C** I then sent Kim to block them from returning towards me. **D** Ban, Kim and Mac then drove the ewes steadily along the path while I guided them from the opposite bank.

(opposite page) **E** Unfortunately, recent floods had caused the bank to subside and the sheep tried to jump to my side of the stream. **F** I was worried that the ewes may hurt themselves by jumping from a height and so I called Mac and Kim to my side to block the sheep and keep them on the far bank. Throughout the rest of the episode, in order to stop the stock thinking about coming over, I maintained the pressure on my side of the stream by keeping Mac and Kim with me. **G** and **H** I sent Ban through the trees to get ahead of the sheep. **I** One sheep thought about confronting Ban and so I helped him exert pressure on her. **J** Ban and I worked together to encourage the sheep to turn back on the narrow path and return to first ford and safety.

CHAPTER 4
WORKING BORDER COLLIES

Work on a farm is continuous and there is always something that needs doing. In my experience, a fully trained dog makes the various shepherding tasks so much easier and enjoyable that I do not know how others manage their flocks without one. What is more, my dogs listen to me and have the stamina and enthusiasm to work all day. The Natural Way training method teaches my dogs to develop a thorough understanding and feel for their sheep. They know how to use their own initiative in addition to being prompt to take their commands. Whatever the weather, they adjust to the different daily challenges with a calm, steady willingness and unexcited attitude that does not upset their stock. They have the power and stamina to gather the dispersed flock across rough terrain and negotiate a safe route through small streams or around rocks and treacherous boggy ground. My dogs are also alert, agile and precise when ewes need to be shed and held from the rest of the flock for treatment. They have the determination and courage to stand up to a defiant tup (ram) or face up to a sheep protecting her lamb. Furthermore, they are confident to work in confined pens without stressing the stock. Moreover, they also know when they need to control their energy and they will be particularly gentle when they are required to stop a panicking lamb without hurting it.

I choose to work with Border Collies because they are truly versatile dogs who can complete all these farming tasks and more. I look for a dog with natural ability, stamina and fitness, who has a good temperament and that is also trainable and adaptable. My dogs show me loyalty, trust and respect and I give them these in return.

No two dogs are exactly the same, but whatever your dog's character, if you train The Natural Way then you will adapt the amount of pressure and release you use to suit his temperament and talent. Therefore I believe my training method is suitable for all types of dog.

Natural Ability. Some dogs have more natural talent and innate understanding on how to read, balance and move sheep than others. These dogs make the shepherd's job easier because they are usually in the right place at the right time. In contrast, a dog with little natural ability will probably be in the wrong place and will often make the job harder than it should be.

Feel for sheep
Kim instinctively adjusts her stance to suit the stocks intent. **A** The ewe lambs consider confronting Kim, so she lowers her body and stares at them until they back down. **B** The lambs are more unsettled, so Kim turns her head and lowers her gaze to decrease the pressure on then. However she still blocks their escape with her body.

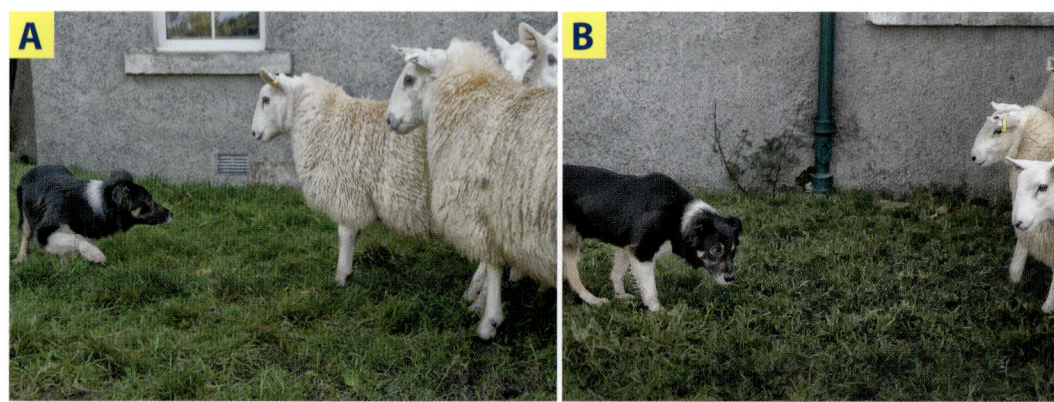

Natural talent requires multiple skills
My dogs need to be versatile and be able to adapt to different situations. They need to be fit, but also show patience when required.

Anecdote. Listen to your dog

One day my dogs and I were gathering strays out on the open hills of Braegrudie in Rogart. I was walking along the ridge and sending my dogs down along the slopes to collect the ewes and bring them up to me. Suddenly Molly stopped and looked under a bush. She remained standing there and no command would pull her off despite my repeated requests that she return to my side. Instead she looked down at the ground and then back at me. I could not see anything amiss from where I was standing, but eventually I gave in and carefully navigated down the hill to where Molly was standing. As soon as I approached my dog ran to my side wagging her tail vigorously before running back to the bush. I looked down and saw a motionless ewe lying quietly in the undergrowth. The sheep had obviously not been able to keep pace with her fitter companions and had hidden under the bush in an attempt to outsmart my dogs. Unfortunately, she had not counted on Molly's sense of smell nor my dog's understanding that I wanted all the sheep. It was worth the additional effort I had to make to reach the ewe to show Molly that I respected her judgement and demonstrate to her that we were indeed a team.

As well as natural ability, I also need a dog that is versatile; can adapt to different situations; use his initiative and is also willingly to take my commands. You can train a dog with less natural ability and a clever trainer will overcome several of his deficits. Some people call this a 'man-made' dog. Although, a dog like this may be good on a trial field and helpful around the farm, he obviously does not carry this training in his genes and any offspring will probably have the same faults.

Moreover, like all things, natural ability is not just black and white, there are different degrees of capability and there are very few dogs who are exceptional in every trait. For example, you may have a dog who can do everything, but has a stubborn attitude and believes that he is always right. Alternatively, you may have a dog with a natural wide cast, a good lift and great natural balance. Despite this, the same dog may never look at lambs or have the guts or strength of character to stand up to a determined ewe who is protecting her lamb. At the end of the day, you need to decide which characteristics in a dog are important to you, which faults you can accept and which you cannot.

Julie's Tip. Not all dogs are equally talented and many cannot reach an advanced stage of training. However, A good handler should be able to bring out the best in any dog, support him it where it is needed and help him reach his full potential.

Fitness and Stamina. Humans make stupid errors when we are physically exhausted Your dog is the same and as he becomes tired, he too will start making mistakes and may either no longer take his commands properly or else do silly things for no obvious reason. Similar to any highly skilled human athlete, a dog needs both fitness and stamina in order to manage all the physical and mental work required on a hill farm. To me, stamina is the dog's innate endurance, resilience and tenacity to work all day. It is passed through the dog's genetics and breeding. No matter how fit the dog, lack of stamina will show up as a weakness when he is under pressure. However, stamina alone is not enough, and just as a top human athlete has to train regularly, so you need to ensure your dog gets sufficient exercise to keep fully fit.

Appearance and Build. Traditionally the working border collie has been bred for its natural working ability rather than for a standard physical appearance and therefore they can vary greatly in their look: from long to short haired, pricked or droopy ears, athletic and whippet-like to solid, sturdy, heavy bodied dogs. Their coat colours can also range from black and white, through tricoloured to the more unusual blue or red merle. As my main considerations for choosing a dog are its character and natural ability rather than how it looks, I have had good working and trial dogs of almost every size, shape and colour. However, if pressed about which build I prefer then I think this has to be a short haired, pricked eared, athletic whippet-like tricolour dog similar to my Tess.

Anecdote. Kim gets on with the job

At Carcant we have a regular routine in the morning. After letting the dogs out for a run and giving them a bite to eat, Bobby and I will feed the sheep that are in the fields near to the house. This is an ideal opportunity to give our young dogs some experience in gathering stock in a work situation, but as we both have our own youngsters to train, Bobby and I will take it in turns to take the feed out to the sheep. On the days that Bobby is feeding sheep, I will usually do odd chores around the farmyard and I often will have one or more of my dogs loose with me as I complete my various tasks. When Kim, my main farm dog, sees Bobby going to get one of his young dogs, she will quickly jump the fence, efficiently gather the sheep to the feed troughs and return to me before I realise that she has left my side. She never does this at any other time of the day. However, her intelligence and experience means that she knows our routine and, as she does not believe that another dog can do the job as well as she does, she just gets on and does it herself. I think Kim is great, but not everyone appreciates her independent spirit.

Temperament can also vary greatly between working border collies. Similar to humans, some are sensitive whilst others are stubborn and hard headed, some are timid and others sulk or are lazy.

You could also have a dog that is keen, but this does not mean that he is determined to fight against the handler, rather he just requires strong handling. Then, there are innately dominant dogs who wish to take control all the time. If you have a dominant dog who does not respect you, then you could have a significant problem on your hands. In this situation, it is important that you interact with your dog away from sheep and establish yourself as the Alpha in the relationship. You need to earn your dog's respect, trust and loyalty by using the communication skills that I described in the previous chapter. In contrast, if you own a submissive dog, then you need to use a gentle approach with minimal pressure that encourages him to gain in confidence as he learns how to work sheep in an appropriate manner.

Trainability. It will make your job as a trainer much easier if your dog has a bubbly personality and wishes to please you, rather than sulk or fight you all the time. Some dogs appear to learn very quickly whilst others take a long time to understand what is required of them. I have trained dogs who seemed to take forever to learn how to flank or drive, but once they realise what is required, they have become very capable working and trial dogs. If your dog is struggling to understand what you want, then it is especially important that you are patient, calm and consistent in your commands and that you do not put undue pressure on him.

As I train each dog, as well as adapting my method to suit his character, I also continually reassess how far I think each can progress and modify my expectations accordingly. Some dogs are definitely more talented than others and a good trainer will take a talented dog to an advanced standard. Personally, I think it is better to accept a dog's limitations and train it to its own limit rather than push it beyond this point. If you attempt to train a dog beyond

his ability, then both your dog and you may become angry and frustrated with neither of you enjoying your work. It is also important while you train that you never ask a young dog to do an old dog's work. This is called **over-facing** the dog, and an example would be when a young inexperienced or timid dog is asked to confront a stroppy ewe. If the dog is uncertain and the ewe comes forward to butt him, then the youngster may lose his confidence to confront sheep in future. If you find yourself in this situation, you should support and encourage your dog by standing nearby and helping to turn the ewe back. Alternatively, you could use a more experienced dog alongside the youngster to give him courage and to show him how to deal with this situation.

Terminology associated with working sheepdogs

Every dog has its own **style** (manner) when they work sheep. There is no absolute specific distance that a working dog should be from his stock, rather the dog needs to position himself at the appropriate place so that he can work his sheep in a controlled yet calm manner. This distance will be determined by the dog's innate level of energy and intent, the type of sheep being worked as well as the weather conditions and the type of terrain that needs to be crossed.

There are a number of terms that are often used to describe a dog's style. Some of these are discussed here while additional terms can also be found in the glossary at the back of the book.

A dog with a **good feel** for sheep instinctively knows how much pressure to apply in different situations and they will adjust their body stance, intent and energy appropriately without command.

Balance is the natural ability of the dog to position himself at the right location and distance from the sheep so that they are held or move at a steady pace in the direction that you want the sheep to be taken. This is often towards you, but could also be towards a gate or a pen. The balance point is often not directly behind the sheep, but rather to one side. The dog will position himself at the **heavy side** of the sheep so that they do not **draw** (pull) along the route they would go if no dog were present. The dog will counteract this draw by positioning himself at the balance point. This way he ensures that the stock move in a straight line in the required direction.

A **good wearing dog** is one that can read the reaction of sheep and work to hold, balance and move (wear) them in the desired direction. This type of dog positions himself appropriately and maintains the correct pressure on the sheep so that they are kept under good control and are kept as unstressed as possible. A dog like this comes into his own when you need to shed one or more sheep away from the flock.

The **eye** of the dog is the instinctive stare that Border Collies and other herding dogs have towards stock. It is this that makes the dog lower his head and front legs into the distinctive 'hunting' crouch as he works his sheep. A dog with plenty of eye seems to control his sheep just by looking at them. Dogs with eye often have balance and look more stylish. A sticky-eyed dog refers to one that has too much eye. This can cause the dog to pull up during his outrun and stop (stick) as he approaches his sheep. Both dog and sheep appear to become transfixed on one another which can make it difficult for either to move in any direction. This type of dog needs to be encouraged to keep moving. This can be done by giving him more freedom on his flanks. It can also help to work him on a larger group of sheep because when he does this, the dog has to continually flank all his sheep in order to cover them and keep them together. His need to do this will motivate him to continue to move more freely and naturally. Too much eye may also make the dog refuse to pull away from the sheep's heavy side. With dogs like this, the more that the sheep draw in a particular direction then the more the dog will become engrossed in them and the less he will listen to his handler's commands.

In contrast, a **loose-(or plain-) eyed dog** tends to flank more easily and is freer in his movement. These type of dog sometimes look less stylish as their eye does not draw their head down. Shepherds who have plenty of flock work sometimes prefer a looser-eyed dog because of their free flanking movement. However, for the same reason, a dog that has little or no eye may find it hard to find the balance point and may require more commands when precision work is required.

A **weakness** is any fault that becomes apparent (or more apparent) in the dog's natural ability or innate character when he works stock. A good trainer will be able to improve many of these, but they will still remain in the dog and can often be observed when the dog is put in a stressful or difficult situation. If the dog is bred from, then these traits may be passed on to future generations of working border collies. A really **weak dog** will keep his distance from sheep because he wants to avoid the possibility that the sheep may confront him. With this kind of dog, the sheep will soon realise that they can please themselves. If the sheep run, then the dog will run behind them. However, the reality of the situation is that the sheep are leading the dog rather than the dog driving the sheep. A very weak dog will find it hard to take control of his sheep and he will find it difficult to turn the sheep when required.

Power is the ability to move any type of sheep in a quiet calm controlled manner without significant aggression. A dog with power rarely has to grip sheep as he will use his eye, stance and energy to convince the stock that he is in command. You cannot predict how much power a dog will have towards his stock from the way he behaves towards his handler and other dogs. Some easily handled dogs have a great deal of natural power and will face up to any stock animal. By using steadfast non-aggressive persuasion this type of dog will stand and convince the sheep that he is boss. In addition, a good dog will also use his brain. He will not just be able to fetch sheep to the handler in a straight line, but where necessary, will take command of the flock and guide it around a bog or ditch rather than mindlessly driving the stock into the hazard.

A **strong dog** is one that is hard to hold back from sheep. This type of dog likes to get on with his work and you need to be a sufficiently dominant handler who has his wits about him to handle this kind of dog. However, for reasons given above, a dog that just continually pushes on his sheep regardless to his surroundings are of little use on the hill. If your dog keeps pushing forward and upsetting his sheep, then you need to apply appropriate pressure to teach him to control his energy. However, if you find you are unable to change this, then you need to convince him that he should work at a greater distance from his sheep.

A strong dog is not necessarily a powerful one. Sometimes a dog will continually push on to his sheep to mask the fact that he does not want to let them stop in case they challenge him. Some handlers are surprised when the dog that they thought would confront everything suddenly turns tail and runs from a charging ewe. Alternatively, when a sheep stands up to this type of dog, he may respond by gripping the sheep. However, gripping can also be a sign of weakness in the dog rather than an indication of strength.

Timid dogs. Some dogs are naturally timid. In addition, any dog that has an unpleasant experience at any stage of his life may become excessively wary if put in a similar environment again. Similarly, puppies that have limited exposure to different stimuli when they are young may also become excessively timid to new things in later life. I want my pups to be well socialised and confident as they grow up. They are therefore allowed in a run in the centre of the farm where they can safely observe and interact with people and older dogs. If you have an older timid dog then you need patience to improve the problem. It will take time to address the issue, but you need to let your dog experience a range of different situations whilst you reassure him in a calm, consistent manner. You will probably have to do this many times and your dog may always have a timid tendency. If your dog is nervous about coming onto his sheep, then you need to encourage and support him to gain confidence. As long as he is not put into situations where he is **over-faced**, then this problem should improve with time and age.

A **sensitive dog** is not the same as either a timid or a weak dog. Instead these dogs have a deep intuitive understanding of human body language and so require very little pressure from the handler to get an appropriate response. Moss, the dog with whom I won the International Supreme Championship and two of my current dogs, Mac and Ban who together have won both the Scottish and International Brace Championships all have a sensitive side to their nature and are also very respectful to humans. Dogs like this require consistent and appropriate communication: they certainly will not tolerate being around an aggressive or angry person who puts too much pressure on them. Despite this sensitive nature, my dogs show great power, natural ability and determination when working stock. They are excellent workers and successful trial dogs. I am glad I train The Natural Way because it has enabled me to encourage and bring out the best in these brilliantly talented animals; I certainly think that my working life would have been less fulfilling without them.

Many of the descriptions I have given are extreme examples. Most dogs fall somewhere in between and each has a combination of traits that make him unique. I strongly believe that in order to protect the work ethic, ability and versatility of the working border collie for generations to come, we need to be careful which dogs we select to breed from. We should focus and breed from those dogs who possess the innate traits we wish to promote. No matter how skilled he appears to be on the trial field, a man-made dog with limited natural qualities cannot pass on his training to the next generation.

Moving on

You must always remember that you are working as a team with your dog. It is the partnership between handler and dog that is important. Not every dog will suit every handler and vice versa. If the partnership is mismatched then neither dog nor handler will show their full potential. When I sell a dog, I always try to match the dog to the handler and the type of work that he will be doing. This way I try to ensure that both dog and purchaser will benefit.

When working sheep, I believe that the dog sees the handler and himself as the predatory hunting pack with the sheep as the prey. In order to fully understand the dynamics of the predator / prey relationship, it is vital that you have sheep-sense and this is discussed in the next chapter.

Fact Box. Advantages and disadvantages of buying dogs at different stages of their training

	Advantages	Disadvantages
Fully trained	Dog is experienced and able to do all jobs, making the shepherd's work more efficient. Dog has stock sense and decreases stress for all concerned, including the sheep.	More expensive. Handler needs to learn the commands that the dog recognises. Some dogs take longer to get used to a new handler.
Semi-trained	Can assist with some work tasks. Is less expensive than a fully trained dog. Buyer can develop the training as he desires because the dog is not fully set in his ways.	Not as much experience as a fully trained dog. Needs time to be trained to do difficult tasks. Dog will take time to learn handler's commands or handler needs to learn commands that the dog recognises. Some dogs take longer to get used to a new handler.
Showing interest, but had no training	Buyer knows that the dog is keen to work and so is paying for the dog's potential. Dog is a blank canvas to work with. Buyer can develop training and use commands that he prefers.	Dog still needs training. Dog is not ready for any difficult work situation. Some take longer to get used to new handler.
Farm dog with experience but knows minimal commands	Can work a full day. Not too much additional training required for more precise work. Dog has experience and often knows what is required of him.	Dog may have developed bad habits. If the dog has no commands on him, then he may not readily accept direction from the new handler. Some take longer to get used to a new handler.
Pups	If home bred, the breeder can choose the pup with the personality he likes. Pup develops under the handler's influence. Bond between pup and handler develop faster. Easier to train correctly (rather than having to correct unwanted habits). Can use training method that the handler prefers.	It is a gamble on how capable the pup will be as an adult working dog. May become apparent that as the dog develops, he does not have the appropriate character to suit the handler's requirements. Need to invest time to train pup properly.

Anecdote. Buyer beware

Soon after I started, I bought a dog called Mirk that I had seen run at the English National Sheepdog trial. He was a big, upright, black, white and tan dog with pricked ears. To my mind, he was complete poetry in motion and one of the most beautiful dogs I had ever seen working. Back then I only had a small flock of sheep of my own, but I sold all of them in order to be able to afford to buy him. I did not think there was any need to have his eyes tested because all dogs have this procedure done in order to be eligible to compete at the ISDS National trials. However, after owning him for a few weeks, I decided that Mirk could not see well enough to spot sheep and if there was not a fence to follow then he would often pass ewes at the top of the field. I had him re-eye tested and was told that Mirk had gradually been going blind for years because of an infection he had picked up when he was younger. As this condition was not hereditary, he had been allowed to run in the National trial. I phoned Mirk's previous owner and explained the situation, but to no avail: the dog was now my problem. This was a very expensive mistake from which to learn.

Chapter 5
Sheep Sense – Understanding your flock

The shepherd's role is to ensure high standards of sheep welfare. In days gone by, the traditional way to check a hill flock regularly was to 'turn' the sheep twice a day. To do this, the shepherd and his dogs would roam the tops of the hills in the morning driving the sheep down the hill as they went. In the afternoon they would walk the valleys to send the sheep back up to the hilltops. This ensured that the ground was evenly grazed. Importantly, it also meant that the sheep would be properly checked. The experienced shepherd would seem to develop a sixth sense and be able to detect any problems with his stock that could easily have been missed by someone with less sheep-sense. At the height of summer, before modern dips and sprays were available, it was imperative that all the sheep were checked twice a day to ensure that there were no eggs or maggots on an open wound or soiled fleece. In addition to the damage and suffering this can cause, fly strike can kill a sheep because of the toxins released from the maggots into the bloodstream. The only way for the shepherd to deal with a maggot infestation is to catch, hold and treat an affected ewe. On an open moor or rugged hill, this is only possible with a good dog who willingly works in partnership with his shepherd to catch any sheep that needs attention.

Today, most shepherds use quad bikes to get their job done quicker. However, even if they have a good dog, they often no longer have the same contact with sheep. When walking, a shepherd will hear a lost bleating lamb that is trapped in an open ditch. This sound would now be masked by the bike's engine.

In addition, dogs are now often encouraged to run alongside and keep up with the bike, and so they too may miss the bleating lamb: something a good dog would not do if he had been given time to use his senses. Similarly, the added noise and speed of the motorised bike also means that the shepherd misses what Nature is telling him. Crows picking at a dead ewe or lamb would warn the shepherd who was walking quietly that there may be fallen stock hidden in the heather. Now, the noise of the bike can scare the birds away before the shepherd is even aware that there may be a problem.

Although we have many advantages from modern technology, I find it sad that we are losing the old skills and feel for the flock that shepherds used to have. In previous times, this expertise would have been passed down from generation to generation. Now there are too few who are interested in learning these ways, and as the older shepherds retire and die, so a way of life is dying with them.

Anecdote. Be stockwise and check your fences

Soon after I had started working with sheepdogs, a local farmer asked me to help him train his dog to work cattle. I took Meg, my very first bitch, along to help because she was always keen to work anything that moved. However, after I had spent several minutes explaining *come-bye* and *away*, the twelve cows took fright and ran through the fences with the farmer and me following in hot pursuit. Regrettably, the original field was close to the local town and to make matters worse, instead of keeping together, the herd split. I followed two of the cows that ran straight into somebody's back garden and towards the house's patio doors. I still remember cringing at the possibility that they might decide to run through the glass and into the unfortunate occupier's home. Eventually, with the police's help, we managed to get all the cows safely rounded up and loaded onto a lorry, but after this incident it was a long time before I was prepared to work with cattle again. The episode taught me two valuable lessons: firstly, if you are going to work stock then you need to be stockwise and secondly, make sure your fences are secure before you start!

Respect for Sheep

Sheep are prey animals that are driven by their survival instinct. They are social animals and even when grazing out on the moors, apparently alone, they will usually still be aware of where others are. They have excellent senses, with mobile, sensitive ears and a wide visual field. However, they cannot see completely behind them, so several sheep together will enable them to cover the full 360° field of view.

If one is suddenly startled, she blows a warning snort and then flees away from the danger and the others flock with her. Alternatively, if a sheep senses potential danger some distance away, she will stop grazing and raise her head to look, listen and smell before making the decision to flee. If the flock is put into flight, then after the sheep have run for a short while and no longer feels threatened, they will often stop and *look back* to decide whether they really need to continue fleeing. It would not be sensible for a prey animal to just keep running from everything as this would use up precious energy. Therefore, once sheep reach a safe distance they will stop to determine the intent of the potential predator by reading its gestures, body language and energy. They will recommence grazing if they consider they are not being hunted. However, they will remain alert in case the energy of the situation suddenly alters.

As prey animals, sheep show few signs that they are ill because any sign of weakness could be picked up by a predator. A good shepherd should be able to pick up the subtle signals that a sheep maybe unwell. For example, an ill ewe may stand on her own away from the rest of the stock or lag behind with slightly drooped ears and dull eyes as the flock is gathered.

Many people believe that sheep are stupid. This is not true. Their survival instinct makes them want to act as a group and so they flock in a group and tend to follow the sheep in front of them. However, this is not the same as stupidity. In fact, sheep can be very canny and when being gathered, it is not uncommon for ewes to hide in bracken or behind a ridge and stand very still with their heads down. If they get the opportunity they will out-manoeuvre the shepherd and his dog by doubling back behind them in order to head back onto the hill. Moreover, they also quickly learn to predict specific tasks. For example, if they are regularly fed in the morning, sheep will gradually graze their way down to the feed troughs but only at that time of day.

I take advantage of this natural ability of sheep to learn and use it to help me gather a flock. I do this by training them to recognise a specific whistle that I give just before sending my dog. The sheep quickly realise that this whistle means that a dog is about to appear behind them and so they start to flock together making it easier for my dog to gather them. When I was working in the North of Scotland, I also trained the sheep to come down towards the farm on a specific whistle. This meant that any stragglers who may have been missed in the gather would start making their own way off the hill and so they were easier to find. Fortunately, sheep also learn from each other, so if you keep young hoggs and gimmers with their elders, you only have to teach your flock how to react to your whistle once.

Traditionally, ewes are **hefted** onto the hill. This means they know which area they belong to and will not stray from it. Historically, this natural trait was very useful, as it meant that there was no need for boundary fences. However, if a hefting system is used, then it is also important that the flock numbers are managed sensibly so that the stocking density is not too great for the ground to support.

After all the sheep have been gathered off the hill and then let loose, it is a wonderful sight to watch streams of ewes peel off in different directions as they return to their own particular heft. This memory of their location and surroundings is also apparent when lambing hill sheep (hill sheep often become stressed if they are moved into barns for lambing and so these are usually allowed to remain outside during this period).

When ewes are about to lamb, they tend to go back to the same place they were born.

It is not uncommon to find an old ewe, her daughters and any granddaughters all lambing in the same area. It often seems that the older ewe supports her young daughter when the latter gives birth for the first time – though, of course it may be that the older one is just being curious!

Sheep also recognise their friends and close family. For example, if I take a flock of a hundred ewes, each with twins into the pens to mark the lambs and afterwards let them loose into the field, each ewe will have picked up her own lambs in under half an hour. Similarly, if one ewe is separated from her friend during a shed, then, rather than join the group that is being allowed to wander off, she may hang back and stay close to the other group even if a dog is working them.

They can also recognise specific people and dogs who come into the field. If my dogs and I walk calmly through a Carcant field of ewes who are lying down and gently chewing the cud with their lambs nearby, they will remain settled and not be bothered. If another person, with or without a dog, comes into the field, then the ewe will often move her lambs to a safe distance.

Sheep can even predict the weather. When they sense that bad weather is coming, they often head to the place where they are used to being fed or else to a place of shelter. It is not uncommon to see the sheep move to a shielded area hours before any signs of approaching bad weather is apparent to us. Once it is raining, sheep prefer to stand still. This is because as they move, their fleece opens and closes and this, in turn, allows water to soak through to their skin. In contrast, if they remain stationary then their fleece is very waterproof. This is probably why, if there is a storm during a sheepdog trial, the sheep are usually quieter and steadier during and after the rain.

Sheep communication

Sheep are social herd animals that continually interact with each other. A flock will monitor all around to detect potential danger. They read the energy and intent behind dog and human actions. If we are near them, we need to control these so that the stock are not stressed by our presence.

Although the inexperienced handler may think all sheep within a flock are the same, if you spend time with your stock, it quickly becomes apparent that individual ewes have different 'personalities' and within a single flock, one will often take the lead that the others follow. If you can identify the lead sheep, this can be an advantage for both work and trialling. In winter, if you need to move sheep through snow drifts back to the farm, then you can make it easier by encouraging an old ewe who knows her way home to go to the front of the flock. Alternatively, if the snow is very deep, then having a strong ewe leading the flock can be advantageous.

Why sheep sense is important

Sheep sense is the ability to read sheep, and, by watching them then understand what they are about to do and why they do it. Understanding this will enable you to predict what probably will happen rather than just reacting after the sheep have responded to a situation. Sheep sense will enable you to place your dog and yourself properly and also determine how much pressure both of you need to exert on the stock in order to achieve your goal.

When I first started running at sheepdog trials, I thought that my poor runs may have been due to the sheep behaving badly. After watching some of the more experienced handlers, I realised that this was not the case: it was my lack of experience, both with working my dog and reading the sheep.

Like me, if you have not been brought up with stock, then sheep sense is something you have to learn. If you get the opportunity to help a farmer with his sheep then I recommend that you jump at the chance. By working and moving sheep yourself, without your dog, you will get some idea of what your dog has to contend with.

It will depend on the individual farmer's nature as to how lucky you are and how much instruction he gives you. But any comments including a brusque 'Get out of there', 'You're in the way' or 'Stand back' will help teach you where to place yourself.

A well-known sheepdog breeder and trials man who would often torment us all, made a joke at my expense by saying 'How the heck do you expect to get sheep in the pen, when you're standing in the way?' Well, obviously you don't, but comments like that did me good, because it helped me learn from my mistakes. As you start to understand why your sheep respond to your position and gestures, you will gradually find yourself being in the correct position more often. This, in turn, will help your dog do his job.

Fact Box. Dog and sheep body language 1

		Appropriate Signs	Inappropriate Signs
The dog		Body relaxed, but ready to respond, moderates pace appropriately.	Tense body and / or dropping shoulder on turns, speeding up inappropriately.
		Eyes soft and focused and also flick across all the sheep demonstrating that he is paying attention to the whole flock.	Eyes staring.
		Tail down and calm.	Tail flicking.
		Ears relaxed but twitching to listen for commands and to hear any sound from the sheep.	
The sheep		Head not too high.	Head held high.
		Ears relaxed.	Ears back.
		Body relaxed.	Nostrils blowing and snorting. Panting with tongue our and / or chest heaving.
		Eyes soft.	Eyes wide open and staring.
		Pace should be steady (slow jog).	High stepping or fleeing.

The body language is the same for all sheep: a stressed or panicked sheep will show the same signs no matter what breed they are. However, the breed and sheep's previous experience will determine how they will react when they see a dog. **Light sheep** (e.g. native breeds such as Scottish Blackface, Swaledale or Shetland) tend to have more instinct to run from the predator and herding these breeds in the correct manner will teach your dog how to work at a distance away from his sheep so that he does not scare them. Other docile breeds (e.g. Texel and Suffolk) hold different challenges for the dog as they are **heavy** to move and require more pressure from the dog.

If stock have never seen a dog or have only experienced being tormented by them, then again they are more likely to flee when a new dog approaches. In contrast, if sheep have been worked with well-behaved dogs for long periods then some breeds of sheep can become very tame and will tend to stick close to the handler's knees. These are called **well-dogged sheep**.

The predator / prey relationship

You always have to remember that sheep are prey animals and when you are working with your dog, you are taking advantage of the predator / prey response to move the flock.

Your dog (the predator) will use his hunting instinct around the sheep (the prey). Therefore, in order to control him, you need to first understand this instinct.

You also need to understand the three-way communication that passes between yourself, your dog and the sheep and respond appropriately to the situation. If you understand this interaction, you can take control of the predator / prey interaction and become the leader of 'the hunt'. This will allow you to manage your sheep in a stress-free manner.

Not only do you (the human handler) need to develop stock-sense, but it is also important that you also teach your dog to develop a good feel for his sheep so that he knows how to control and move them appropriately. Some dogs have more 'feel' than others. As I've already said, in order to teach your dog what is required, you need to appreciate the dynamics of a predator / prey interaction. As well as flocking, prey animals have other methods to evade predators if they feel threatened. One of these is to split up into smaller groups and some primitive breeds do this more frequently than other quieter sheep breeds. This split may confuse the predator because the short moment of doubt as the hunter decides which sheep to chase may make the difference between life and death.

The predator / prey interaction

My dogs automatically position themselves around sheep in a manner reminiscent of a hunt. **A** Gathering a small flock. **B** Helping me catch a lamb. Notice that even though the ewe is facing me, her ears indicate that she fully aware of Kim's presence.

If the ewe is startled or pressurised too much, then she will get a burst of adrenaline that stimulates the fight-or-flight response. The adrenaline surge will also cause extra energy resources to be released and these fuel her muscles as she flees from danger. The flight response is a panic reaction and whilst the ewe is in this state, she is unable to think clearly and so may rush headlong into fences, rivers or bogs in her effort to escape. When all her energy is used up, the ewe may suddenly pull up, exhausted in both mind and body. In this state, the sheep seems to have a glazed look as her brain has 'shut down' through too much stress and she may *lie-down* and refuse to move. The only way to get on top of this situation is to completely remove the pressure caused by the threat and allow the ewe time to calm down and settle her mind. Her reactions will return to normal once she has relaxed. This is one of the reasons why it is better try to work calmly and authoritatively rather than rush and upset your flock.

The other option that sheep can use to protect themselves is to turn and fight the dog. This tends to happen if a sheep is pushed to exhaustion or is backed up against a fence. It can also happen when the dog's energy indicates to her that he wants to provoke a reaction. The ewe is also highly likely to stand and confront the dog when she has a young lamb (as it would be impossible for the lamb to outrun the attacker). If she has learnt that this is successful way of deterring a dog, then a sheep can become wise enough to turn and challenge the dog even when she does not have a lamb at foot. You do not want to put a dog into a situation of confrontation until he has experience in working sheep and has gained sufficient confidence to deal with this situation. It depends on the dog's natural temperament on how he deals with this challenge, some will instinctively retaliate and hold their ground. However, others may be intimidated by a sheep that is heading it. If stock confront your dog and he does not know how to respond, you need to move next to him to help and reassure him. This support will give him courage and tell him that you approve of him dealing with the sheep. Alternatively, you can work an older more experienced dog next to him so that the young dog learns from his elder's example. This is one of the very few occasions when it may be appropriate for the dog to give a well-timed nip on the sheep's nose to indicate that he means business.

Fact Box. Dog and sheep body language 2

Dog Behaviour	Sheep Responses
Dog uses his eye and is calm working at a distance from the sheep. He correctly balances them by working at the sheep's heavy side.	Sheep move steadily and calmly in the direction that the handler commands the dog to take them.
Dog chases sheep for a period of time.	Sheep either flock or break into small groups and flee in blind panic.
Dog pressurises sheep by pushing in too close to the sheep's personal space. Dog may have excited eyes as he attempts to provoke the ewe to react.	Sheep stands her ground to eye the dog down. She may butt the dog. Sheep are especially likely to fight a dog if she has a young lamb
Dog with a predatory-killing state of mind, will use his eye to shed off a single sheep. This is often an ill or weak member of the flock. Once he has separated off the sheep, the dog brings her down with the intent to kill. There may be intensity in his stare and extra tension in his body, but detecting this state of mind prior to the events unfolding is mainly from knowledge of how the dog has behaved previously.	Sheep panics causing her to flee.
Dog shows weakness by backing away from the ewe. He may eventually flee from her.	Sheep stands her ground and eyes the dog down. She may stamp her foot. She may charge and butt the dog.
Dog's tail is waving above his back as he barks. However, he is standing still.	Sheep are unsettled and alert, but do not necessarily enter a fight-or-flight mindset.
Dog runs around excitedly but not actually chasing sheep.	Sheep become stressed, scatter and flee.

As a sheepdog handler, you need to be aware of the ewe's body language to determine whether the sheep is <u>about</u> <u>to</u> flee and time your commands to pre-empt and control this, rather than just respond once the stock has actually reacted and ran. Moreover, when you train your dog on sheep, it is important that he also learns how his intentions and movement create different reactions in the sheep. Your dog will instinctively use pressure / release to move his sheep and with training and experience, he will learn how much and when to use these in order to control his sheep calmly. In turn, you need to use the methods discussed in chapter 2 to teach your dog when he is correct i.e. when he is using an appropriate amount of pressure and has a steady mindset whilst working his sheep (see page 17). If you do not do this, then your dog may always unsettle sheep when he works them.

When training your dog you also need to give him the opportunity to work naturally so that he can also figure things out for himself. When you let your dog work naturally, you should let him move the sheep around on his own with minimal command. However, when doing this, you should still use sufficient and appropriately timed pressure / release to help him understand how his movements effect the way that sheep behave. Remember, it is important that even when working naturally, your dog should not be allowed to unduly upset his sheep.

There are occasions when sheep may behave very differently from how they normally would. These include when a single sheep is isolated from others; when they are being worked in pens and when they have lambs at foot. Your dog will pick up on the ewe's altered energy levels and he too will respond differently. You need to be aware of the altered dynamics so that you can pre-empt an unwanted event.

Working a Single Sheep

As I have already said, sheep feel more comfortable when they are in a group. If you want your dog to single a sheep either for work purposes or in a trial, you must remember that the predator / prey dynamics will be considerably amplified. A sheep that is isolated from others will panic more readily. As a prey animal, all her senses and survival instinct will be sharpened. She will hold her head up with wide eyes and her ears will twitch more as she determines both your dog's and your energy and intent. Your dog will pick up on the sheep's distress and his predatory instinct will be further aroused by the very fact that the ewe is on her own. If she runs, he may be very tempted to give chase, but he must not succumb to this. Instead, your dog has to control his energy, intent and excitement.

A couple of circumstances when sheep behaviour alters
A A single ewe is more edgy when she is on her own so I ask Mac and Ban to remain behind me so that the Blackface ewe does not feel unduly pressurised and remains calm as we direct her back to the rest of the flock. **B** Young Ruby (dog on left) has only just started working in the pens. She feels slightly pressurised by the proximity of the ewes and moves from side to side. Experienced, steady Kim is on hand to give her courage and show her how to manage the stock.

He also needs to learn how to sit back on his hocks and arch his body to block the sheep from moving in any unwanted direction. If managed correctly, the ewe will understand that the only option is to move in the direction that is not blocked by your dog. If your dog puts too much pressure on her, then she may consider that she cannot outrun the danger and has no option but to turn and fight.

Sometimes my dogs and I come across a solitary ewe standing on her own. In these situations, I will usually approach her to assess whether there is a problem or not. If the ewe is not injured or ill, then rather than stressing her further by forcing her to move alone, I often will gather a few nearby sheep and bring them to her. In this way, she will relax in her friends' presence and will be content to be herded with the rest.

Working in Pens

When you work in a pen, the enclosed space inevitably means that the dogs and sheep are in close proximity with each other. This is not a problem as long as they both respect one another.

It is important when your dog works in a sheep-handling pen that he has the patience to lie and wait until you need him to calmly move the sheep. Often you will need your dog to move between the fence and the sheep and the manner in which he squeezes through this small gap will affect the sheep's behaviour: any erratic movement, noise or unwanted energy from either you or your dog will stress the ewe.

An inexperienced dog will often also find the closed confines of a pen very intimidating. If you make a lot of noise or wave your arms about in order to stimulate the sheep to move through the pens, then this can further compound your dog's concern and he may become anxious or overexcited. The whole situation can prompt some dogs to grip. This will obviously increase the sheep's stress levels further.

All my dogs work in the pens with sheep, but I only introduce them to this aspect of their work when I consider they have developed sufficient confidence to work stock in a relaxed, calm fashion. This is especially important when I have heavily pregnant ewes in the pens.

Lambing

During lambing it is even more imperative that my dogs and I work together as a closely bonded team. At other times of the year, as I ride on the quad bike, I often allow my dogs to range a short distance from me so that they can look out for anything unusual. In contrast, at lambing I keep the dogs close by me or have them riding on the bike with me.

I regularly check the pregnant ewes in the fields at one to two hourly intervals, A sheep that is about to give birth will often isolate herself from the rest of the flock.

The signs of lambing are usually obvious. However, sometimes they can be subtle, especially if the lamb is incorrectly positioned in the womb or if it has died inside its mother. If a sheep is struggling to give birth and the flock is gathered together, then as a prey animal, she will try to hide her symptoms from me and my dogs (the potential predators). I therefore prefer to check my ewes and young lambs by quietly driving around the flock without disturbing them.

As I have already said, I have my dogs with me when I check my stock and in order that they do not upset the ewes, it is vital that they control their energy. However, when I need to help a sheep, my dogs have to move purposely and swiftly to corral and hold her so that I can use a leg cleek (crook) to catch her. At this time of year, I therefore only use my more experienced dogs.

There are other things that I need to keep an eye out for. One of these is when a sheep who has not yet given birth tries to pinch a new born lamb from its mother. She does this because her surging hormones make her believe that she has already given birth. I need to work out which is the real mother and which is the pincher. However, the thief can be very determined to keep the lamb and she usually needs to be separated from the mother and her youngster.

If this is not done, then the lamb can get confused as to whom it belongs to. It then risks being rejected by both its own mother and by the pincher when the latter gives birth herself.

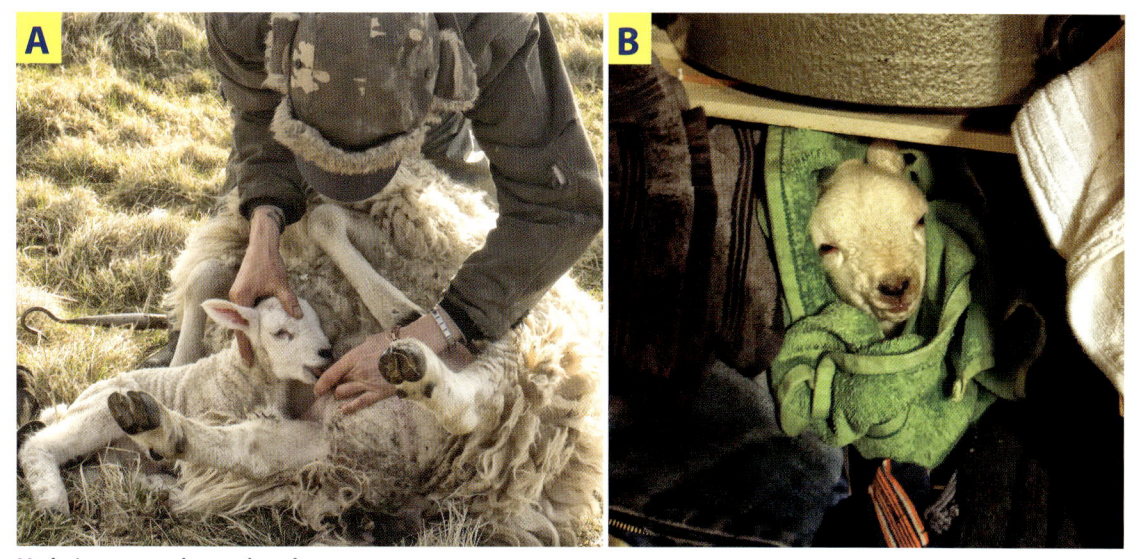

Helping new born lambs
A Lambs need to suckle as soon after birth as possible in order to benefit from the colostrum (the first milk). Some lambs who have had a difficult birth need help with this. **B** Other lambs may need more intensive treatment. This one needed warming up so I put it in the farm airing cupboard.

As I do my rounds, I also check the young lambs. In the first few days after a lamb is born, the rich milk from its mother can make its poo (meconium) so sticky that its tail can become stuck over the anus causing it to become blocked. If not removed, this blockage can kill a young lamb. Again, I rely on my dogs to help me catch the youngsters.

However, some dogs just ignore lambs, not realising that when you want to move the ewes, their offspring need to come as well! Alternatively, other dogs have their hunting instincts fired by lambs as they are small, fast and run past the dog's nose without realising the potential threat. At Carcant, if I need to move my stock when the lambs are very young, I usually guide the ewes and lambs myself and position my dogs so that they block the ewe from running in an unwanted direction. If the ewes feel pressurised by a dog, then in an attempt to save their young, they will take their lambs away from the rest of the flock in order to confuse the predator. Alternatively, if a sheep has a young lamb that is not yet able to run with her, she has little choice but to stand and fight if a dog puts too much pressure on her. Some ewes are so protective they will even run across the field to confront the dog. The dog needs to have plenty of quiet assertive power to manage these situations.

The ewe's strong survival instinct can make it difficult for someone without sheep-sense or an inexperienced dog to move a group of ewes and lambs. I find that it is often better to remove all pressure from the ewe, block the direction that you do not want the sheep to go and let the mother and lamb think they are 'getting away'. They will then move easily in the correct direction.

My stock are getting quieter and calmer the longer I am at Carcant. All the lambs born here now are offspring of ewes that I have also lambed. I believe that my flock is more passive and less stressed than others because my sheep know and trust my dogs and me. I think this is partly because when I check and feed the ewes and lambs, I always have my dogs with me.

Importantly, my dogs are trained The Natural Way and so they know how to control their energy appropriately. Therefore the lambs learn from a young age to respect rather than fear them. However, although my stock are comparatively quiet with us, if a strange dog comes in with an excited, intense energy, they will panic as fast as any other prey animal. This is why I am always cautious about letting other people work their dogs around my flock especially when the ewes have lambs at foot.

Moving on

Everyone has their own reasons as to which sheep they use. Most people who are interested in sheepdog trials and who do not have daily sheep work, will often try to give their dogs as much experience as possible with different types of sheep. In contrast, sheep farmers will have their own particular preferences for what type of sheep they keep. It could be that their terrain suits a certain breed, or they are breeding for a certain type of fattening lamb.

If you are new to working dogs and stock and intend to buy some sheep of your own, then seek advice from someone that has experience of stock as you do not want to buy any in poor condition that are not fit for purpose. This would be unfair for the sheep and frustrating for you and your dog. In all cases, I would advise anyone who wishes to train their dog to a high standard that they start training their dog on a few sheep before working with a larger number.

Remember, you must always consider the welfare of the sheep you are working with. Welfare is more than just feeding and caring for their health (which, of course, are both important). It also means that you should try to limit the stress that sheep may experience when you work with them. Sheep have good memories and if they are handled with care and respect, then they can be quietly and efficiently moved around the different fields, pens and barns on the farm.

You and your dog need to work together as a calm effective team and it is important that your dog respects you as his Alpha so that you can lead the 'hunt'. It is easier to establish this mindset if your dog has been taught to have good manners and respect for humans during his upbringing and so in the next chapter I will discuss how I raise pups.

Dogs need to know how to control their energy when working with ewes who have lambs
A After catching the ewe so that I can help her give birth, Kim knows to stay back and portray a calm energy that does not scare the ewe from her new born lamb. **B** Kim lies in a relaxed fashion and lets a lamb come up and sniff her. I have my back turned as I check the feed in the pens. **C** Kim and I stand back so that the ewes and lambs do not feel pressurised as they head out onto the hill. **D** Mac is about to move ewes and lambs. The horned ewe has lowered her head in defiance in order to protect her lamb. Mac is standing his ground but is not putting undue pressure on her as he does not want to provoke a fight. **E** I encourage the ewe and her very young lamb to move into another field while Mac blocks her from running away. **F** A sheep with a young lamb that is too young to outrun a predator lowers her body in an attempt to go unnoticed.

Cheviot ewes are caring mothers

A When lambs cross a stream for the first time, I make sure that they get across safely. **B, C** and **D** The ewes also encourage their lambs to follow them across and then make sure they have their own lamb with them before taking them onto the moor. **E** When the lambs are a bit older, the ewes are content to let Ban remain close to them while I feed them. This is because Ban knows how to control his energy around stock. The relaxed nature of the ewes mean that the lambs learn to respect my dogs, not to fear them.

Anecdote. An arresting tale

When I lived in Cambridge in the 1980s, I shepherded sheep that grazed along riverbanks. At lambing time, we brought them nearer to home in order to keep a closer eye on them. We tended to lamb mainly mule ewes, but this particular year, my then-partner and I had bought some draft Swaledale ewes to try. They did not seem to like life on the lowlands and tended to be very unsettled. We decided that they would be too stressed to lamb indoors and so turned them out onto a strip of land to graze. The majority decided to accept the situation, but one old persistent escape artist never seemed to be in the same place twice. One morning, she was missing again and I spent the next few hours combing the neighbouring fields trying to find her, but without success. I stopped for lunch and as I was eating the police phoned to ask if I had lost a sheep. The ewe had apparently walked five miles and wandered into the police station itself. Because the sheep had horns, all the officers had taken bets on whether the animal was male or female. However, the answer became obvious when she started lambing. Evidently, they had been very concerned by this turn of events and had rang a local vet who informed them that an experienced ewe would manage by herself and just to let her get on with it. A short while after this call, the officers delivered the proud mother and her newborn lamb back to the farm. They even returned to visit a few weeks later to see how they both were: now that's what you call a good follow-up service.

Anecdote. Don's seal adventure

The Nene River that winds its way through the flat fenlands of South East England, has strong tidal undercurrents that make it dangerous, and sometimes impossible, to cross. In the 1980s, I used to shepherd a flock that grazed its grassy banks and, unaware of the danger, the sheep would often venture close to the edge of the bank. I always used to walk the water side of the field first as it was safer to turn sheep up away from the waterside (rather than down towards it). On the day in question, although the water was flowing rapidly, everything seemed fine as I and my dog, Don walked our normal route. As I moved around a bend in the river, I suddenly startled a sheep who moved closer to the edge rather than running up the bank to safety. Now I have sufficient sheep-sense to appreciate that I should have stopped in my tracks. However, back then, I hurriedly sent my dog to run to turn her, never realising in my inexperience that Don could not manage to do this in time. Now I realise that this increased pressure panicked the ewe and put her into flight mode and I do not think she even saw the water as she fled into it. For a moment, I stood there aghast, with my mind racing as I desperately tried to work out what to do. Would the weight of her sodden wool drag her under and drown her? Could I wait to see if she managed to get to the other side? However, if she managed that then would she continue fleeing into the busy main road that ran next to the river? Don was a strong and determined dog, he had swam on many occasions in deep water and I knew he would give me everything he had. So, despite my misgivings about the fast current, I decided I had no choice but to send him to swim out past her and turn her back towards me. He swam strongly and gradually managed to push ahead of her. Just as I thought he would succeed in turning her, the sheep seemed suddenly to lift slightly out of the water and glide through it at a speed of knots. Don pulled up and started treading water. His look seemed to match my own open-mouthed bewilderment as the ewe shot off down river. The next thing I knew, the sheep lunged at the bank on the other side and she scrambled onto solid ground. The water rippled in the middle of the river, and a seal raised his head out of the water as he stared back at me. His eyes were wide and gleaming and I could have sworn that he blinked at me before rising further out of the water and then diving back down out of sight into the murky depths. I was amazed by what had happened. The seal must have come to the sheep's rescue, though how it had perceived that the ewe was in danger is anyone's guess. Whatever the reason, I was grateful that it had saved my sheep and I marvelled at the wonderful rare sight I had seen.

The episode taught me a valuable lesson: If sheep are in a dangerous position, it is usually better to pull back, remove the pressure and wait for them to move on their own accord rather than rushing in and making the situation worse.

Chapter 6
Building a foundation for training

A farm dog will face many different challenges during his working life. In order to be able to cope with these he needs a steady mindset, a confident nature and a willingness to please combined with respect for humans and other more dominant dogs in his pack.

The pup's place in the pack

An adult dog's behaviour and mindset are products of both nature and nurture. The 'nature' part are the innate traits that he will inherit from his breeding and these were discussed in the earlier chapter on working border collies (see page 42). However, the 'nurture' part is also very important and you need to bring up your pup so that he develops into a balanced, stable, respectful, confident, integrated pack member.

A pup continually learns through play by stalking, pouncing, chasing and tumbling with other pups and older dogs. From this he learns how to fit into the pack hierarchy and starts to develop his skills as a future hunter. As he grows, older pack members show him the ropes and introduce him to different situations. They are quick to discipline any disrespect, but they will also encourage and reassure him as he experiences different challenging events such as crossing streams.

It does not matter whether you wish your dog to work or just want him as a pet, when you buy a pup and he moves into your 'pack', he will feel very vulnerable and insecure until he becomes familiar with his new surroundings and settles into his new environment. As well as providing a safe, dry kennel and a balanced healthy diet, it is important that your pup knows where he fits within your pack and accepts that you are his pack leader.

You need to give your pup encouragement when he is correct, reassurance when he is feeling insecure and affection when he is calm. You must also let him experience as many different situations as possible. These include things like walking on a lead, traveling in vehicles, introducing him to different noises, children and other dogs. Although your pup may be young, he has to realise what is acceptable and which behaviour (e.g. biting) is not.

His real mother and other higher ranking dogs would always chastise the pup for any disrespectful behaviour and they would do this in a timely fashion by using appropriate pressure. You need to do the same, but remember that the pressure you exert must be appropriate. You want your pup to trust and respect you. He should not fear you.

It is important that you are consistent in what you consider unacceptable behaviour because otherwise your pup will become confused as to what is and is not allowed. You must also remember that if you do not tell your dog that he is doing something wrong, then he will interpret this to mean that his bad behaviour is permitted.

Fact Box. Pups in the house

Some trainers bring their pups up in the home. This is a personal choice. If you use The Natural Way of training correctly, it should not make any difference whether your dog lives in the house or not. A more submissive dog can often gain confidence through living in the home and interacting with family members. However, if you have a dominant dog inside, it is important he knows his place in the pack. In order to maintain harmony, you need to set rules and boundaries and ensure that all family members are consistent in using pressure / release appropriately. Remember, dogs also need 'down time' when they can be alone so that they can relax and sleep without interruption.

All dogs use the same language to interact and The Natural Way described throughout this book provides a system that we humans, can use to communicate with any dog. Having said that, a detailed description about living with domestic dogs is beyond the scope of this book. Sarah Jenkins and I have set up Groveshill Dog Whisperers to help pet owners learn how to use the Language of the Dog with their canine companions. For more details go to our website www.groveshilldogwhisperers.co.uk.

Developing a respectful and confident pup

I keep all my dogs, including the pups, in kennels. If I have bred a litter from my own dogs then I will start interacting with the pups when they are just a few days old as I believe that it is important that they get used to a human's touch and voice from this young age. From the very start, I sit with them and their mother while I quietly murmur and gently stroke their sides in a manner that imitates their mother's licks. When they start to crawl, I let them clamber over my legs as I continue to touch and talk softly to them.

Once they are strong enough, they will instinctively follow their mother and I intentionally walk with her for the short distance out from the kennel onto the garden lawn. By walking with the bitch, I make use of this instinct and, so even from this very young age, the pups start to understand that they should follow me when I move. These short walks also allow the pups to start to learn that they should empty themselves away from their kennels.

Although the pups are usually weaned off suckling at about six weeks, they will continue to interact with their mother. She teaches them the proper social manners that enables them to fit into the pack. I also continue to interact with the pups and will now lead the pups into the garden and exercise pen but without their mother by my side.

Usually, I prefer to keep just one weaned pup at a time because it allows us to bond closely. I find that if I have more than one similar aged pup around the farm then they can start to rely more on each other rather than on me. If I have bought a young pup in then I have to build a relationship with him. I do this by spending time with him and by gently touching his sides to reassure him that I am someone he can trust. As soon as possible, I encourage him to follow me. This way he joins up with me rather than with one of my other dogs.

Early days

A When the pups are just a day or two old, I gently stroke their faces and sides. Their mother, Kim is lying beside at the front of the picture. **B** When the pups are a few weeks old, I walk with Kim, and her pups instinctively follow. **C** I continue to interact with the pups who are about 5 weeks of age in this picture. I let them climb over me and their father, Ban, who I know will not harm them in my presence. **D** I reassure a young pup who has recently arrived at the farm.

Fact Box. Similarities between human and dog body language towards their young

	Human	Dog
Encourage feeding	Mother shows that food is nice to eat by putting the spoon in her own mouth before offering it to her own child. At the same time, she makes soft 'Yum, yum' sounds to encourage her baby to taste it.	Mother regurgitates her food for the pup. This behaviour is a rare trait descended from wolves (who habitually regurgitate for their young). I have only come across this behaviour on one occasion – the mother of my current brace dog Ban, Socks exhibited this trait among others that showed she was 'close to nature'.
Touch	Mother touches and strokes the child's cheeks. She also pat's the child's back to both calm and soothe him.	Mother licks and cleans the pup's cheeks, ears and belly. She also nuzzles her pup.
Reprimand wrong doing	Adult uses a stare and a stern tone of voice. She may point a finger to put pressure on the child.	Adult stares at the pup in an intimidating fashion and may give a low growl. She may put her mouth around the pup's muzzle to put additional pressure on the pup.
Encourage the child/pup to come	Adult crouches down to make herself small to encourage the child to come towards her for a cuddle.	Adult lies down and rolls over into her back exposing her belly to encourage the pup to come in and nuzzle her.

Dog - Human interactions mimic the pack dynamics

A As Tweed jumps up, I gently squeeze his muzzle to indicate this is unwanted behaviour.
B Alpha male, Tig gently squeezes a pup's muzzle to calm his overexcited behaviour.
C Tweed licks and nuzzles my cheek. **D** Tig (dog on right) is walking with a dominant stance with his tail held up over his back and his chin held high. Elle has to work hard to show her respect and submission to Tig which she does by reaching up to lick his cheek.

Fact Box. Why a mother has her mouth around the pup's muzzle

• The pup has licked the mother's lips and side of mouth for her to open and regurgitate food. The pup may then push his muzzle into her open mouth to look for food.

• A mother may gently reprimand the pup's inappropriate behaviour by placing her mouth over the pup's muzzle. She also uses pressure / release and the 'ask, tell, insist' scale. Initially, she 'asks' her pup to modify his behaviour by gently holding her mouth around his muzzle. If the pup gives to this pressure, she will release. If he does not respond, she will repeat the gesture but now uses a bit more pressure (the 'tell'), If he still is resistant, she will nip the pup to insist that he responds to her request.

When a pup is following me, he will inevitably get distracted and wander off to investigate an interesting smell or object. To ask him to return to me, I make encouraging sounds, turn to the side, lower my body and tap my thigh. If this fails, I move towards him and gently prod his shoulder to exert mild pressure and gain his attention. As soon as the pup looks at me, I release this pressure and turn away whilst encouraging him to follow. If necessary, I repeat this until he pays attention. By doing this, I am subtly teaching him and giving him guidelines to follow. I never use heavy pressure on a pup as it can be very counterproductive. The pup needs to trust me, not fear me.

A dog's mental development may be severely restricted if he is kept locked in a shed or a kennel during his puppy-hood. A pup brought up like this will receive little environmental stimulation from his surroundings and he may develop into a dog who is fearful of new experiences. I therefore believe that it is important that a young dog is exposed to different stimuli if he is going to develop properly. As I am busy around the farm, I cannot have the pups with me, so during the day I keep them in an enclosed area outside the kennels. This is ideal for young dogs because they can see and experience normal farm life from a safe location. In addition, they get introduced to the adults without being knocked over as the older dogs pass through this enclosure as they go to and from their work.

Once the pups are about ten to twelve weeks old, I let them run with the main dogs as they are exercised together. We all walk as a pack along the farm lanes and around some of the fields crossing ditches and navigating gates, walls and streams. The dogs and pups are also allowed to run free in some of the fields. However, I do not let any of the dogs wander too far from me and call them back if any start pushing the boundaries. Obviously I keep a close eye to ensure that the pack behaviour and interactions between the dogs remains stable and that none of the older dogs bully a youngster inappropriately.

Using The Natural Way to develop basic obedience

As I have already discussed in an earlier chapter, dogs communicate with each other using pressure / release body language. A pup is very sensitive and responsive to pressure and therefore only needs very mild levels to get dramatic responses. Therefore, if you use my training method, it is important that you do not put too much pressure on your pup to correct him. Furthermore, it is also vital that you release pressure when he is correct. If you do this in a consistent manner, then your pup will quickly learn and understand what is acceptable behaviour.

During the day, my pups are kept in a run at the centre of the farm
Here, they can interact with people and other dogs as we go about our work and also experience a range of different stimuli from a safe location.

Gentle training with a 12 week pup

At this stage, I have taken on the mother's role to teach and guide the pup to become a stable, confident pack member. **A, B** and **C** Encouraging Tweed to follow and come when called. **D** Praising Tweed is very important. I do this by talking softly to him and gently stroking the side of his face and body. The pup should also receive this praise calmly. This helps develop a balanced mind and also teaches the pup that calmness is rewarded. **E** Tweed is engrossed in an interesting smell. **F** To gain his attention I touch his side. **G** Tweed initially returns back to his smell, so I retouch his side again. **H** When he refocuses his attention towards me, I encourage him to follow by turning to the side and bending as I ask him to follow. **I** This time, Tweed willingly responds to my request and follows. **J** At the gate to the summer house, I gently touch the side of his face to acknowledge and reward his behaviour. **K** and **L** When he is called, Tweed is happy to leave the field when I request it. As he leaves the field I would again reward him by gently touching his side. My calm, confident approach shows the pup who is leader of the pack. He quickly develop a mindset where he wants to please me.

You also want to encourage your pup to develop a calm mind and bond with you. To do this, wait until your pup is quietly lying or sitting by your side. Then gently touch and slowly stroke the vulnerable areas of his body especially along the side of his face, his lower neck and his chest. Whilst you do this, talk to your pup in a quiet, calm and reassuring voice. When you look at him use gentle, soft eyes that demonstrate you are relaxed and satisfied with his behaviour. These gestures and sounds mimic his mother's nurturing licks and therefore reward him as well as reassure him that he is doing the right thing. Dogs love this gentle stroking action, so it is also important to remember not to use it when your pup is showing inappropriate behaviour. If used at the wrong time this will reward an excited mindset and could even encourage your dog to act disrespectfully towards you.

Although I do very little 'formal traditional' obedience training with a young pup, I do encourage him to follow me as I go around the farm yard and fields. I also use pressure / release techniques to show the pup that when he yields to pressure, he is rewarded by having that pressure released. Remember, when you start training your dog, do not expect him to be perfect straight away. It is inevitable that your pup will make mistakes as he tries to work out what you require. It is important that you do not over correct these errors and you must not exert inappropriate pressure on him. As I have already said, pups are very sensitive to pressure and you do not need to use much to get a dramatic response. If you continue to exert pressure on a pup (or any dog) when he is trying to please you, he will get mixed messages. Depending on his character, he may become anxious or dull to your pressure (see page 27).

One of the first things I teach a pup is to give to pressure and lie-down. To do this squat down in front of the pup, but not so close that it makes him feel uncomfortable. Gently place your hand over his muzzle. This mimics his mother behaviour when she is asking him to listen to her. Your pup should relax and submit by lying down to demonstrate that he is giving to your pressure. As he submits release the pressure to indicate that he has made the right choice. Once he has lain down reward him by gently stroking his cheeks and ribs. Over your next few sessions, you should gradually build on this response so that he starts to give to less pressure. Eventually just lowering your hand towards his muzzle will create the correct response from your pup. As you use these gestures and body language, you can also start incorporating the associated vocal *lie-down* command. Gradually, you should decrease the amount of overt gestures that you use and make them more subtle. With time, your pup will respond as soon as you start to put your hand up.

However, as any dog learns to give to pressure, it is natural for him to go through stages of resistance and / or avoidance before he accepts the situation. When your pup resists, you have to hold the pressure and block any forward movement with your body. If he moves backwards in an attempt to avoid you, then you should put a finger through his collar and give it a gentle, short tug forward. This small amount of pressure is saying 'Don't pull away.' Release the pressure on his collar. Now, put your hand over his muzzle again to ask him to lie-down. When he responds by lying down, you must release all pressure as this tells your pup he has made the right choice.

Moving on

When you raise a pup, you are taking over his mother's role. At this early stage, your main aim is to ensure that he develops into a young confident dog with a balanced, steady mind who understands what is required to be a stable pack member. As the youngster grows, you need to continually assess and reassess his nature, his willingness to please and how sensitive he is to soft pressure. Remember every dog is different, so by having this insight into his young mind, you will be able to modify my pressure / release techniques to suit his character and temperament. By using The Natural Way, you will find that you develop a strong partnership with your pup that is founded on trust and respect. This bond will act as a strong foundation when you come to train your dog to work stock.

The way I train a sheepdog to do the different tasks required for both work and on the trial field are described in the next section. This starts with a brief general overview of my training method.

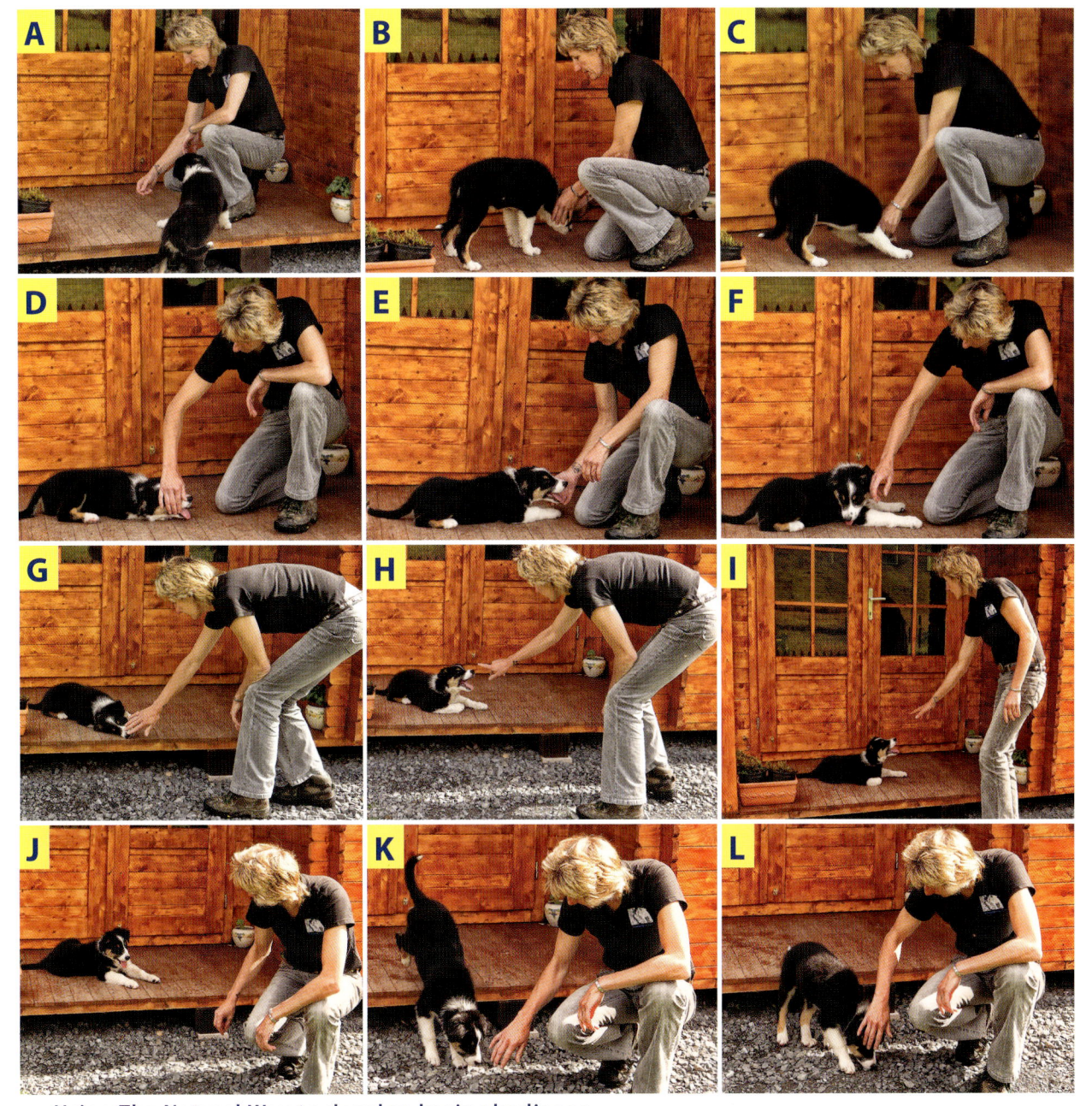

Using The Natural Way to develop basic obedience

I try to spend a few minutes every day having a one-to-one interaction with the pup.
A I encourage Tweed onto the step by kneeling down, turning to the side and clicking my fingers. I intentionally do not look directly at him, as I want him to focus on and draw towards my hand movements. **B** To show Tweed I wish him to lie-down, I put gentle pressure on his forehead to stop him coming forward and gently push him back as he resists my initial request. **C** After gently squeezing his muzzle, Tweed begins to give to this pressure and his body starts to lean backwards. He is still showing some resistance to my pressure, so I continue to gently hold his muzzle until he had completely given and laid down. I make sure that my body is far enough from him to give him physical and mental space. This means he feels comfortable lying down. **D, E** and **F** Tweed has laid down where I want, so I reward him by gently stroking the side of his face. **G** To teach Tweed to stay, I initially touch his nose as I step off the deck. **H** and **I** As he remains lying down as requested, I gradually move away and stand up while keeping my hand in a blocking position. **J** and **K** To call Tweed towards me, I again kneel down, turn to the side and encourage him to come to hand. **L** When he comes to me, I again reward him by gently stroking the side of his face.

PART 2
Training
The Natural Way

Take time to build a strong foundation and use the pressure / release technique correctly so that you do not confuse your dog by giving him mixed messages. Encourage your dog to develop a feel for his sheep and combine this with plenty of natural work. Training this way will let your dog develop into a confident worker who is able to use his initiative and is also willing to take command.

CHAPTER 7
OVERVIEW OF MY TRAINING METHOD

I believe that The Natural Way of training enables me to develop a strong relationship with my dog that is founded on mutual trust, respect and loyalty. In addition, my method allows a dog to build on his natural ability so that he becomes a confident worker who can cope with the different challenges that he will face during his life – both on a farm or when running at a trial.

This chapter provides an overview of how I train a working sheepdog from start to finish. I hope it provides an indication of what you will be aiming for with your dog. You can find more details about all the stages I mention in the other chapters of the book.

Although I will occasionally buy young dogs to train, I personally prefer to start from pups. I either breed these myself or else buy pups whose parents possess the natural traits I want to see in a working dog. By bringing a pup up myself, I know that the young dog will have a solid foundation and will have developed a steady mindset that The Natural Way promotes.

I know that every dog is different and so I will only introduce a young dog to sheep when I consider that he is mentally and physically mature enough to cope with the demands of training. I do not consider that training a dog is a race to get through. Instead, because I know that some dogs will take longer than others to understand what is required of them I pace each one's training to suit his temperament. In fact, some dogs seem to take forever to learn different aspects of their craft, but once they realise what is necessary, they can become very capable working and trial dogs. Moreover, as I train each dog, I continually reassess his ability and acceptance to learn. I also watch carefully how he responds to me and his sheep and constantly re-evaluate the amount of pressure / release that I need to use for him to respond appropriately.

As the dog develops and learns different skills required to manage sheep, I will also often take him back through his earlier lessons so that he does not forget the crucial basics that we have already covered.

Right from the start of his training, I help a dog develop a feel for his sheep so that he learns how much appropriate pressure he needs to exert on his stock to move or hold them in an unstressed manner. It is very important to me that a dog is able to balance sheep and hold them to me properly, so these early formative lessons also ingrain that I am the main focal point that he should bring sheep towards.

Julie's Tip. If you do not use the pressure / release technique correctly, your dog will either resist or avoid you. This will lead to a break down in communication and you will not be able to let your dog reach his full potential.

Once my dog is balancing sheep towards me properly and is also completely concentrating on both the sheep and me, I will start to use body language to indicate the direction that I wish him to flank. I will continue to use appropriate pressure / release to ensure that he takes the natural flank in a semi-circle in a manner that ensures he gives sufficient room so that his sheep are not disturbed. I then move on to small outruns, associating the verbal commands with the correct movement and response. I spend time

---

Fact Box. Training framework

My training method can be divided into three stages. These can be summarised as follows:

Basic: Teach the foundation skills for the different elements.

Intermediate: Develop and expand the dog's knowledge. Increase the distance or difficulty of the task. Introduce natural flock work.

Advanced: Test the dog's skills and understanding plus perform precise work on command when required. The dog should also have a good feel for sheep and be able to use his own initiative around the stock plus be willing and prompt to take commands from the handler.

working on his outrun, lift and fetch, I do this while working close at hand so that I can show my dog how to lift and fetch his sheep with the appropriate calm mindset that does not unduly stress his stock.

As I am keen to promote a dog's natural ability and want him to use his instincts to read sheep, I break up the formal training sessions with plenty of natural fetching and driving. When a young dog is learning to do natural work, I often will walk with him in a relaxed manner that reassures him and encourages him to gain in confidence as he completes his task. If necessary I will remain at this training stage for some length of time until my dog is mentally able to adjust and respond appropriately to further tuition.

Julie's Tip. As your dog progresses through his training you should be able to refine your gestures and vocal commands so that they become more subtle.

Once my dog works well at hand and I consider that he is sufficiently matured to progress further, I introduce the *out* command as he flanks and also gradually increase the distance of his outrun. I also start to drive in a small square, using the natural flank, the flank behind me and the inside flank so that he is able to drive the sheep in a square, initially with me walking with him but then gradually I will stand back so that he learns to drive without me walking along side him.

Hopefully, by this stage, my dog will be running out at least 200m, taking flank commands as well as being able to drive in a small square. This is another point in the dog's training where I often remain for a few months while I wait for the dog's mental capacity to develop as he grows older.

In addition to formal training sessions, I also make sure that my young dog gains plenty of experience from helping with the daily farm chores. This brings its own challenges, as my dog learns to manage more sheep on different terrains. While working at hand with a flock, I introduce simple shedding and the *look back*.

Once I feel that my dog is able to move a flock of sheep and also responds to my commands, I then ask him to gather sheep that are spread throughout a field. Depending on the dog's natural ability, it can take him some time to fully understand how to gather a dispersed flock without leaving any behind.

At this stage as well as giving my dog plenty of natural work, I will also do precision training with him. For example, I teach him to drive different numbers of sheep over greater distances; alternatively, I make the shed harder by asking him to separate out just a few sheep from the flock and to take them away from the rest. I also use the *look back* more frequently. However, even at this point of his training, I ensure that I am sufficiently close to my dog so that I can give support, if and when, he requires it.

Fact Box. Pressure

As I have discussed before, pressure is the positive assertive energy that you, your dog and the sheep portray to each other. When dogs and sheep interact with each other and with humans, they will instinctively pick up and interpret this energy to determine the dynamics of the situation. Although you do not realise it at the time, your behaviour will also be influenced by what is happening around you. Unless you carefully analyse everything, you may not be aware of what your body language and gestures are really saying.

Pressure interactions to consider are:

- **Handler to sheep:** You need to take care how and where you move when you are in close proximity of sheep. What energy level are you portraying? How are the sheep interpreting your intention? For more information about sheep body language look at the chapter on sheep sense (see page 49).

- **Handler to dog:** You need to be aware how your dog reads your body languages and gestures. If you have any doubts, review the chapters on canine communication (see page 6) and how to speak the dog's language (see page 13).

- **Sheep to dog:** Certain types of sheep can be more challenging than others. If a dog lies down, he can be more easily intimidated than one that stands. You need to be aware that sheep will apply pressure / release using similar body language and gestures that dogs and human use.

- **Dog to sheep:** The dog's movement, attitude, energy and gestures will all influence the sheep. Watch how they respond to your dog to determine whether his behaviour is appropriate.

- **Dog to handler:** Look at how your dog interacts with you. If he pushes into your personal space (without you requesting him to do so) then he is attempting to put pressure on you and is showing disrespect.

By the time that my dog is approximately two (Nursery Trial age), I would expect him to be able to gather both a few sheep or a larger flock over a distance of up to 400m. He should take flank commands and redirection well plus be able to drive sheep with confidence. He should also be able to shed sheep and work in the pens. Importantly, he should have the correct mindset, attitude and feel for his sheep so that no matter what task he is required to do, he can work his stock without stressing them.

I only take a dog beyond this standard if I believe he has the natural ability and trainability to cope with the increased demands that further training will inevitably bring. If I think a dog is sufficiently talented and able to progress to an advanced stage, I will use natural farm work to extend his experience further and I will increase the distance, difficulty and precision of his tasks. However, not every dog can be trained to this higher level and I would prefer to see my dog content by being asked for less rather than being pushed beyond his ability so that he starts to resent both his work and me.

Moving On

At the end of the day, it does not matter how long it takes to train your dog as long as you both enjoy the process of working together as a team. A shepherd and his dog should have a close bond built on mutual respect, trust and loyalty. Not every dog can become a superstar, so be happy if your dog is giving his heart to you and trying his best.

In the next chapter I will discuss how to introduce your dog to sheep. You need to read your dog, the sheep and the situation correctly, so that you can apply appropriate pressure when this is required. Do not forget that release from pressure is equally important because this will indicate to your dog that he is acting in an appropriate fashion. Remember, throughout your dog's training you should relay clear simple instructions so that he learns to manage his sheep in a stress free manner.

Fact Box. Setting up a good training environment

Everyday sheep work on a farm tests your ability to read your flock without you realising it. However, if you do not have much natural work for your dog and perhaps only have a few sheep in a small flat field, you can still train to a reasonably high standard by setting yourself different exercises. Once your dog has a strong foundation and is at a sufficient standard, you can start giving yourself tasks to do. Some examples may include.

- Test your dog for all responses including slow flank, fast flank, small flank, longer flank, emergency stop, *steady*, hurry up, *out*, come in, *look back* and *that'll do*.
- Put obstacles in the field to manoeuvre around and through.
- Practice moving sheep from one field to another. If you only have a single field in which to work, then you could set up a gate along a fence. This will allow you to hold the sheep on the fence until you have opened the gate ready to take them through.
- Load the sheep onto a trailer.
- Shed your sheep into different groups around the field and only sometimes ask your dog to gather all of them back together. On other occasions, you could ask him to drive one group near to other, whilst ensuring that the two groups do not join back together.
- After your dog has lifted his sheep, instead of letting him fetch them in a straight line, you could make him drive them across the field to an obstacle before returning back to your side.

Fact Box. Minimum standard to achieve before competing with your dog

In my opinion, a dog needs to be at the intermediate stage of training before exposing him to any level of competition. To me this means that:

- He can manage an outrun of at least 200-300 metres.
- He has sufficient feel for his sheep so that he does not unduly upset them during the lift, fetch and drive.
- He has good, instinctive balance and knows where to position himself properly.
- He is willing to take commands and responds promptly to your voice or whistle.
- He needs to have a good understanding of shedding and is able to exert pressure when necessary to maintain control over the sheep.
- He should be able to pen, or at the very least, be able to hold sheep quietly on a fence. This is the preparatory stage for penning (see page 152).

CHAPTER 8
INTRODUCTION TO SHEEP

An important part of a working sheepdog's job is his ability to work out of sight from the shepherd. It is therefore imperative that he learns how to use his initiative and is able to feel his sheep. This will enable him to gather and bring the whole flock in a settled, calm yet efficient, manner. When you introduce your young dog to sheep, you want these early formative sessions to provide a strong foundation so that he will develop into a confident, thoughtful worker with a calm mindset.

Everyone has their own ideas as to the right age that a dog should be introduced to sheep. When the pup is still quite young (approximately four months of age), it is always nice to see if he shows any instinct to work sheep and it is always a joy to see that a youngster takes notice of sheep rather than just ignoring them. However, at this stage, he is still too young, both mentally and physically, to start his training. If you wish to test your pup's interest, but are unsure of his reaction, especially if he is excitable and strong minded, then you can put three or four sheep safely inside a pen. You can then let your pup loose outside the pen. This way, he can see the sheep and run freely around the outside without hurting them or himself.

Some farmers let their young dogs just run loose around stock. I definitely do not recommend this for several reasons, Firstly, if left to his own devices, a pup can quickly develop bad habits and start to believe he can please himself around sheep. Once your pup believes this, it can take time to sort out. Secondly, a young pup running loose around stock can stress or injure them. Finally, the pup himself could be confronted and butted by a bold sheep, especially if she has a lamb. This could completely knock a young dog's confidence and make him uncertain whether it is safe to approach sheep, which in turn, could hamper his future progress.

To my mind, it is much easier and better to start your pup in a controlled manner where you can use appropriate pressure / release to teach him to have the correct mindset around

sheep. This way your dog learns right from the start that stock are not playthings and when he is near sheep, he should be in 'working mode'.

I normally begin a youngster's lessons on sheep when he is between six to ten months of age. The age I actually start will depend on the young dog's physical and mental maturity. I am looking for him to be sufficiently developed to take some gentle guidance. He needs to be able to physically outrun the sheep and also be mentally ready to receive some tuition.

Short positive training sessions are much more productive than long negative ones. So just ten minutes will probably be sufficient at this stage. It is a steep learning curve for a young dog and he will get tired quickly. I recommend that initially you do not train your dog every day. If you leave a few days between sessions then your dog will have some time to absorb all the information he has learnt in his previous lesson.

Even when you have a well-mannered dog off sheep, he can be very keen when he sees stock. This means your dog may initially be unwilling to listen to you once you enter the training field. It is therefore advisable to have the youngster on a long line of approximately four metres in length that you should attach to his collar before you go through the field gate. The line will let you start and end your sessions in a calm fashion as you can be in control as you walk with him towards or away from stock.

I also recommend, that after you have entered the field, but before you reach the sheep, you ask him to *look*. If you include this at the start of every training session, then he will gradually start to associate this command with the fact that he is about to work and that he should therefore look for his sheep. This will help him later on when he needs to find sheep that are at a distance. However, only give the *look* command when he is calm. This will also encourage him to move into the appropriate mindset when he hears this command. If your dog is overly excited and pulls when he enters the field give the line a short tug to remind him of his manners. If he is over stimulated, do not give him the *look* command because otherwise he may start to associate the word *look* with excitement.

Many people find that a large round pen of about twenty to forty metres in diameter is a very good place to introduce your young dog to sheep. You will find it easier to be close at hand and you can then use The Natural Way to gently and quietly choreograph your dog into the correct position. Another important advantage of the round pen is sheep welfare. A sheep being chased down the field by an excited dog will quickly become stressed. Remember that a panicking sheep fleeing from a potential predator is unable to think clearly and she might easily break her neck if she runs into a taut fence.

This is also why I try to use **dogged sheep** for training. These are sheep that are used to being worked by a dog and are quieter and less likely to be stressed by the situation. In addition, they are more likely to flock together plus they have often learnt that it is safer to remain close to me as I will protect them from an overenthusiastic youngster!

You do not need to use aggressive or excited commands when training your dog. Instead calm, quiet body language with blocks and gentle nudges will tell him to move out of your space and around to the other side of the sheep. When used correctly, with appropriate timing, your manoeuvres will stimulate him to go around (and not through) the sheep. It can be difficult for some dogs to work in a round pen because inappropriate pressure from the novice handler forces him into a situation where he feels uncomfortable or intimidated by the sheep, for example being forced to go along the fence line when the sheep are tight up against it. This can encourage gripping, excitement or avoidance.

At these early stages, you should try to stay close to your sheep to protect them. If the sheep move away from you then your dog may be tempted to rush into them. Moreover, you may actually cause him to do this because your proximity to him may exert (unintentional) pressure that encourages him to run towards the sheep.

You therefore need to continually monitor the relative position of yourself, your dog and your sheep to determine how much pressure you need to apply. You also need to watch your dog's body language and gestures as these will indicate whether he is feeling relaxed, excited or anxious about the situation. You want to vary the amount of pressure / release that you use so that he develops a calm focused mindset as he holds the stock to you while you walk backwards away from him.

Start and end in a positive fashion
I often use a long line for young dogs when they are first introduced to sheep.

Working in a round pen with a young inexperienced dog 1
I keep close to the sheep so that I can protect them whilst I communicate with
Gyp. Initially, I encourage Gyp to move so that the sheep are held on the fence.
A My stick is down but slightly pointing towards her shoulder to keep her
moving anticlockwise. **B** I have raised my stick slightly so that it is now held in a
block position. In response, Gyp has lowered her body stance and has stopped.
C I have moved to the other side of the sheep. In response, Gyp has mirrored
my movement to balance the stock towards me. I hold the stick slightly higher
to ask her to *steady* her pace.

With my own dogs, I tend to only use the round pen for the first few initial introductory sessions. As soon as possible, I prefer to work with a youngster out in a field. This is because there is more room here, so the young dog can learn to use his natural ability to determine the appropriate distance that gently controls, but does not unsettle, the stock. However, when I work out in field in this way, I use a more experienced dog to hold the sheep close to me. If you intend to use a second dog to do this, then it is important that both dogs consider that you are the Alpha of the pack. Otherwise the youngster will start to balance his sheep towards the older one rather than towards you. Even worse, if the dogs do not respect you as leader, then two or more dogs together can hype each other up. This can lead to the dogs becoming overexcited and they could goad each other to start chasing or even harming the stock. For this reason, if you are a novice handler and do not have an experienced dog available, I advise that you continue working in the round pen or in a very small field until much of the foundation work has been established.

However, if you do not have access to a round pen and cannot stop the sheep from fleeing when you try to work in the middle of the field, then an alternative approach is to allow the sheep to settle close to a stock proof fence and to use this as a physical barrier to stop the sheep running off. You can then encourage your dog to hold the sheep to the fence. You should then stand either behind or beside the sheep in a position that allows you to encourage the correct movement from your dog. When he is moving correctly and the sheep are nicely settled, you can walk backwards along the fence-line whilst encouraging the dog to fetch the sheep to you. However, if he keeps coming in towards the sheep, then you need to stand between your dog and them and use sufficient pressure to push him off in order to re-establish a respectful, calm mindset.

Once you feel confident that your dog is listening and responding well, you can start to move away from the safety of the fence. To do this, start as before, but now reposition yourself and move backwards into the field, again encouraging your dog to fetch the sheep towards you. The sheep should now be in the open. Use your body language to push your dog away from you and encourage him to run to the heads of the ewes. Then reposition yourself to help him balance the stock as he fetches them towards you (see page 84).

At the end of a session, reward your dog by gently stroking the side of his face and neck as he sits besides you. This soothing touch is praise enough and helps to reinforce and cement the bonds between you and your dog. Pick up the long line to stop your dog running back towards the sheep and leave the field in a calm manner.

Fact Box. Working with a long line

A long line (approximately 4m in length) can be a useful aid when starting your dog on sheep. It will stop the youngster from bolting towards the stock before you have the sheep settled and you are ready to start. Start by holding the rope as a long lead (with most of the line lying behind you on the ground) and position yourself to one side of the dog. Consider wearing gloves so that if your dog does pull the line through your hands, you do not get a rope burn.

Ensure that you get close enough to the sheep that you can position yourself to help your dog. Ask your dog to bend out by gently tugging him away from your body while at the same time applying light pressure on his shoulder by pointing with your other hand (or pipe). Combined this will encourage him to give to your pressure and start to flank around the sheep. As he bends outwards, you can feed out the line and then let go. However, if your dog is not paying attention to you and rushes straight towards the sheep, then, because you have hold of the line, you are in a good position to give a short tug to correct him.

When you want to finish your training session, pick up the line to make sure that your dog responds to your recall. This will let you finish your session in a positive way.

Remember that release from pressure is an important part of training the Natural Way. If you continually keep pressure on the line, then eventually the dog will pull back in response. Therefore you should make sure that the line is not taut when your dog is behaving properly.

Once I feel Gyp has settled and is responding to my body language, I ask her to move between the sheep and the fence. A young dog may find this manoeuvre difficult because such close proximity to the sheep and the fence puts pressure on him. In response to this additional pressure, the youngster may either be intimidated or excited depending on his natural temperament and confidence. **A** My left hand is slightly out and putting pressure on Gyp's rear in order to drive her forward. My stick is lowered, but positioned opposite her shoulder to encourage her to move correctly round towards the fence. The stick is not raised because this could intimidate her at this crucial moment. **B** As Gyp reaches the small gap between the sheep and fence, I encourage and support her forward movement by gently coaxing her with my left hand which is pointed behind her rear while my stick continues to guide her shoulder and body movement outwards. **C** As Gyp successfully moves through the gap, I relax my body whilst ensuring that she still covers the final sheep. **D** As I let sheep out of the pen, I block the gateway to stop Gyp rushing after them and ensure that the session ends in a positive fashion.

Problems

Insufficient respect

If your dog does not have sufficient respect for you, then he will please himself. In this situation you will find it difficult to train your dog because you will always be fighting with him to prove you are in charge. In contrast, once you have gained your dog's respect, you will find training becomes easier and feels more relaxed. This is because your dog acknowledges you are his pack leader. This means he will want to work with you and will try harder to please you. I believe that you need to give as well as take, so it is important that you respect your dog in return. I have discussed how to use The Natural Way to build respect from your dog previously (see page 19). If you promote this mutual regard, you will develop a strong partnership and bond with your dog.

Excitement

This can be sparked in your dog from a variety of causes. These include the sheep themselves, you as the handler, or from other people or dogs in the vicinity. Even adverse weather conditions such as a very windy day can create this unwanted mindset in your dog. You need to analyse the situation to determine the cause.

- Is it the sheep? Perhaps they are bolting or confronting your dog.
- Is it your dog? You need to determine whether he is anxious or lacking confidence.
- Is it you? Your dog could be sensing your own anxiety or perhaps are you using inappropriate pressure on him. You may be waving your arms around and unintentionally encouraging him to think you want to play with him.
- Is it the situation? Perhaps, your dog is becoming anxious when he is asked go between the sheep and the fence?

Once you have found the cause you can start to address the problem. It often helps to stand closer to your sheep. You also need to watch your dog's body language carefully. Then use pressure / release properly to settle his mind and encourage him to think about his sheep in a calm fashion.

Avoidance

Although some dogs display excitement in response to anxiety and inappropriate pressure, others display avoidance behaviour for example sniffing the ground, exhibiting a lack of interest or losing contact with his sheep and going into orbit. As in all canine communication, these signs need to be taken in the appropriate context and can mean different things depending on your dog's innate mentality and the circumstances.

Often the handler has used too much inappropriate pressure for that particular dog. Think about what your body language is actually saying to your dog. If you are using an artificial aid such as a pipe then lower it to the ground. You may even decide not to use one at all. Instead, encourage and support your dog to give him confidence when he works his sheep.

Remember, an important part of training The Natural Way is to release pressure appropriately so that your dog knows when he is doing the right thing.

Sheep too fast

Working an excitable young dog around sheep can stress the stock and they may try to flee to escape the pressure. However, running sheep can stimulate your dog's chase or hunting instinct. As the working border collie's natural instinct is to attempt to outrun and turn his stock, it is not surprising, if your dog becomes frustrated when he is unable to do this. This frustration can make some dogs cut in and grip the sheep.

Before attempting to deal with this problem, make sure that your dog is physically able to outrun his stock. Your dog also needs to be mentally old enough to take some pressure from you.

If he is sufficiently mature, but still insists on cutting in, you should move forward to block him and then push him out using appropriate pressure. This is explained in more detail in the chapters that discuss the outrun and the *out* command (see pages 93 and page 134).

Fact Box. Use of artificial aids

People often use a variety of items during training. These can include a plastic pipe, rolled up plastic bags, a crook etc. These items should only be used as an extension of your arm in order to help you put pressure accurately and precisely on your dog, for example, by pointing at his shoulder. They should be used with care because otherwise you can do more harm than good. Misappropriate use can result in your dog becoming anxious about working with you. Alternatively, he may become hardened and immune to the desired effect (equivalent to a human who has stopped listening to somebody who continually nags them).

Watch your dog's body language and energy levels

When I use a stick, I routinely raise and lower it depending on the dog's behaviour and energy. **A** Gyp is a young dog who is very sensitive and responds to light pressure. Although Gyp is some distance from me, she feels the pressure of the raised stick and tells me so by licking her lips. In response, I lower my stick. **B** However, because of her sensitivity, she still feels the influence from the previous pressure. This means that when I just slightly raise my stick, she uses diversion tactics and starts sniffing the ground. This is her way of telling me she is not a threat and also indicates her anxiety. At this point I would remove all pressure by lowering the stick, turning to the side and dropping my gaze whilst encouraging her to move back onto the sheep. **C** A young bitch being handled by her owner shows excitement and her body language indicates she is in 'play mode'. **D** Dogs playing together with raised tails and excited eyes. If a dog has this attitude around sheep, he is likely to start chasing and may grip the sheep if he is not kept in check. **E** When I use appropriate pressure / release on the same bitch as shown in C, she relaxes and focuses on her sheep. She has a relaxed lowered tail and portrays a steady attentive energy. She now has the correct mental attitude that I wish to encourage in order to ensure the sheep are not stressed.

Taking sheep off a fence

If sheep are close to a fence, it can be very intimidating for a dog to run between them. This manoeuvre puts a lot of pressure on the dog and in response some may respond by doing something silly. This can include gripping. So, do not just send an inexperienced dog to take sheep away from a fence and expect him just to be able to do it. If you do this, you are setting your dog up to fail. You need to show him what is required.

In reality, taking sheep off a fence uses the same basic technique as asking your dog to flank around sheep, the only difference is that, in the former the dog has to push between the sheep and the fence and as I have just explained this makes it much harder to do. The best way to teach your dog to take sheep off a fence is to build up to it. Start by flanking your dog in the middle of the field as described in the next couple of chapters. Then repeat the exercise, but gradually move the sheep closer to the fence. The dog will get used to moving through successively smaller gaps. Eventually, you and your dog will be confident enough to let your dog push past sheep that are standing tightly against the fence. Remember every dog is different and each has their own level of confidence. Sometimes you need to leave the dog until he has matured and become sufficiently self-assured to be able to manage to do this.

If your dog still refuses to take sheep off a fence then you can use a long line and walk with him to help guide him between the sheep and the fence. Once he has started to move between the sheep and the fence, you should reposition yourself back towards the middle of the field (dropping the rope, if necessary). Your dog can then bring the sheep towards you and he will learn that you want the sheep brought off the fence. However, I find that instead of moving into the middle of the field, many novice handlers often continue to move forward with their dog in an attempt to push him around on a flank. When the handler does this, the dog tends to run to head the sheep and then hold them back onto the fence. The result is that everyone ends up in the same position as they started in!

Gripping

Many young dogs will try to grip sheep and there can be a variety of reasons for this including youthfulness and the excitement of trying to keep up with running sheep. However, a grip is usually telling you something about the dog and the sheep. A dog that just snaps a sheep on the nose and leaves go immediately is a confident dog who is sure of himself. In contrast, a dog that dives in, grips and runs away, is usually one that lacks confidence and is anxious about something. This could be the sheep, the situation or his handler. Situations that can promote this kind of gripping can include taking sheep off a fence, putting the dog in a confined space with sheep for example working in pens and inappropriate pressure from the handler. So although some people call a dog that grips a powerful dog, this is often not true.

Another type of grip that some dogs use is to hang on to the sheep's flank (sometimes called 'running with the sheep'). These dogs often have some guts and they are willing to please, but, at the same time, they may also be tense because they lack some confidence. Alternatively, they may have a bit of a temper or are not sufficiently agile and are unable to outrun the sheep and so grip out of frustration.

Furthermore, there are times when a working dog has to defend himself against a challenging sheep. In these situations, he may need to use appropriate force that could include a deserved, timely, short, sharp grip on the nose. As there are times when I need the dog to grip in order to move a recalcitrant sheep, I often will give my dog a specific command so that he knows that on that occasion it is okay to give a timely nip.

You need to recognise these many different types of grip and understand the basis behind them. You then have to decide whether they need to be addressed firmly, moderately, gently or not at all What you do not want to end up with is a 'dirty gripping' dog that is only interested in hunting. This type of a dog will take every opportunity to attack sheep rather than work them. He is a headache for the shepherd and the flock as you could never trust him to work safely at a distance away from his handler. However, a dog like this can still be very suitable for other jobs, for example, working with cattle.

Moving On

You cannot predict how your dog will react to stock from the way he behaves around humans or other dogs. When you introduce your dog to sheep you will gain more insight into your dog's nature, ability and trainability. This in turn will help you make decisions about how much pressure / release you will need to use to encourage your dog to develop the appropriate mindset and to stimulate his natural talent and feel for sheep. However, remember that you are dealing with a young

mind and using too much inappropriate pressure may cause as many problems as using none at all.

Do not worry if your dog displays unwanted behaviour at the start of his training, this does not have to become a habit. However, you need to identify the cause and confront the problem in an appropriate manner. Although many issues should be addressed as they arise, not every one needs an immediate solution: some just need to be noted and dealt with at a later date when the dog is able to understand why you are applying corrective pressure.

At these early foundation stages, you need to concentrate on nurturing and controlling his hunting instinct and in the next chapter I will discuss how to encourage your dog to balance his sheep correctly.

The position of the dog and handler affect how sheep behave

A The position of the dog and handler pressurises the sheep. Moreover, the dog has an intent eye and energy which adds additional pressure on the ewe and prompts her to break away from the others. **B** The dog is not in the correct position to head the fleeing ewe back towards the others and so goes to grip her in a fit of temper. **C** Diagram shows how the pressure from the dog's eye (blue line) combined with the handler's position pushes the single ewe away from the others. **D** If the handler and dog had positioned themselves further away and had properly covered the sheep, the pressure points on the stock would have altered and they would have remained grouped together. If the ewe had still fled, the dog would have been able to move to turn her (yellow arrow) without resorting to a grip.

Introducing Tess to sheep for the first time was quite an eye opener. Tess was a slim, agile dog who was built like a whippet with the speed to match her looks. She was fast not only in movement, but also in mind. She was desperate to work sheep from an early age so I started her training when she was just a few months old. At her first session, we worked in a relatively small field and I gathered and held some quiet Cheviots with another dog. Although she was eager to start, she waited until I drew closer to the stock. I put slight pressure on her shoulder to encourage her to move in an arc around the sheep. Timing was correct and as I released the long line, she was around the sheep like a bullet out of gun. She completed a few nice turns, then before I even had chance to blink, she shed one of the ewes off from the group and chased it up the field with me in hot pursuit. Thankfully the field was flat and small, otherwise I would not have managed to catch her up.

We had a further couple of sessions similar to this, but each time I managed to stop her a bit sooner. I knew this behaviour was a family trait as both her mother and sisters before her had done the same thing. However, since I believed that Tess was quite sensitive I did not want to overdo the pressure. It was therefore the third episode before enough was enough. This time I immediately gave her a firm warning with an accompanying growl in a similar manner as bitch will reprimand her unruly pup (see Anecdote of Kim disciplining her pup on page 11). This made her realise that working sheep was not a game. It was also the only occasion that I had to rebuke her more firmly than I really wanted to. Tess developed into a very willing and clever dog who gave me everything she had. She became one of my main work and trial dogs and was brilliant and successful at both.

From the Clinic

Handler: My young dog has a tendency to grip and this is gradually getting worse. When I put pressure on him, I seem to gain control because he moves away from the sheep and flanks around them. However, after a short while, he comes in and tries to grip again.

I observed the dog being introduced to sheep. He walked onto the field without pulling on his lead. However, I saw that although he remained by his owner's side, his body was crouched down and slightly tense. He was also staring intently at the sheep. When she let him go, she stood by his side to send him. He rushed straight towards the sheep and gripped one. In response to this, the handler chased after her dog and shouted at him to get off. The dog flew out so that he was a long distance away from the stock and started to flank widely around them. Whilst doing this, he did not look toward the sheep at all. After the session, I asked the owner what she thought had just happened. She believed her dog was relaxed at the start because he did not pull on the lead. She also considered that by forcing him to stay off his sheep, she was doing the right thing. She thought that the dog had a major problem but that she, herself, was not handling him inappropriately.

My opinion: The owner set her dog up to fail because she knew that he would probably grip if he was given the opportunity. By standing at her dog's side at the start of the session, she had let his head and body point directly at the sheep. Rather than blocking his direct route to them, the position of the owner's body meant that she had inadvertently encouraged him to run directly toward them. Although the dog had walked onto the field without pulling on his lead, his whole body and eye contact were telling me 'I'm going to get those sheep'. These signs are often subtle and can be overlooked by someone who is not used to reading a dog's body language properly.

My advice: Before sending her dog, the owner first needed to change his attitude by blocking him from the sheep. She should do this by standing in front of him with a dominant stance to push him out of her space. This would remind her dog that she was his Alpha. Before progressing further, her dog had to indicate that he had calmed down and respected his handler. For example, he needed to relax his body, soften his eyes and slightly turn his head to the side. Once the dog had relaxed, the handler should reposition herself closer to the sheep. This would indicate to the dog that she was declaring her 'ownership' of the stock and that she was protecting them. Once in this position, the handler should lean forward slightly and ask the dog to give to her pressure before she allowed him to move. The dog should give to this pressure by moving his head and shoulders slightly back (and maybe licking or chewing) to show submission. These signs would indicate that he now had the correct mindset. Only then, should the owner release pressure and allow her dog to start his flank around the sheep. In this mindset, he will be listening to his handler and no longer focused on chasing sheep. If the handler, then positioned herself correctly as he flanked, she can continue to influence his movement (see later chapter on the Natural Flank and Outrun (page 90)).

In addition to the problem caused by starting her dog incorrectly, the handler had also inadvertently pushed him out of contact with his sheep. Because this issue relates also to teaching the flank correctly, I will discuss how I helped resolve this on page 103.

Chapter 9
Balancing and Wearing Sheep

Moving sheep requires the dog to take control of their direction and their speed. He needs to read their responses and then adjust his own energy and movement to put the correct amount of pressure on his flock so that they remain settled whilst he works them. Sheep which are not stressed are easier to move and quieter to handle. This makes the shepherd's work more efficient and effective. In contrast, sheep that are stressed are more likely to be anxious and flighty. This can cause them to get injured and in the longer term lose weight and condition.

A dog will read the situation much better than most humans; not only is he often physically closer to the sheep, but he is also much more aware of the subtle signals that stock inevitably give out. A dog that is encouraged to have a good feel for his sheep and understands how to use his instincts appropriately will be much more useful to the shepherd than a dog that has to wait for command or else pushes onto the stock with little thought for their well-being.

Balance is the dog's ability to read the reaction of the sheep and then alter his own energy as well as position himself at the right location and distance (**the balance point**) from the sheep so that he is able to move them forwards (**wear**), or hold them at, the point of interest. This point of interest could be you (the handler) or any other place such as a gate.

Julie's Tip. When you initially train a dog, make sure that he knows that you are the focal point that he needs to balance towards. This needs to be ingrained and well established before you start introducing the concept of balancing sheep towards another point of interest.

In order to balance properly, the dog should manage his sheep in a controlled manner. He needs to exert this control without using excessive pressure because it is important that the stock do not become unduly stressed. The balance point is not always when the dog is directly behind the sheep – often the sheep move to the side and the dog has to move further out to push the sheep heads (and their direction) back toward the point of interest. In addition, if you want your dog to balance sheep towards you, then as you move, the dog should continue to hold the sheep to you, no matter what direction you take.

A dog's ability to feel his sheep properly is different from obedience. When a dog feels the sheep, he is thinking for himself and will position himself appropriately and promptly to pre-empt any unwanted movement from the stock, for example turning a sheep back to the flock when she attempts to break away. In contrast, a dog that is heavily under command will wait for the instruction from the handler before moving. If you decide to use obedience training to do this, you need to see and understand the sheep's intention as well as give a command before your dog will respond. If you train your dog this way, he will not know what to do when you cannot see him and / or the stock: an event that can frequently happen while working on the hill.

Moreover, a dog that is not used to making his own decisions may become anxious and lose confidence when he has to rely on his own resourcefulness. This may cause him to become confused and act erratically. Furthermore the novice handler may reinforce this confusion by then using inappropriate vocal and physical pressure in an attempt to control the situation. Not surprisingly, the dog then believes that it is wrong to use his initiative and so he becomes even more dependent on the handler telling him what to do.

Rather than disciplining and formally training a young dog, I use The Natural Way to develop the dog's innate instinct to feel, read and respond appropriately to the sheep. This uses appropriate pressure / release to encourage the dog in a relaxed manner to think about what he is doing. As I have just explained I am looking for much more than my dog just being on the other side of sheep from me: I am developing his feel for sheep as well as encouraging him to respond promptly as soon as the sheep signal their intent to move.

When I have a young dog, I use another trained dog to keep the sheep close to me. This means I can work in the middle of a field. If you do not have another dog, then you can continue using a fence as a barrier. However, once your dog has a calm mindset and the sheep are settled, gradually move towards the middle of the field.

Julie's Tip. When you walk into a field with your dog and as long as he is calm, ask him to look for his sheep. This will prepare him for the outrun and will help later with the look back command.

When you start with a new dog it is useful to have quiet sheep. Take him out to them on a long line. This will allow you to have control and you should be able to walk with your dog up towards the stock. Sheep are very sensitive to energy. Any dog that has not learnt how to control this hunting energy will send out signals of his intent to the sheep even before he enters the field. You need to educate your dog how to control this inner energy. A dog pulling the long line is telling the sheep 'Beware, I am coming to get you.' If your dog does this, then you need to put some pressure on him by positioning yourself between the sheep and him. You then need to use body language and gestures that suggest he had better back off and settle down. You will not change his attitude immediately. However, you need to work consistently with your dog and gradually he will start to understand that it is counterproductive for him to upset sheep. Remember in a pack, the youngster would be educated by the higher ranking dogs, otherwise his over-excitable behaviour would alert the prey and ruin the hunt.

Once you are close to the sheep, position yourself between the sheep and the dog so that you can use body language and gestures to indicate what you want him to do. At this early stage, you are aiming to keep your dog on the opposite side of the sheep from you so that he can begin wearing them towards you. To make him move out in an arc to balance to the other side, you need to stimulate his movement by driving him forward and lifting his shoulder in a similar fashion as you used in the round pen without sheep. Do not worry whether your dog runs left or right: at these early stages this does not matter. Keep repositioning your body to move your dog. There is an invisible line between the dog and the sheep. If you cross over this, either intentionally or inadvertently, the dog will feel that you are putting pressure on that side and it will block his intended movement in that direction. In response to your block, he may move the other way.

Occasionally your dog might find himself in the middle of the sheep. If this happens, move forward to push him back out and encourage him around the sheep once more.

Training The Natural Way uses the same body language that you use with your dog away from sheep: moving towards your dog will apply pressure. Conversely, when you move away from him, then you are releasing pressure and this will make him feel comfortable. Even standing still is communicating with your dog: the way you stand and look at him, whether you are leaning forward, backwards or to the side plus whether you have your hand raised or not are all indicating different levels of pressure / release to your dog. You need to consciously use your body language to have an on-going discussion with your dog. Use the graduated scale of 'ask, tell, insist' and give the dog time to work out what is the right thing to do.

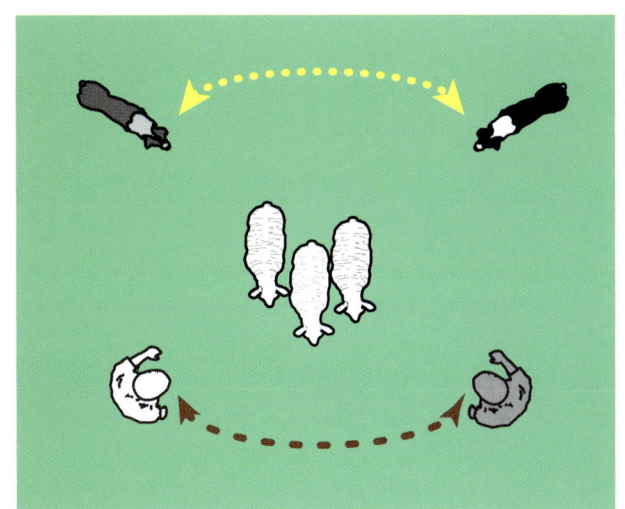

Balance

When you train your dog, you nurture his natural instinct to balance sheep to you. As the handler moves, the dog should counterbalance this while also taking the stock's movement and intent into account.

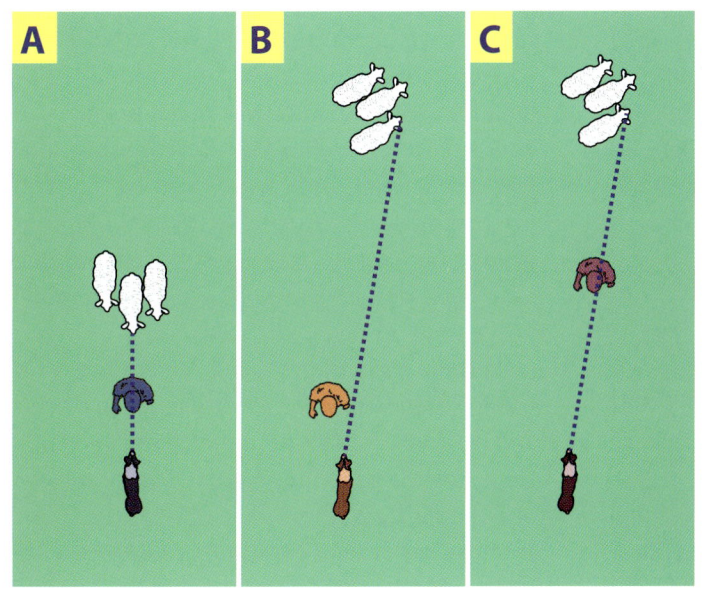

Read your sheep and be ready to adjust your position appropriately

The amount of pressure your dog feels from you will vary depending on how far the sheep are from you. **A** If the sheep, dog and you are close to each together and you are standing on the 'invisible line' between your dog and sheep, then you will block all your dog's movement and he will stop. **B** If the sheep move further away, then even though you remain at the same distance from your dog, you will now exert pressure on him and he will want to move. In this example, the handler is no longer standing on the invisible line and blocking the route to the sheep, so the dog will probably run towards them. **C** In order to continue to block your dog's movement when the sheep are at this distance, you need to move closer to the sheep and again stand on the invisible line.

The balance point is not always directly behind sheep

A The balance point depends on the draw of the sheep indicated by the purple arrows. The draw is the direction, speed and intent that the sheep are moving towards when the dog fetches them towards the handler. The diagram shows where the dog should position himself as the sheep move in different directions. **B** Ban naturally balances himself to turn the ewe lambs so that they are brought towards the camera.

> **Fact Box. The graded scale of 'ask, tell, insist'**
>
> **Ask:** Physically, take one step forward and lean your body slightly forward towards the dog, then release. Vocally, use a quiet voice.
>
> **Tell:** Physically, step forward and hold pressure for longer until the dog shows submissive gestures. Vocally, add a soft growl.
>
> **Insist:** Physically, stalk the dog and dart forward as if to strike so that the dog perceives that you will attack if necessary. Vocally, add a deep, brusque, firmer growl.

I spend months educating my dog to think about his attitude towards stock. By nudging him with appropriate pressure for example by blocking or perhaps leaning towards him, I am saying 'Hey, this is not correct'. I do not ask for a stop, instead I let the dog turn and try again. It is only when the dog appropriately approaches his sheep with a calm attitude that I walk back and release the pressure showing him that I accept this movement. By not stopping him, but instead moving him and encouraging him to try again, I am saying 'Think about this' and when he gets it right, my walking backwards is saying 'Well done, you can have your reward and so can continue to work your sheep in a calm fashion.'

Julie's Tip. Watch the tail. It will indicate what your dog is thinking.

However, I only move back and release pressure when I am happy with his actions. If you do this at the wrong time; when the dog has the wrong attitude or is in the wrong place, you are telling him that you are satisfied with what he has done. This misuse and releasing of pressure at the inappropriate time can cause the dog to become confused. It is also why the handler needs good sheep-sense so that he can help guide the dog and show him when he has made the correct decision.

The amount of pressure / release you need to use will depend on your dog: how natural or how strong willed and resistant he is. You need to be alert and ready to react because the situation can change rapidly as both sheep and dog can move quickly. Do not expect things to be perfect immediately: you have to build towards the outcome you want.

It may feel as if you spend much of the training session standing still, but you must remember this block is communicating with your dog; asking him to consider his actions. You only increase the pressure to a 'tell' if the dog does not respond or if he continues to behave inappropriately. Once the dog responds properly you should go back to an 'ask'. If the dog remains resistant, then you may need to use an 'insist' amount of pressure. However, you must analyse the situation, either during or after your training session, to work out why your dog is being resistant. Is your body language really saying something different than you intend? Are your voice commands and gestures sending mixed messages so that you are confusing, exciting or worrying your dog? Remember that the way you speak to your dog as well as your movements can either stimulate or calm your dog.

At these early stages you should only ask for a stop when your dog is ready to listen to you. You need to watch for signs that your dog's body movement is becoming more relaxed and his attention is focused on you as well as the sheep. It is also easier to ask your dog to stop once he has turned the sheep towards you. When the dog is balancing sheep to you, he knows that the sheep are under your control and because you are the Alpha, this relaxes your dog and makes him more likely to listen and respond to the *lie-down*.

In contrast, if you ask the dog to *lie-down* before the stock are settled, it gives the sheep a chance to flee. This encourages the young dog to chase after them. If sheep are bolting and your dog is chasing them then it may be very hard for you to be able to stop him by vocal command alone. In this situation, if you keep shouting *lie-down*, he will just learn to ignore it. Instead, you need to move quickly to block him and use assertive body language to make him listen to you. If possible, you should try to avoid this situation happening by pre-empting the event as your sheep will indicate whether they are feeling stressed. This is another reason why you need to develop sheep-sense. You need to use pressure / release to keep the dog sufficiently back from the stock so that he covers his sheep on both sides. This will encourage them not to flee and give them a chance to settle.

Some types of dog have sufficient eye to hold their sheep steady. This type of dog can cover both sides of his sheep without much sideways movement. Instead he uses his eye and body stance which may sway slightly as he holds the sheep together. In contrast, other dogs need to move back and forth to tuck the outlying sheep back in.

Points to work on

Encourage your dog to move to the balance point, that is the point where the sheep's' heads turn towards you. When he has reached this point, continue to encourage him to walk towards his sheep so that they move in a straight line towards you. However, similar to a snooker ball, if the sheep have pressure applied in the wrong place with the wrong speed, they will move out of control in the wrong direction. Use appropriate pressure / release to show your dog what is acceptable movement on sheep and what is not. You need to help him develop a feel and correct attitude for his sheep. He needs to be able to move them appropriately with the least amount of stress. Never forget that this

is a predator / prey situation. Use appropriate gestures and body language to talk to your dog and ask him to move correctly. How you communicate to your dog will depend on what your dog is saying to you and how he is responding to the sheep. If necessary go back and re-read Chapter 2 (page 13) as this explains how to work with a dog that is resistant, disrespectful, worried or avoiding the situation.

Julie's Tip. Spend time building a strong foundation. Nurturing balance and developing the appropriate mindset are crucial keystones.

Moving On

At this stage you are not looking for perfection. Allow your dog to learn from working the sheep and use a combination of work on-command and natural work. You can improve your dog, but every dog has his own particular set of talents. He cannot be perfect in every aspect of training, but the more you work to help him, the better. Everything you teach your dog is working towards him becoming a very willing assistant. I cannot emphasise the importance of this strongly enough and it is why I personally spend months building up this strong foundation. If your dog is trained to a high standard, he can save you hours of work. In the next chapter I will describe how to teach your dog the natural flank, which in turn is the start of the outrun.

Using a second dog to hold sheep
A I use a more experienced dog to hold sheep to me when I train a youngster in an open field.
B At the end of a session, always reward your dog by gently and calmly stroking his side and face.

Fact Box. Using a second dog to help train a youngster

I often use a second more experienced dog to hold sheep to me when I train a youngster. If you decide to do this, you need to know the individual temperament of your dogs and be fully aware of how they will influence each other's behaviour. Points you need to consider are:

- When working with two or more dogs, it is vital that they all respect you as their leader because otherwise they may overexcite each other and start chasing stock.
- The experienced dog will often give the youngster confidence to deal with tricky situations such as working in pens or when a sheep turns and confronts him.
- If the two dogs have very different temperaments, then you may find that the older dog is more of a nuisance than a help. For example, the experienced dog may be stubborn and want to take control of the sheep rather than let the youngster learn how to manage them. In response to this, you will need to put increased pressure on your older dog to make him listen to you. If your young dog is sensitive, this increased pressure may upset him and decrease his willingness to work with you.

From the Clinic

Handler: My dog is keen, determined and stubborn. He is fast and strong on his sheep so I always seem to have to fight to control him. How can I calm my dog down, stop the stubborn behaviour and gain better control?

I observed that the handler walked out to the field in a confident manner. However, the dog at his side was desperate to work, his eyes were staring and his body looked tense like a coiled spring. When he was standing near to his handler, the dog would react suddenly and edgily to even the slightest movement. Once released from his lead, the dog ran quickly towards the sheep. He made a number of sudden tight turns and erratic moves as he approached them and completely ignored all attempts by his owner to slow and stop him. Once the dog had settled slightly, the handler managed to gain some control of his dog, but it appeared to me that neither the dog nor his handler were comfortable.

My opinion: The dog's behaviour, stance and staring eyes indicated that his mindset was not balanced. However, before jumping to conclusions, I took over handling the dog to gain a better insight into the underlying problem. I found that the dog not only resisted pressure but he had also ignored it and ran through all my signals as if I had not given any. This habit had been inadvertently taught by the owner because he had not confronted his dog and told him that this behaviour was unacceptable. This lack of clear guidelines from the owner had resulted in the dog believing that he could behave in this fashion.

My advice: When I started to work with the dog, he had wild staring eyes, I therefore initially maintained a quiet, but determined and assertive posture. I did not ask him to stop by using the *lie-down* vocal command. Instead, I solely used body language to block his movement. As the dog's previous experience had meant that he had become dull to pressure, I found that I needed to maintain focused pressure to enforce the block. Eventually, he stopped and then he turned his head slightly away from me. This subtle gesture indicated that he was starting to submit to my authority. As soon as he gave this signal, I released pressure by stepping back and standing side-on with a relaxed posture. This told the dog that I was happy with his decision.

Because I used the pressure/release technique properly, he quickly understood what I required from him. Once, this link was established between us, I moved slowly forward to gradually increase pressure on him. By doing this, I was requesting that the dog take a natural flank and because he now understood what I required, he responded appropriately. I then repeated this exercise with the other flank. Because I was using the pressure-release technique in a manner he understood, the dog quickly relaxed and became willing to give to my pressure. Furthermore, because he realised that I was consistent in the way I gave my requests, rewards and corrections, he quickly developed a desire to please me.

This dog was not dominant, instead he was eager to work. The eagerness had resulted in the handler using exaggerated commands and sudden movements as he fought to control his dog. These actions, had, in turn, made the dog worried and as his anxiety increased, the dog had found it increasingly hard to think clearly. The only way he had been able to cope with the situation was to ignore his owner. With this type of dog, it is important that his handler did not incite him in this fashion. Instead, his owner needed to portray a strong, assertive but calm presence. When pressure was required, it had to be applied firmly and promptly so that the dog did not have time to become over-stimulated. It was also important that the handler released pressure when the dog started to respond appropriately. Once the handler used pressure/release properly, the dog became more settled. He started to understand that it was better to give to pressure rather than fight it. The overall result was that he stated to want to please his hander and work with him.

Fact Box. Some key commands

Lie-down: This command is initially taught away from sheep. Preferably start when your dog is a young pup (approximately three months old). Teach your dog to *lie-down* in response to slight pressure exerted on his muzzle. Once the youngster has learnt to give to this physical touch, you should ask him to respond when your hand is held a short way from him. Start to introduce the vocal command. Gradually, move away from your dog and continue to use the same signal with the *lie-down* command. Eventually, your dog should respond to just the vocal command or when you slightly raise your hand or point your finger. Remember, your dog should always feel comfortable when you ask for a lie-down. If he feels uncomfortable when you give the command it may make him worried or else he may resist you.

Steady: Initially teach this when your dog is nearby and balancing sheep towards you. Use a quiet, calm, assertive tone. Your body language should be a half-halt block meaning you lean forwards slightly. Your dog should respond by sitting back on his hocks for a couple of seconds. When you see this, your body should rock backwards to release the pressure. If you need to enforce the *steady* command, then ask him to *stand* (see below). If the dog totally ignores your request, you need to reassert your authority by driving him away and changing his attitude so that he wants to negotiate with you.

Stand: Use the block to teach your dog to *stand*. If he lies down, take a step back to release the pressure and ask him to get up and then soften your block and ask for a *stand* again. Your tone of voice should be slightly sharper than that used for the *steady*.

Walk-on/Get up: As you move backwards, you should relax your posture slightly so that your dog is invited to come forward onto the sheep. Your vocal request for the *walk-on* should mimic your gestures and should also be soft and not excitable or demanding. If your voice is assertive and your posture is dominant, your dog may either resist or avoid your pressure. If you ask for a *walk-on* after giving your dog a sharp correction for not steadying appropriately, do not be surprised if he hesitates before doing this. Give him time to respond. When the situation requires a faster response you should both sharpen your vocal commands for the *walk-on* and at the same time, move back more quickly. Both of these will stimulate him to move forward. However, you should take care to ensure that your tone does not unduly excite or worry your dog.

Balancing sheep to the handler

A and **B** Ban is aware of all the sheep in the group as he wears them to me. A dog needs to learn how to feel sheep, so that he automatically adjusts his energy and distance. This ensures he controls his flock whilst ensuring that the sheep remain calm and unstressed. **C** Mac is calmly balancing a group of ewes with lambs, ensuring they all remain with me. **D** As I lead, my dogs automatically take up a formation which surrounds the sheep and balances their movement towards me in a controlled manner. This formation is reminiscent of a pack hunting and so it is important that I lead the 'hunt'.

Chapter 10
The Natural Flank and Outrun

A well formed flank and outrun are two key fundamental skills that any good working dog should possess in order to manage his flock in a calm, steady manner. They are both important assets in sheep welfare and management because, when properly performed with the appropriate energy levels, the dog will not stress the sheep and send them unduly into flight. A dog that has a good outrun and can take direction at a distance is a tremendous asset for the lone shepherd and together they will often be able to work more efficiently than several men working on quad bikes. A fully trained dog should be willing to pull out during his outrun to gather dispersed sheep across rugged terrain. In addition, he also has to be versatile enough to come in when required to pick up just a few that may need attention.

When your dog is flanking, he needs to move smoothly around the sheep at a sufficient distance from them so that they are not disturbed. However he should not be so far out from the flock that he loses contact with them. The **natural flank** is so-called because the dog is instinctively (or naturally) drawn to the **pull** or head of the sheep. As I have previously explained, the best team between man (or woman) and dog is achieved if we humans do not stifle these natural instincts by over-control. Instead you are aiming to harness and develop your dog's understanding so he appreciates when, why and how he should flank.

The natural flank is essentially the same as sending your dog on a short outrun. Therefore as well as being important in its own right, it is also the basic stage for the **outrun**. Moreover, the same arcing movement is also used in other manoeuvres, for example, during the unnatural flank (see page 122) and when the dog is penning sheep (see page 152). Therefore, if you take the time at these early stages of his training to teach your dog to perform a natural flank properly, you will find it highly beneficial later on.

Start in the same way as you did in the earlier exercises and ask your dog to lie-down. Position yourself between him and the sheep and decide which side you want to send him. You encourage your dog to take the natural flank by using your body language to provide pressure / release as necessary.

As I have previously described, there is an invisible line of contact between your dog's eyes and the sheep. The position of this line will alter as the sheep and dog move. By watching your dog's eyes you will be able to see where the sheep are pulling towards, and you will be able to position yourself so that you can encourage the reaction that you want from your dog. So, if you want your dog to run on a natural flank in one direction then you need to stand on the other side of the invisible line and block your dog from running that way. The release comes when you allow the dog to run in the direction intended. Remember, especially with a young dog, to give and take—he does not have to be perfect every time.

The body language you use is the same as in the round pen without sheep. When you use your body to block the dog, you should step to the side and there should not be any forward or backward motion – unless the distance between the sheep and dog has altered (see diagram on page 85).

If the block is timed and positioned perfectly then you are <u>asking</u> your dog not to go in this direction. It is quite common that an inexperienced handler unintentionally steps forward as he moves to block. This forward movement is really saying 'Move out of my space' and the dog may perceive it as a more forceful <u>tell</u>. As fight often creates fight, some dogs will resist this. The handler then responds by putting yet more pressure on the dog and the problem just escalates. In contrast, other dogs can become anxious and uncertain from this additional pressure.

Alternatively, if the dog is putting pressure on the handler and the handler moves backwards whilst he attempts to block the dog, then the dog may read this as a submissive retreat and believe that he can keep acting as he (the dog) wishes. Remember, the block is a neutral position that is used to negotiate.

When teaching your dog to flank you do not want him just to circle you endlessly, so at the same time you will also be teaching the basic stages for the lift and fetch which are described in more detail in the next chapter (see page 104). When the dog reaches the balance point, ask him to stop. This makes sure he is listening.

However, once you feel he has learned to listen, you will not have to stop him completely every time. Just use the *steady* command so that the lift is smooth. Use your voice to ask him gently to come forward. At the same time, walk backwards. This will invite your dog to come forward balancing the sheep towards you. After he has fetched them a short way, stop him again and reposition yourself to set him on another flank.

> *Julie's Tip. You need to be in the correct position and also control your energy levels appropriately if you wish to communicate effectively with your dog.*

Although it sounds obvious, you must remember that sheep are not static objects, and their movement and stress levels will alter the dynamics between themselves, the dog and you. It is important that you are always aware of where your sheep are. If they change direction

and you have your back to them then your dog's reaction might not be the one you intend or expect. I often find that inexperienced handlers just concentrate on their dog and forget about the sheep that they are trying to work. For example, the handler sets up a situation for the dog to run to the right. However, by time everything is ready to start, the sheep have moved and the handler is now in the wrong position to ask the dog to do this. Try to keep one eye on what the sheep are doing. If for any reason you cannot see your sheep, then the dog will indicate where they are by the direction in which he is looking. It is often worthwhile for beginners to work the sheep themselves without their dog. This helps them develop a feel for sheep and gain some sheep sense.

I introduce voice commands as soon as I think my dog is ready both mentally and physically to start serious training. Again it is a gradual process to wean your dog off body language and onto these. Start with the natural flank, as this is what you have already been working on. Use body language to encourage your dog to run in the direction that you would like and give the voice command for that particular flank. At this stage, you are only saying the command at the same time as the dog flanks. Repetition of the command will enable your dog to start to understand that this sound means for him to flank in a certain direction. Some dogs will pick this up more quickly than others, but do not be disheartened if your dog takes a long while. Training a working sheepdog is not a race, and patience and perseverance will conquer. You introduce your whistles using quiet tones close at hand in a similar fashion.

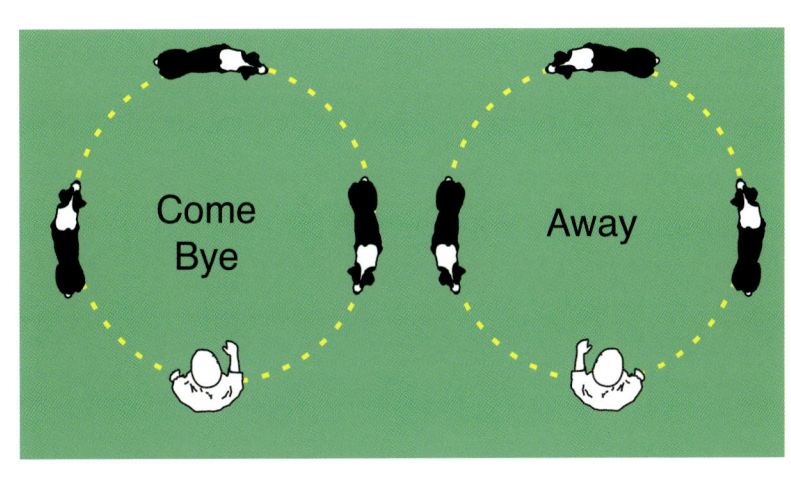

Direction that a dog moves in response to *come-bye* and *away* commands

Come Bye

Away

Consistent communication
The movements I use with the dog on sheep are the same as those used in the round pen. Here I block Ban's movement in **A** The round pen and **B** While working sheep.

Teaching the natural flank
A There is an invisible line between the dog and the sheep (blue dotted line). The dog will react differently depending on where you stand in relation to this. **B** As I stand on the invisible line and hold my hand up, I block Mac's forward motion. **C** and **D** By moving to the side of the line, I block Mac from moving in that direction and I use my body language to encourage him to start to flank in the opposite direction.

It is also useful to start using the *out* command at this stage as you can then teach your dog to move out whilst flanking (see page 134). If taught correctly, the dog will understand that you are asking for a wider command and will not consider it as a correction. The wide flank can be very beneficial in farm work.

Moving on to the outrun

Once you are happy with how your dog is flanking and balancing his sheep, then you have managed the basic stage of the outrun and it is now time to develop it further.

The whole picture for the outrun is of a dog that looks for sheep on entering the field and then runs out in the direction required by the handler. The run should be wide enough not to disturb the sheep. It needs a natural bend at the top that gives room to the stock before he makes first contact with his sheep. The dog then needs to gather any dispersed sheep, balance and lift them so that they move at a steady pace towards the handler.

The best line (**cast**) for the outrun is often, but not always, a pear-shaped one. Remember, think practically whenever you judge your dog's outrun. You do not want him to take short cuts and run too tightly as this may upset sheep and put them into flight. In contrast, you also do not want him to take all day to get to his sheep and cast out so wide that he takes ages to find them.

In order to prepare your dog's mindset for work and before you send him on his outrun, it helps if you ask him to look for sheep. Some dogs are better at spotting sheep at a distance than others. You have a height advantage and will probably be able to see sheep that he cannot, especially if the stock are up a hillside and your dog is used to working on the flat. You can help him learn where to look by stopping the dog at your side (either in a lie or stand) and position your body so that it is facing towards the sheep. Ask him to *look*. At the same time, glance at the dog and then use an obvious movement of your head, so that you now look at the sheep. If necessary, repeat this head movement and command a couple of times until he looks in the direction you are looking and sees the sheep. Do not expect him to understand immediately what you are asking him to do. However, with time and patience, your dog will automatically look for sheep in the direction of your gaze.

To extend the outrun, you need to gradually increase the distance. Initially, position yourself between the sheep and the dog and face the dog in a similar fashion as you did to start the natural flank. As he should now know his voice commands, you should use the appropriate vocal command to send him right or left. If he does not respond, try again and take a step or put out your arm to cross the invisible line between the dog and sheep so that you block the direction you do not wish him to go. In order to release the pressure, the dog will set off in the correct direction.

Julie's Tip. From the moment you start teaching voice and whistle commands, concentrate on the tone and pitch that you use and watch how your dog responds. Stimulating tones will increase the urgency of your command and make him go faster.

As your dog learns that he needs to cast around the sheep rather than running straight towards them, you will find that you no longer need to stand in front of him. Instead you can start the outrun with your dog by your side. You should stand so that your body blocks the side you do not want your dog to run and this subtle body language stimulates him to run out in the opposite direction.

Starting a short outrun
Note how the position of my outstretched left hand encourages Ban to move forward in a clockwise (*come-bye*) direction. Teaching both the natural flank and outrun uses the same movements, but as the dog progresses through his training, the distance he is sent is gradually increased.

Different dogs will instinctively cast out along different lines toward the sheep. If your dog tends to cast out very wide, then you can encourage him to draw inwards by setting him up so that he is slightly in front of you and facing more tightly towards the stock.

In contrast, if your dog wants to take a straighter line, then you can set him up so that he is slightly behind you and his head is pointing more towards the side. This will encourage him to move outwards.

Julie's Tip. Do not rush to get the finished article. You need to gradually build up your dog's understanding of what is required.

When you train your dog you always need to consider the big picture. I need my experienced dogs to know that they have to fetch sheep back towards me even if they cannot see me when they lift the stock. Therefore when I initially teach the balance (see page 83), I ensure that my young dog knows that I am the main focal point that he should always balance and fetch sheep towards.

As I have explained, when I start teaching the outrun, I position myself between the dog and the sheep before I send him. Once I have sent my dog, I walk backwards to his starting point. As my dog knows that I am the focal point that he balances towards, the fact that I have moved to this position teaches my dog that he has to fetch sheep back to where he started from.

If you have imprinted the same idea on your dog, then as his outrun extends, he will also lift his sheep to bring them back to his starting point. You will find that he will only alter from this routine if you give a command or if he realises that you have moved to a different location.

However, if you do not consider the final picture at these early stages of training and also do not realise how your movements can influence your dog, then you may unintentionally introduce problems. For example, if you send your dog on a short right hand outrun, but then you move to the left, the correct balance point to lift his sheep is actually at a point that may not allow him to easily cover all his sheep.

If you regularly move in the opposite direction when you send your dog, then as a consequence he will learn to expect this. Before you know it, you will have inadvertently ingrained the idea that he should always lift his sheep before he has covered them properly.

You may find that when you ask your dog to lift sheep from a greater distance, he may lift them too soon and then push them in the wrong direction (across the field rather than towards you). If you have imprinted this error into your dog's brain during his early training (but you do not realise it until later on) then you may find that it takes time and patience to correct.

In contrast, if your dog needs to be encouraged to cover his sheep properly then you can move in the same direction that he is running. The correct balance point is now further around the sheep. In order to reach this, your dog will need to continue on his outrun. So, this time your movement pushes your dog to cover his sheep. This can be useful if your dog needs to learn how to manage all his sheep and tuck them together.

However, you still need to remember that once your dog is in the proper position that you need to move backwards. This release of pressure tells your dog he is correct and also asks him to walk forward onto his sheep.

Be careful that you time when you release pressure correctly. If you do not, then you may make your dog over-run at the top of his outrun. In the worst case, your initial movement may put too much pressure on your dog and he may run into orbit and lose contact with his sheep.

As always you must watch how your dog responds to your body language and gestures and adapt the amount of pressure / release you use so that they are appropriate for your dog's temperament.

As your dog becomes more experienced and depending on his natural cast, you can set him up at different angles so that he achieves different types of outrun. For example, if the sheep are spread out across the field, you need to position the dog so that he will cast out wide enough and far enough so that he covers all the stock. As he runs out, the sheep will start to flock together. Once he has covered all the sheep, he should double back to tuck in any stragglers and then move to the point of balance to lift the sheep towards you.

When gathering a field of sheep, an inexperienced dog may pull in and attempt to gather the nearest sheep whilst ignoring the others. You need to be aware of this and look for cues from your dog that he is turning in prematurely, for example dropping his shoulder and moving his head inwards. If your dog does this, then you should help him by moving forward and putting pressure on his shoulder. Teaching the *out* command will also help solve this problem (see page 134).

A dog at the intermittent training stage should be able to gather a field of sheep, work on different terrains and with more testing sheep. He should also respond appropriately if asked to continue to flank further round the stock. He should also be able to respond to the *out* command.

When the dog reaches the advanced stage, he will be able to work even greater distances (400m or more), over very challenging terrain. He needs to be able to gather sheep that are out of sight of the handler. Therefore he has to be able to pace himself at the top of his outrun without command. Whilst on his outrun, the advanced dog will also take additional commands. For example the shepherd may need to guide him to find sheep that he may not be able to see or else require him to gather a few specific sheep that may need attention. The dog therefore needs to respond willingly to commands to send him out wider, to bring him in or even to intentionally leave the stock in front of him and gather others that the shepherd needs.

Fact Box. Communication through whistles

If you are going to work at a distance then it is advisable to communicate through whistle commands. To teach these, give the voice command followed by the whistle of choice or vice versa. It is important that your whistle commands are consistent, otherwise you will confuse your dog and make it almost impossible for him to learn the connection between the two. If you cannot whistle through your fingers, then you can use a plastic or metal whistle. It is best to practice your whistles when your dog is out of earshot.

I personally introduce the *stop* whistle first. Once established, I follow with a *steady* and a *get-up / walk-on* whistle. When my dog fully understands these, I move on to the flank commands. Try to keep your whistle commands as simple as possible and ensure the flank whistles are distinct from each other. For example, use a single low tone for one direction and two tones for the other. Decide which tones and sound to use, and how to give both a normal and an emphatic whistle. When choosing what sound to use, then I recommend that you try to give 'steadying' whistles with a fast dog. In contrast, slow dogs need sharper whistles to quicken their responses.

Your voice and whistle commands should be quiet when you are close to your dog, and use louder ones when he is further away. This will give you more flexibility and a better range for your dog to respond to when he is working at a distance.

Fact Box. Taking your dog onto the hill for the first time

Sheep that are found out on the open moors and hill are often much wilder than those kept in fields. In addition, the terrain itself can also make jobs much harder. So, perhaps it is not surprising that dogs who are used to working in fields, suddenly find it much more challenging when faced with this new situation. When you take your dog out onto the hill for the first time, give him every opportunity to succeed and start with easier tasks. For example, do not expect him immediately to be able to manage the same length of outrun as he does in a field. Also remember that when he is working in these types of environment that he will not always be able to see either his sheep or you. The dog will swiftly learn to listen to his shepherd because he will realise that he may not find his stock without his handler's guidance. Furthermore, if the dog is expected to work all day, then he will also learn to pace himself. I find that working on a challenging terrain promotes teamwork because neither the dog nor the handler can work effectively without the other. It is a steep learning curve for a dog and when I worked on the 10,000 acre Braegrudie Estate in North Scotland, I came to realise how in the past young dogs working on those kind of places would gain knowledge far beyond their years.

96

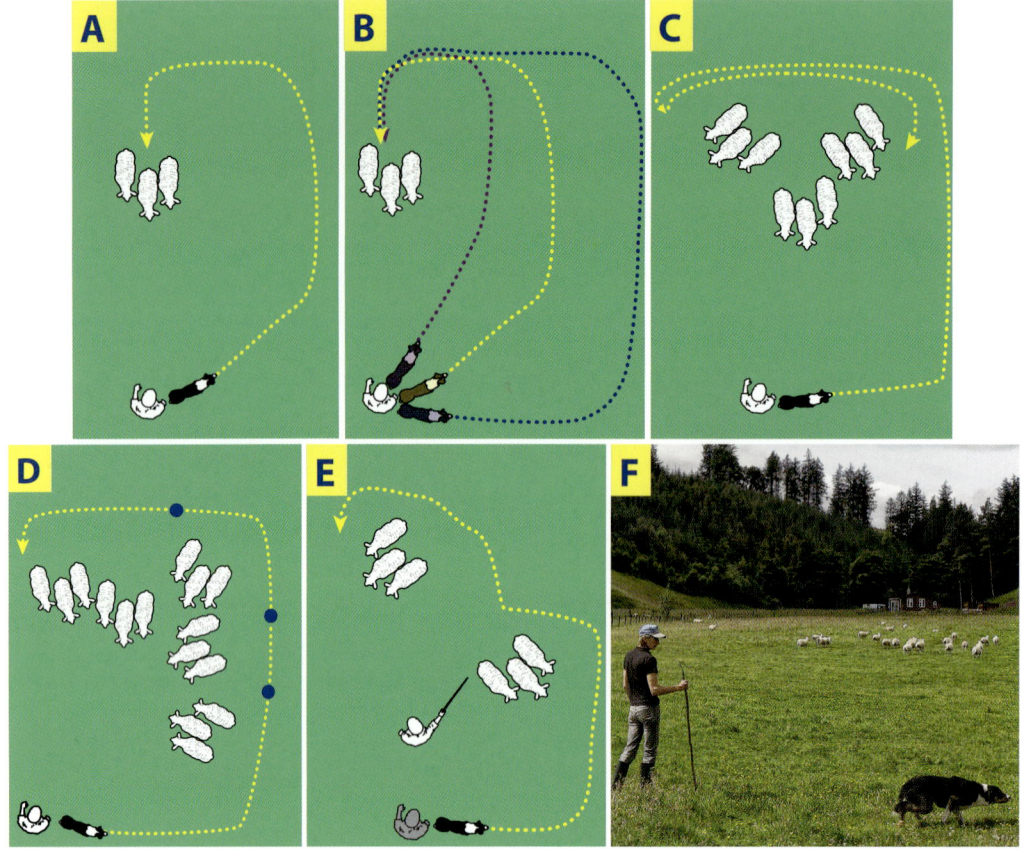

The outrun

A The natural outrun is pear shaped and gives enough room so the sheep are not disturbed as the dog goes around the field. **B** You can set your dog up at different angles depending on its natural ability and how many sheep he needs to gather. If your dog naturally tends to run wide, you can draw him inwards by setting him up at a tight angle and slightly in front of you. (purple dog) This will encourage him to draw inwards, but still give enough room at the top. If your dog tends to pull in tight towards the sheep, you can start him at a larger angle to encourage him to run out wider(blue dog). This angle is also used if you want to gather a field of sheep.

C When gathering sheep that are spread out across the field, your dog should initially cast out wide enough and far enough so that he covers all the sheep. As he runs out, the sheep will start flocking together. Once he has covered all the sheep, he should double back to tuck back any stragglers. **D** When gathering a field, an inexperienced dog may pull in and try to gather the nearest sheep whilst ignoring the others. You need to be aware of this and look for cues from the dog that he is turning in prematurely. The blue spots indicate where he may pull inwards.

E If your dog does try to pull in after the first group, you can help him by moving towards him and putting pressure on his shoulder. Teaching the *out* command will also help solve this problem. **F** I set Sam off on a wide outrun so he can gather a dispersed field of sheep.

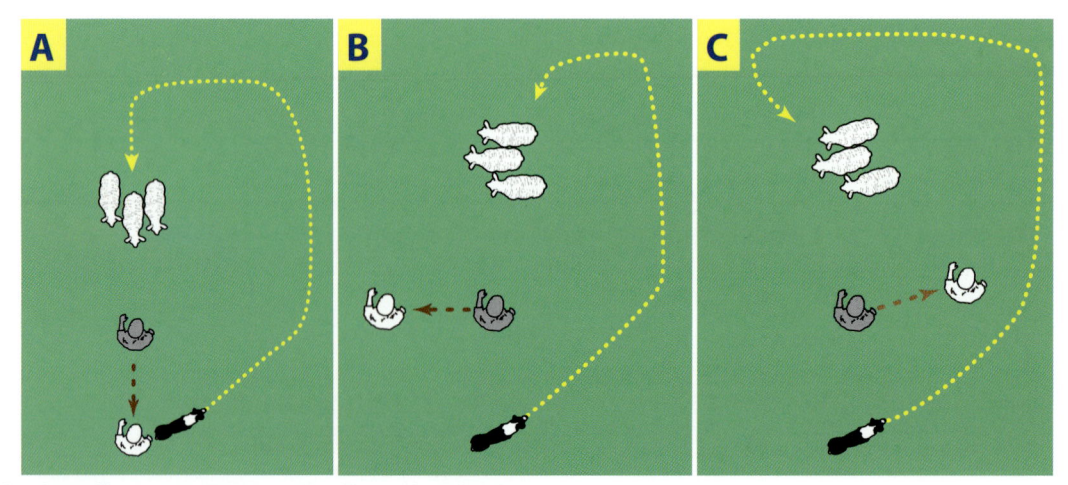

The handler's position will effect the dog's outrun

If your dog has learnt to consider his handler as the focal point to balance sheep towards, then you can use this to help him during the outrun. **A** After sending the dog on his outrun, you should return to the point where your dog started from. This helps him understand that he is expected to bring sheep back to this point. **B** If you move away from the line that your dog is running, then he will balance the sheep to your new position. This may pull him in too early at the end of his run and he may not cover all his sheep properly. **C** If you move towards the line that your dog is running, it will encourage him to flank further around the sheep.

Summary of the training stages required for the outrun

The basic stage. The dog should:

- Outrun a short distance for just a few sheep.
- Flanks and lifts sheep correctly so that they are not unsettled.

The intermediate stage. In addition to the basic stage, the dog should:

- Gather sheep that are up to 250m away.
- Work a flock as well as a few.
- Cover all sheep.
- Be introduced to the *out* command.

The advanced stage. In addition to the basic and intermediate stages, the dog should:

- Gather sheep from over 400m.
- Gather a flock that is very dispersed.
- Work on varied terrains.
- Respond promptly to all redirection commands.

Problems

There are several reasons why a dog has a problem with his flanks. You need to identify the underlying cause before you can rectify the problem. In order to do this, you must be able to read your dog correctly. Moreover, think about the whole picture of the flank as this will remind you of the movement you are trying to promote. Finally, remember that a dog will learn that a behaviour (e.g. a tight flank) is acceptable if you do not address the issue but instead continually let him get away with it. The inappropriate behaviour will then become ingrained. As the way a dog flanks and balances sheep are such fundamental building blocks for so many different aspects of a sheepdog's work. I strongly recommend that you spend time trying to iron out these issues early on in his training. You will also often find that if you over-exaggerate the training manoeuvre you need to use in order to address the problem, then when you ease-off after these sessions, your dog will have improved.

The dog decides what to do

I often find at clinics that the dog responds to the sheep more quickly than the handler can react. This means that the dog is deciding which side he will go, and the handler is just following. Very soon the dog will not listen to any commands at all and become engrossed in 'his' work. If you are aware that this is happening, you should try to correct it. Stop your dog at a point where you are sure he will listen (for example at the balance point or when he is near to you) and quickly give the flank command (using voice and body language) before he has time to make the choice for himself. You are now starting to take charge. Keep positive, and your dog will soon learn that he has to listen rather than resist you. Remember fight creates fight.

The dog rushes straight up the field with the intent to chase or grip the sheep

As you extend the outrun, your sheep will be more vulnerable the further you are from them. If your dog runs straight up the field, you need to return to working closer to the sheep in order to guard them. Go back to basics. Stand between the dog and the sheep and block your dog from coming in too close. It is important that each time you block, as well as stopping him from coming forward onto the sheep, you use sufficient pressure to make him rethink the situation so that he wants to negotiate with you. Once he shows the correct attitude keep close to the sheep and ask him to flank the sheep once more. This time he should show a different and more relaxed approach to his work. Once he is behaving appropriately, gradually extend the outrun. However, only move to longer distances once you know his attitude has definitely changed.

The dog has a tight flank

This is sometimes also called **cutting the flank**. In these cases, the dog runs or spirals closer towards the sheep as he flanks. This causes the stock to be disturbed. Some dogs only have the problem when flanking in one direction. Often, the dog's body is slightly stiff and he seems to lean inwards into the flank in a manner that is similar to a motor-bike cornering. If not corrected early in a dog's training, it can become a habit as his muscles become accustomed to working with his inside leg leaning inwards.

In my experience a dog cuts the flank because the handler has not spent sufficient time building a strong foundation and has not taught the dog to flank in a proper semi-circle motion. Frequently, the underlying problem is that the handler has not used the pressure / release technique correctly and the dog does not feel his sheep properly.

In order to solve the issue, you first have to analyse why the problem exists. You may need to go back to basics and work on changing your dog's attitude towards you. In these cases, your dog has to acknowledge that you are his leader. If you have to gain your dog's respect, re-read the chapter on communicating with your dog (see page 13). You also should work on using pressure / release technique correctly so that your dog understands when his flank is too tight. Importantly, you must release pressure when your dog attempts to flank a bit wider. Do not expect an immediate improvement. If cutting the flank has become an ingrained habit, your dog will need time to learn how to flank correctly. Remember to reward any small attempt that he makes as this will help him appreciate that he is acting correctly.

If he has become used to dropping his inside shoulder, you need to spend time helping him become comfortable when he keeps his weight onto his outside leg. Go back to working close at hand. Ask your dog for a flank and watch his movement carefully. As soon as he starts to drop his shoulder and spiral closer, apply pressure to his inside shoulder by pointing at it. As he gives to your pressure, he will inevitably have to put weight on his outside shoulder. With practice, he will start to feel more comfortable putting his weight on his outside leg. You may also find that it helps to teach your dog to exaggerate his flank (also called **square flanking**). Use the *out* command (see page 134). Once you see a response to the *out* command and he is square flanking then you are well on your way to improvement. Ease back and your dog should now flank in the correct semi-circle direction.

Pushing a dog out during his outrun
A The direction of a dog that is coming in too soon on the outrun causing the sheep to be lifted in the wrong direction. **B** To correct this the handler should move towards the dog and use pressure to push him out during the last part of his outrun. This will encourage him to give more room and cover the sheep properly. It is important that this command is timed correctly. **C** A dog that is tight from the beginning of his run, needs to be pushed out from the start and may need to be reminded by additional pressure during his outrun. Again this needs to be timed correctly.

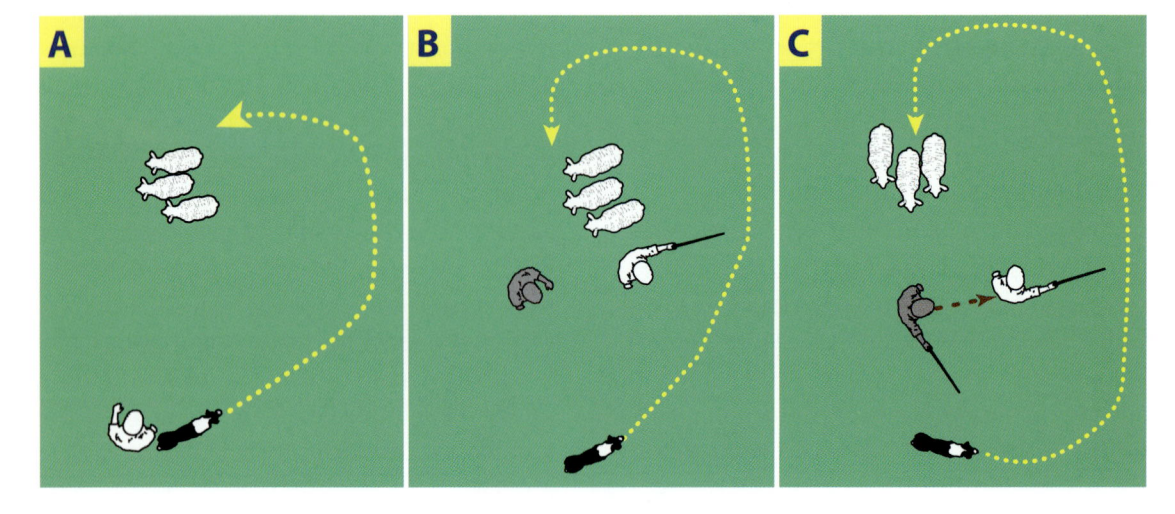

The time taken to correct a tight flank will depend on how tightly your dog arcs around the flock, his innate character and his trainability. If your dog is very sensitive to pressure and has also learnt that it is acceptable to flank tightly, then you need to be careful as to how much pressure you use to correct this fault: too much pressure could send your dog out of contact with his sheep.

The dog is off contact from his sheep

Every dog is different in the way that sheep react to him. Some dogs have to be close to move sheep whilst others need to work further off. A dog's instinct can tell him what sort of sheep he is approaching. It is amazing the distance that a dog can sense this. The same goes for the sheep, they pick up the dog's energy and different breeds will be more sensitive and responsive to this than others (see page 53). So **contact** is the distance that a specific dog needs to be for that type of sheep to move them in an appropriate manner. When a dog works **off contact**, he gives too much ground to the sheep, and lets them decide the direction they want to move in. The dog prefers not to be close to sheep and every flank he takes will often make him turn off and away from the sheep rather than move round them in a semi-circle. This kind of dog usually lacks confidence and is avoiding a situation. The problem is normally exacerbated if the handler has used incorrect pressure during training.

To solve this problem, you need to encourage your dog to move forward onto the sheep while, at the same time, ensuring that he does not feel pressurised from either you or the stock. You need to show the dog that he can feel comfortable working close to you. If you use a training aid, such as a plastic pipe, keep it lowered or even stop using it. Ask for small, close flanks. You should also try to work him faster and encourage forward movement to keep his attention on his sheep. When you give flanking commands, try to use calm, positive, encouraging commands. Do not emphasise them too much. As soon as the dog starts to move wider and lose contact with his sheep, call him back closer. Gradually as you

show him what you want, he should start to relax and understands what is needed of him. You will then start to see a change. However, it may take time and patience.

If the changes that you have made with your body language and voice are not helping, then you can try putting the dog on a long line to reinforce your command. To do this, you need to give the dog a calm tug at the point you want him to make contact with his sheep (the balance point). Using, the long line in this fashion, will show him that he gets pressure (a tug) when he tries to move off his sheep, but has a reward (release of pressure) when he comes onto his sheep. This will ensure that he has to work close to you and his stock. It will also give him the opportunity to re-think what you require from him. You will then be able to start addressing any concerns that he may have about you and / or the sheep.

Personally, I find that it is often harder to call a dog back onto contact, than it is to push a dog out. This is because a dog off contact is out of reach in an attempt to avoid confronting the problem.

The dog flanks too quickly

I do not feel that a fast flanking dog is a problem unless he is also tight or overexcited and so unsettles the sheep. However, a fast dog requires, you as the handler to be on the ball. In general, as the dog learns, his speed will often slow. A dog with plenty of natural work will be tired at the end of the day and will learn to ease up sooner than one that does not have much work to do.

Some dogs flank too quickly and also upset the sheep. Nine times out of ten it is not the speed itself that is the problem, but rather that the dog is not paying attention to the handler's wishes. Sometimes he will not even wait for a command before rushing the flank and because he has not waited, he then may flank the wrong way. The way you ask for a flank (or any command) will affect how the dog responds. If the dog starts running out of hand, you will need to assert your authority and re-establish respect. Once respect has been re-established, then ask the dog for his flank and if you see any sign that the dog is testing you, then warn him with appropriate body language. Watch that you do not exert too much pressure or you make your dog worried and over-cautious. As with any problem, you need to find the correct balance that suits the dog and the situation.

The dog does not take his flank commands

There are a number of different causes for this and the way to resolve the issue will depend on what the underlying issue is. Causes include 'shutting out' the handler; being too focused on his stock to listen to commands; getting his flank commands mixed up; not hearing the command.

If the dog is stubborn and shuts out your commands, then you need to ask yourself why? Is it from lack of respect? Have you used incorrect pressure and nagged your dog, so that he now just ignores your wishes? In these cases, you need to gain your dog's respect and re-educate him to accept pressure / release.

Alternatively, a dog can become engrossed in what is ahead of him for example, if the sheep are pulling in a certain direction. In these cases, you need to gain the dog's attention.

First block and stop him. Then insist he backs out of your space as you move into his. Hold the pressure using a stare and stiff dominant body language until you see the dog licking, chewing or turning his head away. All these indicate that he does not want a confrontation with you and acknowledges your presence. Ease the pressure by relaxing your body, facial gestures and lean backward sufficiently to acknowledge his uncertainty.

However, when you release pressure do not give too much or dog may read this to mean that you are submitting to him. Now, ask for the flank command. If the dog hesitates, keep relaxed and block to stop any forward movement and again ask for the flank command. Remember that if a dog is worried or insecure then he may not respond immediately. Give him time to absorb what you have asked and this will help calm his mind and allow him to concentrate on what you have asked.

If your dog has a lot of eye, he may become so engrossed in his sheep that he only makes small flanks before sticking. You need to encourage more movement on his flank by giving your command in a manner that may motivate him to respond more quickly. Asking for large flanks will also help him to loosen up. In these situations, working a larger flock of sheep often helps as the dog has to move more to keep the flock together.

With a dog that is confused and keeps mixing up his flanks, you first need to ask, is it your fault? Are you giving inconsistent commands? For example saying *come-bye* when you mean *away* and vice versa. If this is not the case, then the dog needs relaxed training, with plenty of natural work. He needs to be given time to work out what you are asking. Sometimes, this confusion is caused by the dog's immaturity and all that is needed is time for him to develop mentally.

If he does not hear your commands, look at how you are communicating. Does your voice carry well? Is your whistle consistent in pitch and tone? If your communication is the problem, you will need to improve it, before you will see an improvement in the dog.

The time it takes to see an improvement will depend on the underlying reason. In general, however if you confront and address the problem early in a dog's life then the problem does not usually persist for long. The older the dog, the more he will become set in his ways and the harder it can be to sort.

The dog is too slow

Again there can be a number of causes for this. These can include the dog's physical build and fitness; how much eye he has or his mental attitude to work. If your dog is unfit then you need to work on building this by increasing his exercise and perhaps altering his diet. If the problem is his build and he is still slow once fully fit, then you will find no further improvement. I have discussed strategies of working with a dog with too much eye in the section above. The amount of improvement will depend on just how sticky he is and if he has good trainability.

However, sometimes the dog can slow down because of his mental attitude to work. For example, the dog may pull back on his pace because he has been over-controlled or has had too much inappropriate pressure from the handler. In these situations, the dog does not feel he can use his own initiative and so feels insecure that he may be flanking incorrectly. If this is the case, you need to assess how you are communicating with your dog. Some dogs have talent, but do not wish to use it because they have a lazy attitude towards their work. The only way to deal with a dog like this is to make sure he enjoys his work and training. Other dogs tend to sulk. If your dog has this trait, then again you need to adjust your handling so that he does not feel over-controlled. This should make him happier in his work and he should become freer in his movements.

The dog is tight on the top of his outrun

This means the dog usually sets off well, but starts coming in tight towards the sheep at the end of his outrun. I find this a common problem at training clinics, especially if the dog does not have a strong foundation but instead has been asked to run out too far, too soon in his training. To solve this, you have to stand nearer the sheep and leave the dog lying down some distance away. Before you allow your dog to move and to start on his outrun, use assertive body language to indicate that he needs to give to your pressure. Ask your dog to begin his outrun and as he starts, you need to move towards the area where you know that your dog will try to come in. Use the *out* command and at the same time point your arm (or plastic pipe) towards the dog's shoulder to push him out. Timing for this is critical. If you move too soon then you will block and stop the dog. If you move too late then you will put pressure on behind him and push him faster and tighter onto the sheep.

The dog crosses over or runs straight up the middle of the field

I would tackle this in the same way as that used for the dog that is tight at the top. The only difference is that you and your dog would both need to be closer to the sheep at the start of the outrun so you can keep more control at this point.

When you send your dog, position yourself between him and the sheep, and make sure that he starts his outrun correctly. The direction that of his head will often indicate the direction that he intends to move.

You need to make sure you put enough pressure on the dog to move away from you. It is easier to keep a dog out if he sets off wide than it is to push him out once he has started. When you think that your dog is running wider, try to extend the distance from the sheep.

The dog runs very wide at the start of his outrun (rather than running in a pear-shape)

You can often help the dog by the way you set up your outrun and also by teaching him to look for sheep.

When you want him to run out, set him slightly in front of you and angled more tightly towards the sheep. Then, when you want him to start his outrun, ask him to take a couple of steps forward before starting on his flank.

The dog runs wide during his outrun

If this is caused by a lack of confidence then you should read the section above about how to deal with a dog that runs off contact. Alternatively, your dog may have a natural trait to run wide or it may be that he does not know where his sheep are and has run very wide in an attempt to find them.

To help your dog, you should ask him to look for his sheep.

Once he is on his outrun then you should use a voice or whistle command to draw him inwards (for example *get up* or *here*).

The more quickly you see the problem and respond to it, the easier it will be to rectify. Once the dog is coming in, give another flank command just at the right time to direct him onto the path you have chosen. Watch that you do not emphasise the flank, or he may bend out wide again.

I have found this is very successful on most dogs once they understand that you want them to come inwards on command as well as to go out wider on command.

The dog misses some of the sheep on his outrun

Some dogs seem to have this problem more than others. To me, when you are busy gathering sheep, there is nothing more frustrating than a dog that leaves some behind when it is clear that he has seen them.

Obviously if the sheep are masked by the terrain and your dog cannot see some, then you need to use a prompt *out* command to tell him to go out further to look for sheep. If he does not respond, stop him and ask again. If he still will not run out wider, make him lie-down, move closer, and push him back out towards the fence. Sometimes sheep hide from a dog and reappear from behind a bush after he has passed. If this happens, I want to be able to stop my dog and ask him to turn round, see the sheep he has missed and re-gather them. For this, you will need a *look back* command, followed by a flank command and, if needed combine it with an *out* command.

Moving On

Now that your dog has an outrun that covers his sheep, he must now learn how to lift and fetch them in a non stressful manner.

Anecdote. Why won't you let me play my way?

Many years ago, when I still had a lot to learn myself, I was training a young bitch who was tough and very sharp. I was trying to stop her from running through the middle of the sheep. She would lie-down and refuse to move, even though I was insisting she respond. She would tempt me closer towards her and then, once I was near her, she would start to take the appropriate flank. However, every time she would take a route that was just wide enough to run past me before she would swing inwards towards the sheep which she would then have fun chasing around the field. It was a battle of wills and I had to do a lot of running to cut her off and block every time she tried to outsmart me and pass me. She stopped this behaviour when she realised that I was not going to let her play the game the way she wanted to. Eventually she did train to have quite a good outrun but it was more man-made than natural.

From the Clinic

Handler: My dog finds it hard to spot sheep.

I observed that every time the handler tried to get his dog to position himself to run wide, the dog would ignore his efforts and bounce around in an excited fashion with a loosely waving tail. The handler did not wait until the dog was settled, but instead moved to the side of him and sent him off on his outrun. The dog set off more in 'play mode' than being focused on his work. This failure to concentrate inevitably meant that he missed sheep that were dispersed across the field.

My opinion: He clearly did not respect his handler. Furthermore, he thought that the handler's gestures were inviting him to play.

My advice: The handler needed to get his dog's attention and respect. When I took over handling the dog, I knew I needed to made it clear to him that I would not let him work his sheep until he started to listen to me. Therefore, I stood in front of him on the invisible line of contact between him and the sheep and blocked his forward movement in a calm, assertive manner. In response, the dog quickly relaxed, and his tail dropped to hang loosely behind him. I then put some additional pressure on him. The dog gave to my wishes and moved backwards. I released the pressure slightly to show that he had done the correct thing, and the dog lay down. I pointed my hand at his shoulder and he slightly turned to the side. I maintained the pressure on his shoulder until he had turned to face the angle that I wanted to send him at. Still facing the dog, I moved to the side that I did not want him to go and directed my other hand towards his rear. The dog responded as I expected and started to flank out widely. He completed his outrun in a calm fashion. I repeated the exercise with his other flank.

Remember, you need to teach your dog to run in the direction he is facing. Therefore, you put sufficient pressure until he turns to the angle that you require. It is only then that you should ask him to start his outrun. The first few times you send your dog 'blind', you may find that you need to keep stopping and redirecting him on his outrun. Once you have practised setting your dog up for different types of outrun and he learns that he is always going to find sheep, he will start to trust your judgement and be more willing to listen to your directions.

Anecdote. An outrageous outrun

Even with a natural dog that you think is on good command you can still have problems with outruns. Unexpected things can happen and looking back I now realise that my inexperience caused many of them. If I only knew then, what I know now.

When Moss was a young dog, I thought I had more control of him than I really had. I sent him on a difficult long outrun to gather some Cheviot Mules that were grazing over a wide area of rough ground. He ran out well and started to balance the sheep towards me when one ewe took flight. In hindsight, she probably panicked because of Moss' excited energy. Furthermore, because he was in this heightened state, he set off in hot pursuit and totally ignored all my efforts to communicate with him. Instead of heading the sheep, he ran with the escapee into some trees, and vanished from sight. I panicked and rushed up the hill to find the ewe at the bottom of a short crevasse looking up at me. My dog was not in sight. He must have stopped in time and decided to hide in some bushes until I had calmed down. It was too steep to reach the sheep, so I had to return to the farm to get a rope. I then climbed down the cliff face, thinking that I would be able to encourage her to move along the stream along a safer route out of the hole. Unfortunately, the ewe had broken her leg in the fall, so I put the rope round her, climbed back up out of the hole and then hauled the sheep up, swearing at every breath.

From the Clinic.

This is the second part of the story of how I helped solved the issues that one owner had with her dog. To recap, the handler was chasing her young dog away after he had rushed to grip sheep (This part is discussed on page 82). In response to these fierce signals, the youngster flew out so that he was a long distance away from the stock and started to flank widely around them. Whilst doing this, he did not look toward the sheep at all.

My opinion: The handler had insisted that her dog move away from the sheep in order to regain control of the situation. However, she did not realise that her dog's wide flanks were actually caused by avoidance as he fled from too much inappropriate pressure. From the dog's perspective, he thought he was not allowed to work sheep because his owner was forcing him to stay away from them. Therefore, when he moved closer to sheep, he felt intimidated by them and also by his handler's panicked demands to keep off. This situation caused him to become anxious and as a result he rushed in and gripped the sheep badly. The underlying problem was that the dog had never been properly shown how to behave and be confident when he was close to sheep.

My advice was that the gripping itself needed to be confronted. This should not be done by pushing the dog so far from his sheep that he lost contact with them. Instead, I put him on a long line. I walked with him close to sheep and gave calming vocal sounds when his behaviour was relaxed towards the sheep. However, whenever the dog displayed any tension or intent, I quickly checked him by giving a short sharp tug on the line combined with a low growl. This training exercise meant that the dog was given appropriate pressure when he started to think about gripping. Moreover, because I quickly released the pressure when he was relaxed, he realised that this attitude was rewarded. Within about five minutes, the dog started to become calmer and more confident.

After this, the handler and I continued to work him with the long line. We ensured that as he flanked around his sheep the dog kept in contact with them and did not flee into avoidance. Gradually this approach let the dog become more comfortable when he was closer to sheep. Although he occasionally showed intent that he might grip, his owner was also able to read his body language faster. She was therefore able to remind him with slight appropriate pressure that this intent was wrong.

After our sessions, the handler understood the underlying cause and felt confident that she now could deal with it. As a result the dog was happier and could progress with his training.

Chapter 11
The Lift and fetch

At the end of his outrun, a good working dog will steady himself without command as he approaches the stock at the balance point. When this kind of dog lifts sheep, he will apply the appropriate amount of pressure in a quiet, composed and assertive manner that will encourage them to start to move calmly towards the shepherd. During the fetch, the dog needs to exert sufficient pressure to ensure the flock move at a steady non-stressed pace along the shortest, safest, most direct route so that they arrive at the shepherd's feet in a settled state.

Moreover, when a dog is gathering stock on a hill farm he often has to work out of sight of his shepherd and so he has to be able to lift and fetch without command. In order to do this, the dog needs to be confident about using his own initiative and be able to read his stock so that he can gather them in a manner that suits both the terrain and the breed of sheep. Despite this ability to act independently, a good working dog also has to be willing and prompt to respond to any commands so that, if required, the shepherd can direct him to navigate the flock safely around hazards. A dog that just pushes on with little regard for his sheep or his handler is of little use on a hill farm because he could easily force the stock into a bog or even over the edge of a cliff.

You have to remember that when you gather sheep with your dog, you are exploiting the dog's instinctive predatory nature. In addition, the 'prey' – the sheep – are driven by their survival instinct. Consequently, the initial contact that your dog makes with his stock has a huge impact on how they will subsequently respond to him. If they are upset at this crucial point then the sheep are more likely to panic in response to any subsequent unexpected or awkward movement from the dog.

In contrast, if the sheep are not startled at the lift, they will not get an adrenaline surge prompting them into flight. Instead, the sheep will be more comfortable and accepting of your dog's presence and allow him to move closer to them.

The **lift** describes the first point of contact that your dog makes with his sheep. If it is too forceful, then the sheep will flee from pressure. This makes it harder for the dog to bring them under his control. At the opposite end of the spectrum, the dog will show weakness towards his sheep. The stock may then take advantage of the situation and they could confront the dog or else continue to graze.

You need to be calm when working with your dog
A As Ruby reaches the balance point to lift her sheep, I ask her to *lie-down* by moving into the block position and raising my hand. **B** As Ban fetches the sheep he automatically adjust his energy and distance so that the sheep remain calm, I release pressure to indicate he has acted appropriately. I do this by walking backwards and keeping my stick pointed downwards.

The lift

A Ban has gathered the flock and is approaching quietly to start the lift. The sheep are aware of his presence (the rear ones having their ears back). However they are still relaxed as they show signs that they are willing to move away from him. **B** Ban has moved to the centre point of the small flock and has proceeded to lift them in a calm manner. Although Ban has acted appropriately, the steep descent has caused the sheep to speed up. Once they realise there is no danger from the dog they will relax and their pace will ease. Notice that Ban's body language is relaxed but focused even though the sheep are showing the signs of imminent flight (their ears are flicked backwards and several have their heads raised).

A dog has to learn to evaluate the situation and use appropriate pressure

A Ban eyes a small group of ewe lambs asking them to move. They face him with raised heads and flicking ears. These signals indicate that they are questioning his authority. **B** In response, Ban makes a sharp movement forward. The sheep closest to him instantly turn as they realise he means business. **C** The next frame in the photo sequence shows that Ban does not grip. Instead, as the sheep have given to him, he sits back on his hocks and starts to move to the correct balance position in order to complete the lift. Ban performs this whole sequence of events without any commands from me. **D** Ban gently lifts a young lamb to return it to its mother. Even though the lamb is facing him, Ban realises that he needs to be careful and has a relaxed face and soft eyes.

Julie's Tip. Every dog possesses different levels of 'energy of intent'. The sheep will sense this energy and use it to decide whether they are in imminent danger or not. As the dog approaches the stock, he needs to control his predatory instincts so that the sheep are not startled into flight.

The **fetch** comes immediately after the lift and this is the action where your dog brings the sheep to you in the most direct route possible. He should not move them from one side of the field to the other unless you specifically want him to do this (for example to navigate through a gate or to go around a hazard).

In order to lift and fetch sheep properly, it is important that your dog balances the sheep correctly and that his energy towards them is calm and assertive rather than excited or menacing. As your dog gains in experience, he needs to become sufficiently versatile to adapt his energy depending on the situation. For example, you many need him to work with heavy, domesticated, stubborn Texels. Alternatively he may be expected to gather wild flighty Blackface ewes who are only rarely corralled or perhaps he gently needs to encourage a young lamb to return to its mother.

When your dog starts to learn to lift and fetch, he will inevitably make mistakes. Be prepared to take time and gradually build on his efforts. You need to use appropriate pressure / release and the graduated scale of **ask, tell, insist** so that he can start to appreciate that some misdemeanours are more serious than others.

Follow the steps: teach, ask, tell and then only enforce if you need to remind your dog that he needs to respect your wishes. Remember, when you are training your dog, you are having a two way conversation with him. To do this effectively, you need to be able to read your dog's body language. You also need to have sheep sense because this will help you determine your dog's intent and mindset. For example, if your dog does not respond immediately to your 'ask', do not instantly think that he is not listening. His lack of movement may be his way of warning you that the sheep will escape if he moves away from his current position. Alternatively, he may pause as he tries to work out what you require from him.

Sheep read a dog's energy levels
Ban's face and posture are very intense. Even though he is some distance from the ewe lambs, they have read his higher energy levels and are running with their ears back and heads raised. These signs indicate that the sheep are unsettled.

I have already briefly covered the basic stage for the lift and fetch in the last chapter. However, because they are such important foundation stones for your dog's daily work, I think it is worth considering them in more detail.

When you start to teach the lift and fetch, you need to be close enough to the sheep to be in control of the situation. As your dog flanks the stock and approaches the balance point, you may need to use your body language and gestures to ask him to think about what he is about to do. If necessary ask him to slow down. If he does not respond, move forward assertively and tell him to give to you. You need to hold your assertive body stance until he gives to your pressure and indicates that he wants to negotiate with you. In response, relax your body and ease the pressure slightly (but do not release it completely). Ask him to *steady*. If he does not respond, move forward and tell him to give to you. Then stand in the block position to stop him and ask him to *lie-down*.

Let your dog wait a few seconds to readjust his mindset. Then slowly walk backwards and allow him to walk forward onto his sheep. If your dog has too much eye or lacks confidence it may be necessary to encourage him forward more so that he is able to move his sheep. These and other issues are discussed in more detail in the problems section on page 112.

Remember that walking backwards is releasing pressure on your dog and therefore by doing this you are telling the him that he has done the correct thing. So you should only move backwards and allow him to lift and fetch the sheep if he has the proper attitude and uses an appropriate method. By this I mean that you need to make sure that your dog feels his sheep and steadies on your request. When doing this, watch that you do not keep your hand (or pipe) raised all the time as you try and steady your dog. Never forget, it is pressure <u>and</u> <u>release</u>.

If your dog is impatient, then you may need to stop him frequently so that he learns the importance of patience. Allow the sheep to move away while you block any forward movement from him. Wait until he settles. Then move closer to the sheep again and flank your dog around them until he reaches the balance point. Hold him in this position using your body language, until his attitude is correct. You need patience because you may find that you need to repeat this many times before your dog works out what is required.

As your dog progresses, try to walk backwards for a reasonable distance and in different directions so that the dog learns to balance sheep towards you wherever you go. When you do this, you may find that you need to block your dog frequently until he starts to reconsider his behaviour. Eventually, rather than stopping the dog every time, you should start to use the *steady* command and, if this is properly taught, the dog will learn to pace with a nice continuous flow rather than a stop / start jerky motion.

As I have explained before, I mingle natural work with my training. For example, after controlling my dog to fetch sheep for a short distance, I often turn round so that my back is to the dog and sheep. I will walk a little faster and at the same time stop giving any commands. This natural work encourages my dog to relax while staying focused on the task in hand: he should continue to concentrate on all his sheep and react to what they are doing. An added advantage of doing this exercise is that I can test my dog to determine whether he really understands how to fetch sheep correctly and calmly while he does not perceive pressure from me. I therefore consciously make myself relax and let my dog work using his initiative. This is something he will need to do in the future when he works on the hill and cannot hear or see me. However, in these early stages of his training, I am still close at hand to correct any problems and if my dog makes an inappropriate movement towards the sheep then I will make a gesture to remind him how to behave.

It is sometimes hard for inexperienced handlers to relax during this exercise, partly because the beginner believes that a dog pushing sheep is inevitably out of control. However, do not assume that your dog is misbehaving even when he pushes sheep past you. Look at your dog; does he have an appropriate relaxed attitude? Look at the sheep; are they showing signs of distress? If all is well then allow him to continue to work.

Let your dog work naturally
A I walk with my back turned to the stock and let Ban fetch the sheep to me. I use minimal commands while I do this, but I maintain an eye over my shoulder to ensure that my dog's attitude and behaviour remains correct. **B** If Ban comes forward too much, I just put my hand back slightly to remind him not to push his sheep too heavily.

If you stop and hold your dog back too much then depending on his character, he may either start to resist your commands or else become too careful and uncertain about what to do. A dog that is never allowed to relax and work naturally may become frustrated. This frustration can escalate to such a point that one day, he may be unable to contain himself any further and he just runs riot.

I recommend that you spend a long time working at hand until you are confident that your dog learns to lift and fetch with the appropriate mindset. By this stage he also should be willing to take different flank commands as well as respond to *steady,* and *lie-down.* He also needs to leave the stock and come back to your side when you say *that'll do.*

> *Julie's Tip. Make sure that your dog fully understands what is required when you are working close at hand. This groundwork will pay dividends later on when you are working with him at a distance.*

With time, you will start to send your dog on longer outruns and you may be disappointed that he no longer lifts and fetches sheep correctly. Do not despair. Instead go back to working at a shorter distance and reinforce the idea that he needs to lift and fetch with the

appropriate attitude and manner. Working on your dog's stop can help remind him that he needs to respect your commands. Once you have re-established your dog's respect, you should be able to ease back on the amount of pressure you need to use to keep him moving steadily and calmly.

Your dog needs to apply appropriate pressure at the correct position in order for the sheep to be lifted and fetched towards you. The correct position that your dog needs to start his lift will vary depending on where the sheep are and also on the direction that they are trying to pull towards. This will become even more apparent when you start to send your dog on longer outruns because the sheep will often be grazing at one side of the field rather than in the middle.

Understanding what the sheep are thinking will help you decide where your dog needs to be in order to balance the stock towards you. Some dogs radiate more predatory energy and intent than others. The sheep will respond to this type of dog when he is further away compared with another dog who has a calmer mindset. Look at the alertness of the sheep's head carriage; the direction of their head and the angle of their ears: all these will tell you what position they want to move in and whether they are relaxed or unsettled.

The sheep may be put into flight if the dog cannot control his energy when he attempts his lift and fetch. When this happens, it is highly likely that an inexperienced dog will run to catch up. Before you know it, the fetch will actually turn into a chase. In response, the sheep may panic and they could seriously injure themselves as they flee to escape. Some novice handlers do not realise that their dog has entered this 'chase mode'.

If this happens to you then the sooner you see what is happening, the easier it is to re-adjust your dog's mindset back so that he works appropriately. If you are quick to notice what is happening, ask your dog to *steady*. However, if you are slow to respond to the situation, then your dog will become more engrossed in the chase and it will probably be harder to get him to listen. You need to escalate the strength of your commands to a 'tell' or even an 'insist'. You do this by using assertive body language, a stern tone and dominant gestures to gain his attention and make him re-focus. Your dog should check his pace and sit back on his hocks. If he does not, block his forward movement and insist that he backs off and then stops. Do not let him move forward until he has settled his mind. Get closer to the sheep and once your dog has relaxed and has the correct attitude, ask him to balance the sheep towards you. Then walk calmly backwards and remind your dog to *steady* as he comes forward.

As well as watching the sheep, you need to understand what your dog is telling you. If your dog has natural ability, you will find that as he fetches the stock, he may move to one side in order to balance the sheep towards you. This is because your dog is instinctively moving to the heavy side of the sheep in order to block and counteract them from drawing away. In fact, your sheep may put so much pressure on your dog in their attempt to escape, that he feels he cannot move from the heavy side without losing control of them. In these situations, your dog may seem to refuse to respond to your commands to move away from this position. As I have said before, do not automatically assume he is being disobedient. Your dog is trying to tell you that he thinks he will lose his sheep if he leaves the heavy side.

The lift position varies depending on where the sheep are in relation to the handler

All three of the examples shown are correct and the arrow heads indicate the correct point of balance where the dog should lift the sheep. If you have taught your dog to balance sheep to you when he is close at hand, he will be able to read his sheep and will lift them at the correct point.

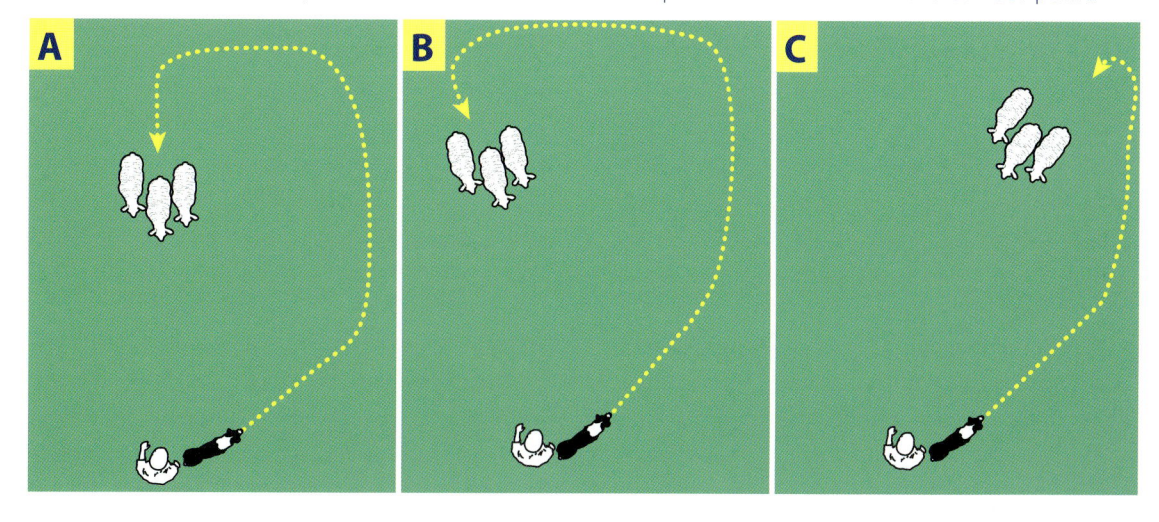

Obviously, there are times when you need the sheep to alter their course during the fetch. For example, you may need to avoid an obstacle in their path or alternatively go through a gate that is at one side of the field. Sometimes, it may be sufficient just to ask your dog to stop. Once he has stopped, you then need to choose the right moment to give him the next command. In order to make this decision, you need to read the sheep and understand how they will respond to your dog. You also need to know how your dog reacts around stock and how fast he can run!

Clearly, stopping your dog will not always result in the sheep going where you want them to. Therefore, you also need to teach your dog to flank as he fetches sheep. However, as I have just explained, you may find your dog unwilling to flank away from the balance point. I will discuss how to get your dog to do this in more detail on page 122.

As your dog reaches the intermediary and advanced stages of training, you should extend the distance that he needs to cover before lifting and fetching sheep. If possible also introduce your dog to different types of sheep and terrains as well as working in different weather conditions. Work him with a flock so that after gathering them, he learns to move to the correct balance point to lift them. Once lifted, he also needs to hold the sheep together as he fetches them to you. It will depend on your dog's particular style, the size of the flock and the type of sheep being worked as to how he does this. Some dogs hold back and use their eye and small movements of their head to hold them all together. In contrast, another dog may need to flank more, weaving from side to side, tucking in the stragglers at the side as he fetches them to you.

At Carcant, I combine plenty of natural work with precision training to extend my dog's knowledge. This way he learns to use different levels of assertion and pace. For example, I will encourage him to push forward when lifting a larger flock as this will prepare him for working with heavy sheep.

However, even when I ask my dog to push on more forcibly, I still make sure that he does not unduly stress the stock. Some sheep need more careful handling than others, but all will become stressed if a dog pushes them too hard. Some ewes learn that if she pulls up or lies down then the dog may ignore her and carry on with the rest of the flock who are willing to keep moving. If a sheep does pull up, then ask your dog to steady or even stop. This will take the pressure off the slow ewe. Allow her time, both to settle her mind and to join up with the rest. If for any reason she does not seem able to keep pace with the others, use your dog to hold a few sheep with her. Then you should walk up to her and check that there is nothing wrong.

If your dog is careless or lazy and deliberately leaves sheep behind even though he has seen them, you need to correct him as soon as it is apparent that he has ignored them. Ask for a *look back* (see page 137). Reinforce this with assertive body language so that he pays attention to your request. It is important that your dog immediately realises that you are not happy that he has left some sheep behind. If you do not correct this mistake, your dog does not know it is wrong to leave sheep behind: Bad habits will not cure themselves: you need to confront them, if you want your dog to improve. Also remember to release your pressure as soon as your dog turns to re-gather the strays because this will reward him for making the right decision.

Sometimes a sheep, for example one with a young lamb, may stand and attempt to overpower a dog. Some dogs who are naturally weak will not be able to deal with this confrontation. However a dog may also lose confidence if his handler has been too hard during training. A dog that has been trained this way may choose to back away from the stock rather than risk being reprimanded for using the necessary force required to turn an aggressive sheep.

I want my dog to be a confident, calm worker. However, I also want him to know that I will accept assertive behaviour from him towards the stock if the situation requires it. Therefore, if one of my inexperienced dogs is uncertain how to deal with a sheep that confronts him, I will often use a more experienced dog to help him exert his authority over her. Alternatively, I will walk up and give him my support and encouragement so that my dog feels confident to turn the ewe. If necessary, I will allow him to give the sheep a quick nip that is definitely not an aggressive grip. By permitting this, my dog learns that he can use appropriate force to move any sheep if the situation requires it. If, for any reason, we still fail to move the sheep, then I will often gather a few others and bring them to the solitary one. Sheep feel more comfortable when they are with their pals and a stubborn or stressed ewe is often more willing to move away from the dog when she is with a group.

Summary of the training stages required for the lift and fetch

The basic stage. The dog should:

- Work close at hand with just a few sheep.
- Lift sheep at the balance point.
- Have the appropriate attitude.
- Lift and complete a short fetch at the correct pace.
- Do some natural work close at hand using very few commands. However, always consider your sheep.

The intermediate stage. In addition to the basic stage, the dog should:

- Lift a few or a flock of sheep up to 250m away from you while still having the correct attitude.
- Lift carefully without becoming sticky.
- Be allowed to push forward when lifting a larger flock in preparation of working with heavy sheep.
- Be able to flank off the balance point whilst fetching sheep. This will ensure that your dog can move stock any direction you require.
- Be introduced to 'different gears' so that he learns different paces and can speed up or slow down as required.
- Be allowed to do plenty of natural work with very few commands.

The advanced stage. In addition to the basic and intermediate stages, the dog should:

- Be able to use his own initiative and work naturally.
- Willingly respond promptly to all commands.
- Feel his sheep and be able to work with different breeds (from heavy to light) using appropriate pressure / release.
- Pace himself and alter his energy levels depending on the situation for example whether he is lifting and fetching some defiant tups, returning a frightened lost lamb to its mother, working with a single sheep or fetching stock that are less accustomed to dogs.
- Lift and fetch sheep from a great distance across different terrains and in different weather while keeping appropriate control.

Ban knows to alter the pressure he puts on the sheep depending on the terrain and weather

Problems

Every dog has his own individual method for working and this will influence how he approaches, lifts and fetches stock. The sheep will often tell you what the dog is thinking. Spend time developing sheep sense and you will be able to help your dog be in the right position at the correct time with the appropriate mindset that will allow him to work his stock with calm, steady authority.

In general, if you have a problem with the lift and fetch then you need to go back to basics and break it down into stages. Go back to working close at hand and focus on altering your dog's attitude so that you re-establish his respect for both you and the sheep. When you see an improvement, gradually increase the distance.

The dog attempts to lift sheep before the balance point

If this happens, the sheep will not be turned onto the correct fetch line. Instead they will run off with the dog running parallel in an attempt to catch them. If your dog gets into this situation, then you need to stop the sheep's forward movement. You do this by asking your dog to flank further around so that he can head the sheep and stop their forward movement. He then needs to turn the stock so that they move back onto the original fetch line.

If the problem recurs then you need to assess the situation and work out why it is happening. Is it an issue with his outrun, flank and balance? If you think one of these is the underlying issue then you need to review the earlier chapters (see page 83 and page 90).

Alternatively, your dog may attempt to lift the sheep early because he refuses to head the sheep. Again you need to work out why. Does he lack confidence? Does he feels threatened by the sheep? Is he unsure how you will respond if he approaches sheep? Perhaps, you are using inappropriate or poorly timed pressure that makes him feel uncertain that he is correct? Does he have a lot of eye that is making him stick as he approaches his stock? In all these cases, you need to go back to basics. Get closer to your sheep and encourage your dog to keep moving around to the balance point by giving an additional flank command as he starts to slow. When he reaches the balance point, do not stop your dog, instead encourage him to walk onto the flock: it is easier to keep a dog moving rather than starting him from a standstill. If your dog lacks confidence, use minimal levels of pressure and try to stimulate his forward movement using encouraging tones. If you have another more experienced dog, consider working them together to help boost the youngster's confidence. Make sure you reward every small try and allow him to make some mistakes. It takes patience to give a dog like this confidence.

The sheep run before the dog is at the balance point

A If your dog is not at the correct balance point, he will not manage to turn the sheep onto the correct fetch line. As a result the sheep run off and the dog runs parallel with them. **B** If your dog gets into this situation, then he has to be flanked further around to stop the sheep's forward movement He can then direct them back to the original fetch line. If this is a frequent problem, then you should go back to basics to address the issue.

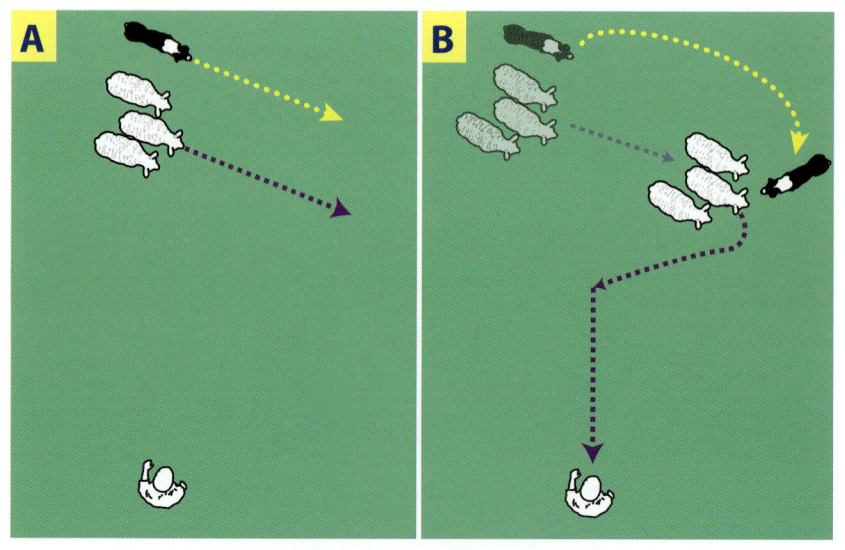

You may also need to consider other reasons why the sheep move before your dog reaches the balance point. If he is physically unfit, your dog will tend to cut in tighter towards his sheep. To solve this, you need to increase his fitness and stamina. Alternatively, the sheep may have been previously chased by dogs. This earlier experience may make them panic whenever they see a dog. If your sheep are like this, you need to spend a lot of time working calmly with them close at hand while you control your dog's energy levels. Gradually the stock will readjust their attitude to your dog and be more accepting of his presence. Both these situations require patience as they will take time to sort.

The dog lifts sheep after the balance point

A dogs that either is not concentrating or is loose-eyed may go past the balance point and push the sheep in the wrong direction. If you have this problem you will have to watch the sheep yourself and decide where the correct balance point is. Then combine vocal or whistle commands with appropriate body language and hand gestures to manipulate his movement in the desired direction. You will need to assess and understand what your dog's movements and how the sheep are responding to him in order to time using the pressure / release technique properly. Initially, as your dog approaches the balance point, give him a *steady* command to ask him to pay attention. If he seems to ignore this command or if he looks as if he is going past the balance point, then use a block to stop any further forward movement. In contrast, if he stops too soon then give him an additional nudge to move further round. When he has reached the balance point, walk backwards to release pressure as this tells your dog he has reached the correct place to lift the stock.

However, when working your dog make sure your interpretation of his behaviour is correct. Some dogs intentionally flank past the balance point in order to tuck in the strays near the edge of the flock. Once they have gathered all the sheep into a tight group, this type of dog will instinctively return to the balance point to lift the sheep. This type of natural behaviour needs to be encouraged and not corrected.

The lift is too fast

A dog which does not feel his sheep can push forward quickly at the lift, startling the stock into flight. You need to go back to basics and move closer to your sheep so that you can control the situation (even if you leave your dog at a distance so that he can still have a longer outrun). Use appropriate pressure to remind him to consider his attitude and take notice of his sheep as he nears the end of his outrun. Some dogs may lift sheep quickly, not out of devilment, but actually because he is concerned about moving stock. This type of dog does not have the confidence to move sheep steadily and instead feels that he can only do it by hurrying forward. His anxiety may also cause him to grip. Go back to basics to build his confidence.

The dog rushes in and grips

As I have just explained this is often due to lack of confidence. The dog often feels too much pressure either from the sheep or from his handler. After gripping, he may flee out of contact with the sheep in an attempt to avoid a severe reprimand from his owner. If your dog is like this, you need to build his confidence so that he feels comfortable near sheep. You also have to inform him that rushing at sheep like this is not acceptable. When your dog reaches the balance point, you need to hold the block position and not allow him to come onto his sheep. This block is 'asking' him to consider his actions. If he drops his shoulder or looks like he intends to rush in, then, you need to increase the pressure by leaning forward and if necessary raising your hand to 'tell' him to think about his attitude. You should only move backwards when he shows signs that he is listening to you and wants to negotiate with you. Remember, that much of this problem has arisen because your dog lacks confidence. It is therefore very important that when he tries to do the right thing and comes forward steadily that you reward his try by releasing pressure and keeping your arm and hand down whilst you walk backwards. If his body language and gestures indicate that he intends to rush in, then move to the block again and ask him to reconsider his actions. It may feel that you do not progress rapidly in sorting this out, but, if you are consistent, fair and appropriate using pressure / release the issue should resolve. Sorting this problem will take time.

The fetch is too fast

A dog that pushes on too much during the fetch may end up chasing sheep if he is not corrected. As the sheep run faster, the dog often tries to catch up. Although some dogs have natural pace, others have to be taught to feel their sheep. To teach your dog to slow down you need to go back to basics. Walk backwards, and ask your dog to check his pace using the *steady* command. If he does not respond to your voice, lift up your hand or a plastic pipe and tell him to check his speed. If this does not work, then you need to move forward to insist that he listen to you. Remember to release the pressure once you see him start to give to your pressure. However, with some dogs, you always have to remind them that it is you that is in charge!

Sometimes the speedy lift and fetch problems are exacerbated because the dog does not have enough work to do. It is perhaps not surprising that when he is given the opportunity to work, he finds it hard to contain himself. I find that a dog will alter his mindset once he becomes tired after working a few hard long days on the hill. When the dog works stock on a regular basis, his excitement on initially seeing them will be moderated as they becomes 'just a job' that needs doing. If your dog is like this but you do not have the option of working stock on a regular basis then take him on a long tiring run before you go to work with him on stock.

The lift is too slow / the dog does not want to walk onto sheep

There are a few reasons why this may happen. Firstly, your dog may have too much eye and freezes as he becomes fixated on the sheep. Alternatively, other dogs do not have sufficient power to assert their authority over the stock. This second type of dog sometimes finds it difficult to move a large number of sheep especially if they are heavy or are confronting him. If your dog is either of these types then I recommend that you do not stop your dog at the end of his outrun. As he is already slow about his lift, you also do not need to ask him to *steady*. Instead, ask your dog to *walk-on* so that he continues to move forward onto the sheep directly from his outrun. This will hopefully make the stock move away rather than confront him. It should also give your dog confidence that he can lift sheep.

If your dog does stop and you then struggle to get him to *walk-on* to his sheep, then ask him to flank slightly before asking him to move forward again: it is easier for a dog to move forward from a small flank than it is from a static position. You then want to keep your dog and sheep moving with a nice steady flow. Be careful, when you do need to encourage your dog to lift sheep, do not use an urgent tone as this may cause your dog to become more anxious. Anxiety or excitement can make a dog grip.

Some dogs do not want to walk onto the sheep but instead shows signs of avoidance such as sniffing the ground or moving out of contact. Often this is because the handler has used inappropriate pressure and the dog does not feel comfortable about approaching him. If your dog is like this, you will need to reconsider how you use the pressure / release technique(see page 16).

The sheep stop to graze

Sheep will graze when the dog does not exert sufficient pressure to move them. They take advantage because they do not respect him. You need to encourage your dog to move faster or closer to the stock to stimulate their sense of danger. Once the sheep have started to move away from him, try to ensure that he maintains pressure on them to keep the sheep flowing. Do not stop your dog too often or the sheep will resume their grazing,

The dog does not want to flank on the fetch

A dog who lacks confidence will not want to move around to the heavy side of the sheep. Alternatively if he has a strong eye, he can become so focused on the sheep, that he sticks and is unable to flank when requested. If your dog is like this then it is important that you exert sufficient pressure through your body language and gestures that you gain his attention and he responds to your commands. As always, remember to release pressure when he does flank so that he knows he has done the right thing.

Some dogs manage to flank but do not go far enough around to turn the sheep in the required direction. This problem may arise because the dog has not been taught to turn the sheep inwards when he is flanking. If this is the issue, reread the chapters on flanking (see page 90 and page 118).

The dog circles the sheep

There are several reasons why this might happen. You need to work out what the problem is before deciding how to deal with it. If it is just a one-off mistake, then you probably can ignore it. However, if your dog often misunderstands you, then perhaps your commands are not clearly distinct from each other. If your dog often mixes up your whistle commands, then you may need to become more consistent or else consider adapting one or more of them so that you no longer confuse your dog. Pay particular attention to the tone your whistle makes.

Another possible cause of circling is when the dog is not sufficiently experienced and is sent on too long an outrun. In this situation, the dog forgets that you are there. Instead, he instinctively tries to stop the sheep who are probably running swiftly away from him. In his attempt to control the situation, he circles to head them off and probably ends up holding them to a fence rather than to you.

If your dog does this, you need to shorten his outrun and stand closer to the sheep. Go back to basics and remind him to balance sheep towards you (see page 83). Gradually extend the distance of the outrun and fetch. If he still attempts to head the sheep, you need to apply pressure to push him back to the balance point and remind him that you are the focal point. However, when doing this you need to have sufficient sheep sense to know where

the balance point is. As I have explained previously, this is not always at the back of the sheep, it may be to one side. You need to watch the sheep to be able to tell the difference between whether your dog is holding the heavy side of the sheep correctly to balance them towards you and whether he is about to circle them incorrectly and head them off in the wrong direction.

The dog weaves during the fetch

Every dog has his own style and method of moving sheep. It also depends on the type and number of sheep that he is working: a dog working a large flock will inevitably have to weave in order to keep the outside sheep tucked in and flocking together.

When working fewer sheep, some dogs use their eye and put their head down and walk directly onto the sheep. Others with less eye or lacking confidence may need to weave backwards and forwards in order to get the sheep to move away from him. In both of these situations, try to keep the sheep's momentum going and do not stop your dog too often. The weaving will often decrease when the sheep move more fluently and as your dog gains in experience and confidence.

Moving on

It is important that your dog knows that he should bring sheep to you in a calm fashion. He must also have the appropriate attitude and respect towards both you and the stock. As you progress and you want the sheep moved in different directions, you will find that the natural flank alone is not sufficient to get your dog into the right position to do this. Your dog will also need to know how to flank in front and behind you as well as flank away from the balance point. These are all discussed in more detail in the next chapter.

From the Clinic

Handler: My dog has no pace on the fetch.

I observed that the dog was not pulling back when he was given a *stand* command. When he did check his pace, the handler quickly asked for his dog to *walk-on*. This meant that the dog only pulled back from his sheep for a second.

My opinion: In reality, the handler was asking his dog to keep moving rather than teaching him to listen and respond to the *stand* command.

My advice: The handler had to teach his dog what the *stand* and *steady* commands were for. He needed to do this by working close at hand. I advised that he walk backwards and let his dog fetch and balance the sheep to him. As soon as the dog started to increase his speed, the handler needed to ask for a *steady* using a quiet, calm and assertive tone. To reinforce his vocal command, the handler had to lean forward slightly to indicate a half-halt block. If his dog had been listening, he would have responded by sitting back on his hocks for a couple of seconds. However, he ignored his handler's request and continued to push onto his sheep. Therefore, the handler had to tell his dog to *stand* in a slightly sharper and firmer tone. At the same time he moved into a block position and raised his hand. This time the dog stopped and acknowledged his handler's presence. I asked the handler to immediately release his pressure so that the dog felt comfortable and realised he had made the right choice. The handler moved backwards and allowed the dog to come forward slowly. By working close at hand and using pressure / release properly, the handler managed to communicate effectively with his dog.

Once the dog understood what the *stand* and *steady* commands meant, the handler could start to extend the distance of the outrun again. As the dog appreciated what his owner's body language meant, the handler could use this to reinforce his vocal commands even when the dog was some distance from him. At the end of the sessions with me, the handler felt capable of dealing with the situation as he knew that if the problem arose again, he just needed to have the patience to go back to basics and work close at hand again to reinforce his message.

Anecdote. A lift too far

Back in my early days, I attended a trial in Derbyshire with my black bitch, Bess. I sent her on her outrun and she ran out wide along the wall. Unfortunately, the Swaledale ewes we needed to gather on the trial were very different from the heavy sheep I usually shepherded. They snorted at her forward manner as she approached her lift and promptly fled. They made straight towards me with high heads, eyes staring and tails spinning. Their curled horns and flaring nostrils made them look like small devils as I narrowly dodged the on-coming stampede. I stood transfixed as a blur of wool carried on past me. Bess stopped at my feet and it felt as if we both had the same open-mouthed gormless expression on our faces as we watched them speed across the hill and vanish out of sight. It took a few moments for me to close my mouth. Laughing as we both left the post, all I could do was look at Bess and ask 'What the hell did you say to them?'

From the Clinic

Handler: My dog is pulling up short on his outrun and stalking sheep rather than running to cover them.

I observed that before the dog was sent, he looked intense and tense, his tail was under his body indicating uncertainty. Furthermore he was walking with a low body position as if he was already attempting to stalk the sheep. The dog started going to the right on his outrun. However he stopped and froze when he reached a point that was almost level with the sheep (I call this the '¾ point'). He then slowly started stalking towards the sheep who responded by moving away in the opposite direction. The handler ran towards her dog waving her stick in the air and shouting the *away* flank command, but, to my mind, there was little intent behind her movement. The dog responded to his handler's actions by becoming excited and with a flicking tail rushed into the sheep.

My opinion: The dog was sticky-eyed and this was inhibiting him from completing his outrun in a smooth pear-shaped arc. Instead his eye is pulling him up short and causing him to stalk the sheep who moved away. The result was the dog was starting to drive the sheep before he had completed a full outrun. The dog then became confused by his handler's subsequent inappropriate attempt to move him around on his flank. Instead, her actions overexcited him which caused him to rush into the sheep.

My advice: When working sheep, the handler's movements needed to be calm, assertive and given with intent. She also had to learn to focus her energy so that her dog had a clear understanding of what he was being asked to do. In addition, the handler needed to break her dog's thought pattern about stopping and encourage him to have a flowing movement that would enable him to complete his outrun. To achieve this, she needed to give her commands before he actually physically stopped.

I advised the handler to go back to basics and return to small outruns. I suggested that she stand between the sheep and her dog before sending him on his outrun. After sending her dog and just as he was coming up to the ¾ point, the handler needed to push him out and around. To achieve this, I advised the owner to move and point her stick at his shoulder (to push him out) and then repositioning her stick so that it was slightly behind her dog. This would stimulate forward movement in him and encourage him to continue on his outrun. The dog needed to learn to respond to his handler's body movements and voice at the same time. Therefore, while she was pointing at her dog, I suggested using the commands *get* and *away* to push him further out and round. She needed to combine these commands with a shushing sound that would encourage more movement from her dog.

By keeping her dog moving on his flank, and giving sufficient pressure with encouragement to cover the sheep, the hander was able to make her dog want to fetch sheep rather than continually attempt to drive them. Once she started to have some success, I suggested that she worked on small outruns with her dog. She should then walk backwards and allow her dog to balance the sheep to her. I encouraged her to move in different directions asking for large flanks that ensured that her dog actually over-flanked the sheep.

Over time, the handler needed to work on the natural fetch and drive. However, she should only allow her dog to drive for short periods before asking him to flank and gather the sheep to her once more. These short drives followed by flanks would test whether her dog was improving or not. At some point, the handler would need to ask him to drive sheep, so I did not want her to stop him driving completely, rather she just had to concentrate more on her dog's outruns.

CHAPTER 12
MORE FLANKS

In order for a dog to be truly versatile he needs to be willing and able to flank in any direction. For example, he may need to reposition himself during a fetch so that he can direct sheep to bypass a hazard or go through a gate. Similarly, he will need to move to the appropriate position when he is driving stock or helping you pen or shed some sheep. As the dog flanks around sheep he must neither upset them nor push them in an unwanted direction. Therefore when flanking he always needs to have both the correct attitude and also move in an arc around the stock.

As I have discussed in Chapter 10 (see page 90), a dog has a natural tendency to flank towards the balance point and I therefore call this the natural flank. In contrast, he does not always feel comfortable flanking away from the balance point and because it is against his instinct I call this manoeuvre the **unnatural flank.** In this chapter I will cover three types of flank: the flank behind the handler, the flank in front of the handler and the unnatural flank. The first two are often used when teaching the dog to drive while the final one is required when redirecting sheep during a fetch.

However, no matter what type of flank you are teaching, there are some basic principles that relate to all of them.

1. Before teaching your dog a new skill, always first go into a block position to make him stop. This will give your dog time to focus on the new command.

2. Remember that there is an invisible line of contact between your dog and the sheep. Think about how you are moving and positioning your body in relation to this line. If you do this correctly, your body language will tell your dog what you are trying to do. However, your dog can easily become confused if you give a mixed message by positioning yourself in the wrong place.

3. Think about your sheep: where they are and what they are about to do. I often find that when a novice handler is teaching a new flank, he will often say to me 'My dog sometimes does what I want, but other times, he just seems to ignore me'. Nine times out of ten this is because the handler has focused too much on the dog and forgotten about the stock. In addition, if the dog does not fully respect his human, his attention will be fully fixated on the sheep. A dog may also appear to ignore his handler, if he feels his sheep are about to escape. In these situations, the dog is fully focused on the stock so that he can instantly react if they attempt to flee.

4. Your dog needs to move in an arcing movement around the stock. If he cuts in too tightly during the flank he can push the sheep in the wrong direction. When you begin teaching your dog a new flank, start with both your dog and sheep close at hand. You will then be better placed to control the situation. Use your body language to ensure that your dog moves around the sheep in an arc and that he controls his energy levels as he does this.

5. Give the dog space to move. Asking your dog to take an unnatural flank may make him feel uncomfortable. This will be exacerbated if you or the sheep put additional pressure on him by standing too close. Therefore, if you want your dog to move behind you, take one or two steps closer to the sheep. In contrast, if you want him to flank in front of you, move away so that there is a sufficient distance between you and the sheep for him to pass without feeling pressurised by either of you.

6. Use consistent voice and whistle commands. In addition, when you are close to your dog, use quiet tones. As your dog becomes more experienced, he should start responding to these and your body and hand gestures should become more subtle.

Flanking behind the handler

The flank behind can be useful when you are close to the sheep and the only way to keep them settled is to ask your dog to flank behind you because flanking in front would bring him too close to the stock and upset them.

Stand on the invisible line of contact between your dog and the sheep and block his movement in any direction. Then move your body over the line to stop his movement in this direction. At the same time, move your arm that is close to your dog behind you and twist round. This body language asks him to move behind you and flank around the sheep. As your dog progresses, you can test this flank by just leaning your upper body over the line whilst holding your hand backwards. The next stage is when you use a more subtle hand signal that does not cross the invisible line of contact. When you are certain that he responds readily to this, you can finally move to just voice and whistle commands to ask him to flank behind you.

Ask for a stop before teaching a new task
I ask the dog to stop by moving into the block position. This ensures that he focuses on the new command.

The flank behind
A I want Mac to flank to the left (*come-bye*), I position myself across the 'invisible line of contact' between my dog and sheep to help guide him in the correct direction. **B** By moving over this line, I block Mac's forward movement to the right. I simultaneously move my arm backwards as if opening a door. This asks Mac to move behind me and take the left flank. **C** Mac responds to my body language by turning towards the left. **D** Mac continues to respond to my body language by taking the left flank. **E** As a dog becomes more experienced, he should listen to voice and whistle commands and the obvious hand gestures should become more subtle. Here I just put my stick and hand over the invisible line while I ask Ban to flank to the left.

Flanking in front of the handler (The inside flank)

Let's consider that you want your dog to take a right (*away*) flank in front of you. In this situation, your dog will start on your left side and you should be facing the sheep. If necessary move further away from the stock to give your dog sufficient room to pass between you and them without feeling uncomfortable. Turn your upper body slightly towards the right and move anticlockwise (the direction you want him to flank). Lower your right hand so that it is just in front of your left thigh and encourage him to focus on this by clicking your fingers. If you have used my Natural Way of training in the round pen then he should associate these gestures with being invited into your space. You can also use the *here* command. However, obviously, you do not want him to stop at your feet, so as he passes over the invisible line of contact you need to reposition your upper body into a half block to discouraging him from coming too close to you. Simultaneously, lift your right hand up to point towards his head. It is important that you time this correctly as it puts mild pressure on him and makes him turn his head inwards. As your dog starts to do this, walk to the right (the direction you want him to flank) and use the *away* command to encourage him to flank inside. You should reverse this exercise to practice the left (*come-bye*) flank.

Julie's Tip. Work with a large group of sheep when teaching the inside flank. Your dog has to move more and this will make him relax as he flanks.

If your dog becomes unsettled by this method or does not understand what you want, then an alternative method is to move behind him and cross the invisible line of contact. In order to re-balance himself, your dog should respond to your movement by taking the inside flank in the other direction.

From the Clinic

Handler: My dog is an experienced worker who has just stopped flanking for no obvious reason.

I observed that he was a very classy type of dog that was keen to work. He did not seem to be stubborn or temperamental. However, after watching the handler work her dog, I realised that I could not understand what she was asking her dog to do. The problem was that she had developed three very distinct flank commands for each side. Many people alter the length of their flank commands depending on whether they require a large or a small flank, but in general they keep the same tone and pitch while they do this. In contrast, this handler varied the pitch and tone so that each flank command was very different from the other (even though they were all supposedly asking her dog to flank in the same direction). In addition, every time her dog made a mistake she would discipline him.

My opinion: The handler had over complicated her commands so that the dog could not understand what he was being requested to do. In addition, she had reprimanded him every time he made a mistake. It was not surprising that the dog had stopped flanking. He did not know what she wanted and was being told off when he guessed incorrectly. The dog's only solution was not to take any flank command.

My advice: The handler needed to simplify her flank commands and not be so quick to discipline an error. These simple changes meant her dog could understand what his owner required and also let him relax back into his work. He was now able to focus without worrying and could therefore make an instant response when his handler gave her flank command.

The take home message from this story is do not make things too difficult for your dog. He will remain willing and responsive if you keep your commands simple and you also use the pressure / release technique appropriately.

The inside flank

In this sequence I want Mac to take a right (*away*) flank moving between the sheep and me. **A** Mac is focused on the sheep and I take a step forward and call *here* to get his attention. **B** I move further back from the sheep and hold my right hand by my thigh and click my fingers. This asks Mac to focus on my hand. **C** Mac starts to draw towards my lowered right hand. Notice that as I have called Mac towards me, I have walked backwards. This encourages him to come towards me and also gives him sufficient space to feel comfortable as he moves between me and the sheep. **D** As Mac reaches a point in front of me, I alter my body language slightly to discourage him from coming to my feet. Simultaneously, I draw my right hand out and back to prompt him to continue his flank to the right. **E** I start to relax my posture as Mac continues to flank towards the right. This release of pressure informs Mac that he has acted correctly.

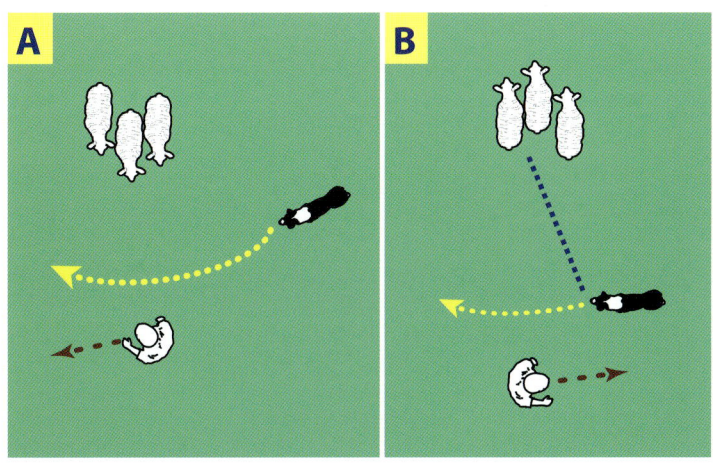

The handler can move to encourage the dog to take the inside flank.

If your dog is unsettled or does not understand what you require, you can move to help him. In both these cases, the dog should flank to the left (*come-bye*).
A Walk to the left and encourage your dog to come to you by clicking the fingers of your left hand as you say *here*. As your dog curves towards you, give the *come-bye* command and use your body language to encourage him to continue on his flank.
B Walk behind your dog to the right. As you cross the invisible line of contact, the balance point will alter. In order to re-balance himself, your dog will naturally wish to take the left inside flank.

Flanking away from the balance point during the fetch (the unnatural flank)

The unnatural flank is similar as the flank behind. The main difference between the two is that the handler is close to the sheep during the flank behind, but further away during the unnatural flank. The dog may need to perform an unnatural flank when he needs to redirect sheep during a drive or fetch, for example to navigate the stock through a gate that it situated at one side of the field.

The full manoeuvre is actually made up of a number of different elements. When you are starting to teach this to your dog, start by sending your dog on a short outrun. Let him lift the sheep and fetch them towards you. When the sheep are close to you (so you can control the situation) with the dog on the other side of the sheep, ask him to stop. If necessary, lean forwards and raise your hand in order to enforce the block. Then still facing your dog, use the flank behind hand gesture to encourage your dog to flank off balance. Use the appropriate command (*come-bye* or *away* as you do this). When the dog is in the correct location to move the sheep in the new direction, stop him again. If necessary move to a block position to stop him from continuing his flank. Then walk with the dog and the sheep in a short drive (see page 125). Stop your dog again and this time ask for a natural flank. As the dog flanks to the balance point in order to lift the sheep, you need to move backwards to give him space to bring the sheep towards you. Remember that walking backwards is releasing pressure and this tells your dog he has acted appropriately.

Let him fetch the sheep to you. Make sure you train your dog so that he can do this whole manoeuvre with both *come-bye* and *away* flanks.

As your dog gains in experience, you will be able to ask him to flank off the fetch line without asking for stops between each element. With time you should also decrease the amount of overt body language and hand gestures that you use so that your dog learns to respond to just your voice and whistle commands. As the dog reaches the intermediary and advanced stages of his training, he should be able to flank away from the balance point at any point along his fetch. Furthermore he should be able to redirect sheep in any new direction you require.

Summary of the training stages required for flanking

The basic stage. The dog should:

• Work a few sheep at hand (but leave sufficient space between handler and sheep for the inside flank).

• Respond to the handler's body language and be introduced to voice commands.

• Flank sheep correctly so that they are not unsettled.

The intermediate stage. In addition to the basic stage, the dog should:

• Flank sheep at some distance away from the handler.

• Respond to voice and whistle commands. However, the handler may still also need to use some hand signals.

The advanced stage. In addition to the basic and intermediate stages, the dog should:

• Combine different flanks as required to move sheep calmly in the required direction.

• Take commands that ask for a small flank or a larger one.

• Be willing to flank in response to the out or in command.

The unnatural flank

A I send Ruby on a left (*come-bye*) flank. **B** As she reaches the balance point, my body moves to a block position and I ask her to stop. **C** After a short fetch, I ask her to stop again. **D** I then use the same arm movements that I would use for the flank behind to ask her to flank away from the balance point. **E** As Ruby reaches the 9 o'clock position, I again ask her to stop and my body moves into the block position. After this I would ask her to drive the sheep for a short distance while I walk next to her.

Problems

Many of the problems associated with these different flanks often also occur during different manoeuvres and so are discussed elsewhere.

If your dog cuts his flank i.e. runs tight on his flank see page 98; for over-flanking see page 113 for under-flanking see page 112; for refusing to take your flank commands see page 100).

When you have a problem with the way your dog works his sheep, remember that he may interpret the situation differently from you. Any single issue, for example, cutting his flanks, may potentially have any one of several different causes. Each of these in turn will have their own solution. Therefore it is always important to analyse the facts and consider what has happened from your dog's perspective. So when you find a problem, always ask some general questions. These include:

- How do you communicate with your dog?
- Does your body language match your voice command or are you giving mixed messages?
- Is your body language and the way you give your voice commands consistent and appropriate for the situation?
- Are you giving the correct flank command?
- Does your dog respect you? Does he consider he is dominant to you? Or does he feel insecure in your presence?
- Are you using pressure / release appropriately for your dog's temperament and nature?
- What is your dog's temperament?
- Does your dog lack confidence? Is this affecting his behaviour?
- How much eye does your dog have? Is this affecting his movement?
- How does your dog react to sheep? Is any grip actually due to insecurity rather than aggression?
- How do sheep react to your dog? Does he calm or upset them?

Once you have decided on the underlying problem, then you can start addressing it. It helps to address most problems by working close at hand with your dog. You may find that you need to go back to basics and re-establish your dog's respect (see page 13) before you properly solve the issue.

Moving On

These flanks will be used time and again during your dog's working and trialling life. Although it will take time, I recommend that you spend time working close at hand so that he learns from the start how to move around his sheep in an arcing movement. If he cuts the corner and moves in a straight line, your dog will almost inevitably push the sheep forward in an inappropriate manner. This can cause problems during the drive or at the pen. In the next chapter I will discuss how these flanks are used during the drive.

From the Clinic

Handler: My dog works nicely at hand, but she will cut off a sheep and chase it when working at a distance.

I observed that when working at a distance, the dog would concentrate on one sheep and keep pushing forward. As sheep are prey animals, the ewes felt threatened by this and would split as they bolted away from her. When the dog created this exciting effect, she inevitably went into 'hunt mode' and chased one of the sheep because she did not know what else to do. The handler considered that she had intentionally done this, and once the chase had started, would start shouting, but to no avail.

My opinion: This dog was not badly behaved. However, she did not realise that she needed to be aware of all the sheep and lacked any understanding of how to keep them together. Furthermore, she did not know how to use her own initiative, so if she could not hear a command, she did not know how to bring all the stock to her handler.

My advice: The dog needed to learn how to be aware of all the sheep she was working. I encouraged the handler to go back to working closer at hand. I showed him how he could use his body language to ask his dog to flank away from the balance point. When a sheep started to drift to one side, the handler could use appropriate gestures and movements to prompt his dog to reposition herself so that she tucked in the straying ewe. After she had done this, the handler needed to ask her to flank to the other side to gather the stock back together and then re-balance to bring them towards him. In order to be able know where to position his dog correctly during these various manoeuvres, the handler had to be able to read both the dog and the sheep, so that he could pre-empt the ewes from drifting too far to the side. When his dog had acted correctly with the appropriate attitude, I suggested that he release pressure by lowering his arm and walking backwards. This told his dog that she had done the right thing. The handler learnt that he did not need to shout. In fact, he discovered that a calm manner and small gestures, were more effective at making his dog understand. He also started to appreciate why it was necessary to teach his dog to use her own initiative.

During the duration of the 3 day clinic, the handler realised that when his dog made a mistake, he could correct her with appropriate body language and not use his voice. He also needed to give his dog sufficient leeway, so that she could learn. He told me afterwards, that this was very useful because he knew he was falling into the trap of shouting and growling a lot. He felt he now had a better way of communicating with his dog.

Chapter 13
The Drive

In olden days, the shepherd would use his dog to drive sheep many miles along ancient routes known as drove roads in order to take them to market to sell. Since the advent of trucks and the railways, many of these old drove roads have become overgrown and lost, but even today the shepherd's dog still needs to be able to move his stock safely from one location to another. At Carcant, my dogs are required to drive sheep during their everyday work. For example after gathering a heft, I may need to take them down to the pens or else move them onto a field nearer the farm. Alternatively, at tupping time, one of the tups may have been enticed by some fertile ewes onto the wrong heft and needs returning to the sheep he is supposed to be serving. An experienced dog who knows the farm routine will not require a large number of commands to drive stock to the correct place. Instead, he will use his knowledge to ensure that there are no stragglers as he moves the sheep at a steady pace along the most direct route to the final destination.

I start teaching the drive, when I am certain that my dog can balance, flank and gather sheep from a short distance. By this stage, my dog should have the appropriate attitude towards stock so that he lifts and fetches them without undue stress.

Similar to all other aspects of sheepdog training, when you teach the basic stages of the drive you should stay close to the sheep so you can then control the situation and guide your dog to be in the correct position. In addition, while your dog learns to drive, remember to continually reuse the other skills he has learnt in order to keep them fresh in his mind. When I first started training sheepdogs, I did not realise the benefit of doing this. Instead, I focused all my training sessions on developing my dog's driving technique. Unfortunately, when I went to gather sheep with him, he started driving them away instead of fetching them towards me. He obviously thought this was the new way of gathering stock! I learnt a valuable lesson from this: no matter what new skills you train your dog, always keep practising those he has already developed.

I find the easiest way to introduce the dog to driving is to make it a direct extension of the natural fetch which I described on page 106. In brief, this is when you walk around the field with your dog working naturally behind you as he balances the sheep. Once you are satisfied that your dog is doing this with the correct mindset, you should slow up and let the sheep pass you. Continue to walk behind the sheep but in front of your dog. Hey Presto, the dog will carry on balancing the sheep in front and he will be driving without realising it – this is why I call this approach the **natural drive**.

Starting the natural drive
A I let Ban use the natural fetch to direct the sheep that are walking behind me. **B** I gradually pull back so that the sheep pass me. Ban continues on the natural drive.

Julie's Tip. Try to keep moving quietly and smoothly while teaching the natural fetch and drive. This will relax both you and your dog.

The advantage of walking slightly in front of your dog is that you can easily use your body language to direct him to take the sheep in the required direction. If he moves away from the drive line, you can simply block this wrong direction by walking across the invisible line of contact. Your dog will re-balance himself back onto the drive line.

Do not expect precision driving at this basic stage. Instead you want your dog and sheep to flow smoothly in a relaxed manner. You should only ask for more precision in the natural drive when you are satisfied that your dog is balancing properly and has the appropriate mindset. Move further to the side, but stay just in front of your dog so that he can still see you. This position again means that you are still strategically placed to ensure that he moves where needed to maintain the drive.

As you continue the natural drive, it is useful to have a focal point that both you and your dog can aim for. This can be anything convenient, for example a barn, a gate or a post.

Read your sheep, look at the carriage and the direction of their head and ears. They should be alert, but not unduly worried. If they move their head away from the correct drive line, encourage your dog to take small flanks to get them back on track. Also keep an eye on your dog's body language. If he starts to push too hard, then ask him to *steady*. In contrast, if the sheep start to graze, then you need to encourage your dog to walk onto his stock. If you also help him move the sheep, his confidence will grow as he begins to understand what is required.

As he drives, your dog will also probably keep flicking his eye or ear towards you to determine what your body language is telling him. So when he is behaving appropriately, it is important that you remain relaxed as you walk alongside. Your calm attitude will reassure him that he is doing the right thing and in response, your dog will also relax as he gains confidence and enjoys his work.

It is inevitable when your start to drive that the sheep will move off the drive line. When this happens do not be tempted to follow them around the field. Instead, you should continue walking along the original line while you send your dog on a flank to bring them back. You do not want him to head the sheep, so he should flank behind them (and you) in order to get into a position that will direct them back onto the correct line. He will need to use both the natural flank (see page 90) and the flank behind (see page 119) in order to do this.

Remember he should flank in an smooth arc and not push the sheep in the wrong direction as he moves to the new position. You can help the dog understand what is required by moving your body slightly over the invisible line first one way and then the other. Your dog will mirror your actions to re-balance the sheep and this in turn will nudge them inwards and keep them moving forward.

Some dogs find it very difficult to learn how to drive and may repeatedly try to head the sheep in order to balance them back towards you. If your dog continues to do this, then you can practice driving alongside a fence with you walking in front of your dog. The sheep will probably attempt to pull off the fence and your dog will pull out slightly to balance them back to the fence. You should ask your dog to *walk-on* but use your body language to indicate that he should stay behind you and not head the stock. Not only will this help your dog understand that he should not circle round to head them, but it will also assist him to appreciate where he should position himself to hold the heavy side of the stock as he drives them forward.

As your dog drives, he will almost inevitably move faster than you with the result that he and the sheep are both in front of you. Some dogs will be tempted at this point to circle the sheep in order to fetch them back to you. Others will take advantage and may start to chase the sheep. A third type of dog may become uncomfortable and *look back* towards you for reassurance.

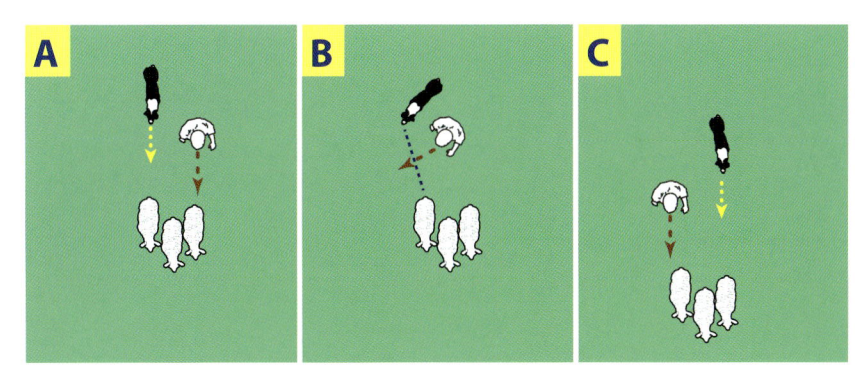

Helping your dog to keep driving forward
A During the natural drive, walk to the side of your dog but just in front of him. **B** Your dog may start to change direction. You need to move (brown arrow) across the invisible line of contact (blue dotted line). **C** Your dog will reposition himself to balance to your new position and continue to drive forward.

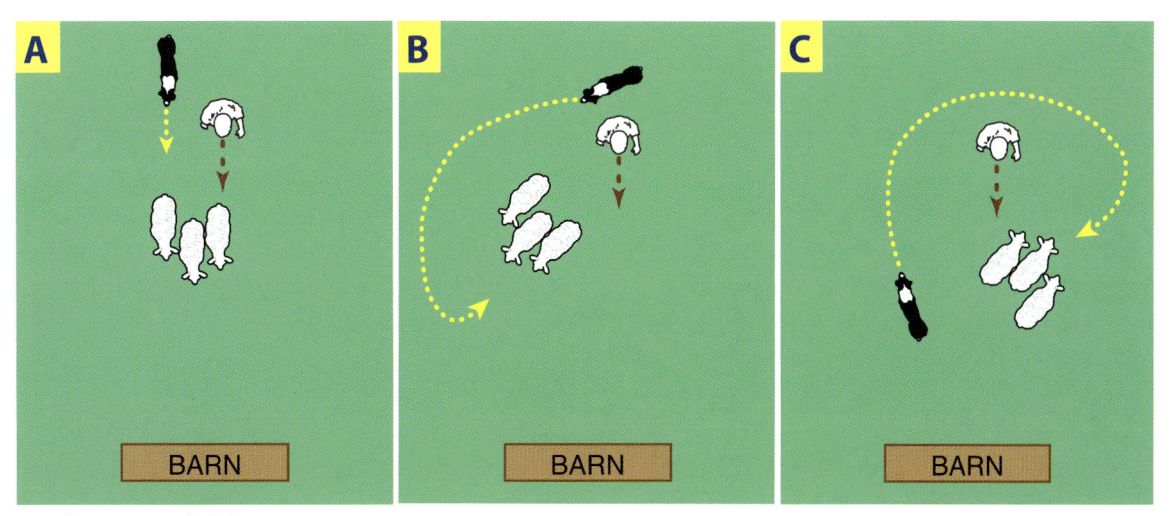

The natural drive
When starting to teach the drive, it helps both the handler and dog if there is a focal point (e.g. a barn or gate) to aim for. The handler should also remain close to the sheep throughout the exercise so he can guide the dog as necessary. **A** The dog starts to drive the sheep. The handler also walks behind the sheep but slightly in front and to the side of the dog. **B** and **C** If the sheep move off the drive line, the handler should use either the natural flank (**B**) or the flank behind (**C**) to bring them back to the correct line. The dog should not circle in front of the sheep.

Driving along a fence
A fence line can help a dog learn how to drive. **A** I walk beside the sheep with my dog behind me. **B** I use my body language to block him from coming forward while also signalling with my right hand to encourage Mac to flank slightly left so that he can tuck the sheep back in.

Obviously, you do not want your dog to do any of these, so I recommend that you teach your dog to drive in a square. I find this method useful for a couple of reasons. Firstly my dog can always see me. Secondly I am always close to my dog whilst he is learning and so I am always in a position to correct any errors. Do not panic over the shape, the 'square' only needs be approximate: it does not need to be precise.

At the basic stage of driving in a square, you should walk with your dog driving the sheep in a straight line across the field. Your dog will find it more comfortable to drive if you are also walking along in the direction he needs to go. After about fifty metres, flank your dog to turn the sheep around an imaginary corner before driving them again along the next straight side of the square. Continue to flank and drive to complete the full square. Remember, when he flanks at the corner of the square, make sure that he does this with the appropriate mindset and in an arc shape so that he does not push the sheep in the wrong direction. If the sheep move outwards during the drive, you need to ask your dog for a natural flank. Alternatively, if they move towards you, then you need to ask your dog to flank behind you. Whichever flank you require, stop your dog in the correct position so that he redirects the stock back onto the original drive line.

The type of sheep used will also influence how easy or hard it is for your dog to drive. Heavy sheep can be difficult to move from your feet and in this situation, walking with your dog will help stimulate the sheep's movement. In contrast, light sheep will probably want to flee at the slightest opportunity. If your sheep are like this, you need to remind your dog to *steady*, mind his attitude and work him at a distance from the stock. Driving in a square can help, because if the sheep start to run, you can send your dog on a natural flank to turn them around the corner of the square.

When driving in a square make sure you repeat this exercise in both clockwise and anti-clockwise directions so that he does not become 'one-sided'.

I recommend that you spend weeks or even months working on the basic stages of the drive. It is much easier to teach your dog to have the correct attitude and manner of work from the start than it is to correct bad habits once they have become ingrained.

As your dog gains in confidence and you want to advance his training further, you need to ensure that he has a good understanding of how to flank inside you (see page 120). Once he knows this, you can move towards the centre of the square. However, still walk with him as this will ensure that your dog can still see you out of the corner of his eye. By continuing to drive in a square, you are still close enough to influence the manner in which your dog flanks and apply appropriate pressure to correct any problems. Be careful that your body language is not unintentionally exerting too much pressure on your dog. If you lean forward when he flanks in front, you will push him tighter onto the sheep. This is something you do not want as it may upset the sheep and put them into flight.

Your dog needs to have a good and thorough understanding of all types of flank before he can increase the complexity of the drive. As your dog reaches the intermediary and advanced stages of training, you should extend the distance that he needs to drive. You, yourself, need to move less and encourage him to work to your voice and whistle rather than to your body language. He should learn to drive away from you and also start to cross drive which he needs to do in both directions: from right to left and also left to right.

Similar to developing your dog's other skills, you should, if possible, also introduce him to different types of sheep and terrains as well as working in different weather conditions. Work him with a flock so that he learns to hold them together as a group. As with the fetch, it will depend on your dog's particular style, the size of the flock and the type of sheep being worked as to how he does this. Some dogs hold back and use their eye and small movements of their head to hold them all together. Others may need to flank more, weaving from side to side, tucking in the stragglers at the side as he drives them to where you want them taken. A dog at the advanced stage of his training should be able to drive sheep for long distances with minimum command, altering his pace to suit the sheep, terrain and weather.

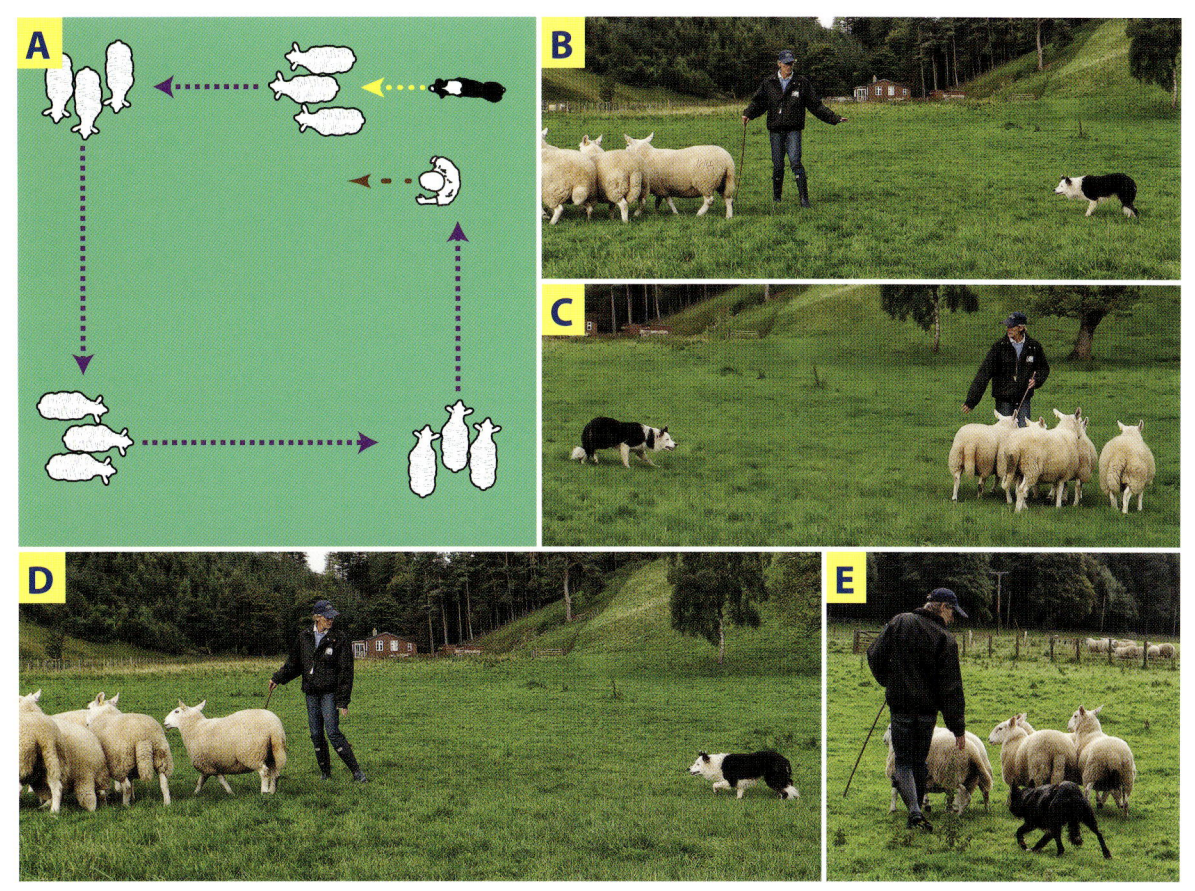

Driving in a square

A Driving in an approximate square enables you to communicate effectively with your dog as he learns all the manoeuvres required to drive. It is important that you face and move in the direction you want the sheep to go. **B** I move to a half block position to ask Ban to *steady* his pace. **C** I ask Ban to come to the balance point which is close by my side so that the sheep will turn and move forward. **D** I call Ban in to keep contact with his sheep and drive them forward. **E** I call Mac in to move sheep away from my legs. A dog has to be calm and confident to be close to sheep. My proximity helps maintain control of the situation.

Turning the corner

A You need to ask for a flank in order to turn a corner. **B** and **C** I send Ban on a natural flank. **D** The unnatural flank can also be used if you need to realign the sheep or if you are changing direction.

The intermediate stage
Ban drives in a square whilst I stand to the side. He uses all flanks as necessary. I remain close enough to help him if I am required.

The advanced stage
The dog needs to adapt his drive depending on weather, type of sheep, terrain, distance from handler and length of drive.

Summary of the training stages required for driving

The basic stage. The dog should:

• Work close at hand and walk with the handler while driving either using the natural drive or driving in a square.

• Respond to hand signals and body language as well as voice commands.

• Be able to perform the natural flank and flank behind to keep the sheep on the drive line.

The intermediate stage. In addition to the basic stage, the dog should:

• Be able to flank in front.

• Drive further away from the handler (who will move less).

• Drive for longer distances both on the cross drive and away from the handler.

• Drive with both a few sheep and a flock.

• Respond to voice and whistle commands rather than body language.

The advanced stage. In addition to the basic and intermediate stages, the dog should:

• Drive for very long distances without stressing the sheep.

• Regulate his pace and energy to suit the stock and the conditions with only minimal commands from the handler.

• Drive across different terrains.

• Drive in different weather conditions.

• Drive with different breeds of sheep.

Problems

There are a range of problems that can happen with the drive. Many will be a result of your dog's innate character. For example he may be naturally assertive, pushy or have a lot of eye. Alternatively, he may lack confidence or have insufficient power to drive the sheep away from your feet. These problems can be compounded by the breed of sheep you use because heavy sheep can be hard for the dog to move, whilst light sheep will flee at the slightest opportunity.

Sometimes, the problem is caused by the dog's immaturity and in these cases it can pay dividends just to wait until he is old enough to understand what is required of him.

In addition to the dog and sheep, often an inexperienced handler may exacerbate the problem by exerting pressure and / or releasing pressure at the wrong time and in the wrong place. Remember, many dogs find it hard to learn how to drive. Do not expect perfection at these early stages. You need to analyse the situation: look at your dog, the sheep and yourself to determine where the problem lies.

The dog runs to the head of the sheep

This is where your dog runs away from the balance point for driving properly and instead fetches the sheep back towards you. There are several reasons why he may do this:

1. Your dog anticipates that the sheep are about to flee and heads the sheep to stop this. You need to watch the sheep and the dog to predict when this is about to happen, Use the *stop* command before he has actually started to run around the sheep. If necessary, reinforce the stop with your body language. If you wait until your dog is running, then he probably will not listen to you until he has reached the balance point to fetch the sheep. It often helps to practice driving along a fence line and use the *steady* command, to remind him to pace himself to suit the sheep. This way your dog learns how to hold the heavy side of the sheep and also that the stock will remain under his control as long as he does not push them too hard.

2. Your dog feels uncomfortable exerting pressure to drive heavy sheep. However, he knows he can successfully fetch sheep. Therefore he releases the pressure on himself by running and turning the sheep towards you. In this case, you need to boost your dog's confidence by walking with him to help move the stock. Encourage him to work naturally and minimise the pressure you exert on him. Let him work the sheep slightly faster as this can also help build his confidence. Use consistent commands and make sure you do not give a command that encourages him to run around the sheep when you want him to drive.

3. Your dog is only used to driving sheep for short distances. When you go beyond this, he considers that he no longer should be driving and so turns the sheep. In these cases, try to gradually increase the length of the drive so that your dog gets used to driving longer distances.

4. Your dog is more of an 'outrunner' than a driver, and finds it hard to grasp how to drive. Practice driving alongside a fence. If he still refuses to drive, then it may help to put him on a long line to guide him.

The dog will not take a flank

Again there are several reasons why this can happen:

1. He may be fully engrossed in driving the sheep and so is not willing to listen to commands. You need to exert sufficient pressure to make him listen. If necessary, move to a block position and stop him. Once he is listening, ask him for the flank.

2. Your body language and vocal commands are giving mixed messages and he does not understand what you require. For example, you may be too close to the sheep and he feels too much pressure to flank in front of you. In this situation, move backwards to give him more space to flank. Alternatively, you may be getting frustrated that your dog is not flanking in front or behind you. Your annoyance is read by the dog as pressure and so he feels uncomfortable approaching you. You need to relax more. Give him more space to flank. Encourage (rather than insist) that he flanks. Reward even a small try to build up his confidence. If necessary use a long line to help guide him. You need to use this properly and you should release

pressure when he starts to flank.

Therefore, only pull on the line when he refuses to flank towards you. Once he starts to move, stop pulling as this will decrease the pressure and he will know he has made the correct decision. Remember to use the 'ask, tell, insist' scale of pressure and start with giving only small tugs on the line. Only give a slightly stronger tug on the rope if he does not respond to your initial 'ask'.

The dog follows the sheep rather than pushes them

Every dog finds different aspects of their training easier than others. Some dogs find the concept of driving hard to understand. This type of dog will follow behind sheep that move easily. However, he will find it difficult to move sheep that are reluctant to go in the required direction. This problem is not necessarily caused by a lack of power. Sometimes, your dog just lacks confidence or does not understand what is expected of him.

In these cases, I suggest going back to the basics of driving and use the natural drive. This will focus your dog's mind on balancing the stock while using the appropriate amount of pressure to move them forward. He will gain in confidence as he starts to comprehend what is required.

Moving On

However natural your dog is at working, you will often need to redirect him to flank wider or come in closer to stock. Additionally, if you work with more than a few sheep there will be times when you need him to *look back* and gather another group of sheep. These redirection commands are all discussed in the next chapter.

Fact Box. Driving ewes with lambs

If you intend to use your dog at lambing time, you need to be aware that a sheep's behaviour will probably change when she has a lamb at foot. It is worth bearing the following pointers in mind.

• New born lambs are best left until they are 3 or 4 days old before you attempt to move them any distance with a dog near by.

• If you are moving young lambs (less than 1 week old), keep your dog well off his sheep. If you let your dog get too close, you will probably find that the ewe will confront him in order to protect her lamb. Instead, you should ease them forward yourself while your dog lies at a distance. To guide them in the direction you want, ask your dog to flank (but still to keep his distance).

• When there are a group of ewes and with very young lambs, each ewe will try to leave the group in order to take her lamb to safety. This action is due to the sheep's survival instinct because splitting up may confuse the predator.

• When the lamb is approximately 2 to 3 weeks old, the ewe will tolerate a dog in closer proximity as long as he reads his sheep properly and is careful using pressure / release on her.

• Once the lamb is about 1 month old, the ewe will be more confident that her lamb can keep pace with her. She therefore will not stand and fight unless provoked. If your dog works calmly and considerately, the ewes and lambs will flow forward without too much difficulty.

From the Clinic

Handler: My dog won't drive sheep away from me.

I observed that this young bitch was very sensitive to pressure. She was eager to please her owner, but was uncertain what she was being asked to do. In an attempt to satisfy her owner, the dog tended to head the sheep and balance them back towards her handler. This felt natural to her especially as she knew that her owner had previously released all pressure when she did this. Now, the handler would get frustrated when his dog did not understand his gestures to flank in front of him. The owner's body language clearly showed his annoyance. Furthermore, he had a bad leg and used a stick as he walked. His limp meant that he tended to lurch unexpectedly on the uneven ground and as he became more angry he subconsciously slammed his stick onto the ground as he moved.

My opinion: The handler's body language was putting inappropriate pressure on this sensitive young bitch. This was compounded by the handler's limp and stick stamping. The timing of these jerky movements was unpredictable and further worried his dog. The result was that the dog did not want to pass in front of her owner. Instead she felt more comfortable when she was balancing sheep to him and so she always flanked in order to head the sheep and fetch them to him.

My advice: The handler needed to relax and overcome his frustration. I politely suggested that he make a conscious effort not to lurch to one side as he walked. He should also attempt to moderate how he used his walking stick. In addition, he needed to soften his stance and leave more space between the sheep and himself. All these changes would reduce the pressure on his bitch when she took the inside flank. I also advised that the handler encourage his dog to come by clicking his fingers and softly calling her name. When she approached, the handler needed to walk in the direction he required his dog to flank. This effectively meant that the handler turned his back on his dog as she approached and similarly acted to release any unintentional pressure on her. As his dog neared him on the inside, he had to give a gentle flank command without exerting too much pressure. The dog responded positively to this and willingly took the inside flank.

The handler understood from my explanation that the problem was his subconscious body language rather than an issue with his dog. Over the next few days, the handler practised softening his manner. In response, his dog started to relax and feel more confident in taking the inside flank.

From the Clinic

Handler: My dog has no pace on the drive. She pushes onto the sheep and does not listen to my commands when I tell her to *steady* or stop.

I observed that although the dog had a lowered tail and carriage, to me it was clear that her body and eye indicated an intense, excited nature as she drove the stock. When she was asked to flank, she cut her corners and instead of making a proper arc when she flanked, she ran in a diagonal straight line. This meant that she pushed closer to the sheep, who quickened their pace in an attempt to get away from her. She responded by also speeding up and because of her intense attitude, she did not listen to her handler's angry shouts and blasting whistles to *lie-down*.

My opinion: It was clear to me that the dog did not respect her handler sufficiently. In addition, she did not have a proper feel for sheep and her determination to work stock meant that she did not listen to her handler. As the dog drove the sheep in front of her owner, she could not see if he was using any appropriate body language to reinforce his voice / whistle commands. She had therefore learnt to ignore his commands. In addition, she needed to learn to flank her sheep in a semi-circle.

My advice: The handler first needed to gain his dog's respect. I therefore asked him to work close at hand and ask his dog to balance the sheep towards him. When she pushed the sheep too hard or her eyes became too excited and intense, I taught him how to use his body language to apply a block that made his dog give to pressure. This reinforced his *steady* and *lie-down* commands. I also asked him to give these commands in a calm, quiet, yet assertive fashion.

I then had them drive the sheep in a square while the handler walked beside his dog. She had to learn how to take the inside flank properly. In order to achieve this, when the handler wanted the dog to flank inside, he needed to slow down and move slightly more to the side. This meant he was slightly behind his dog. While moving slowly forward, he had to encourage his dog to come towards him by clicking the fingers of his hand that he held near to his thigh. As the dog turned outwards and came towards her owner, the handler had to ask for the flank command and then stop his dog once she was in the correct position to continue driving along the next side of the square. He needed to practice this in both directions.

Over the next few days, the communication between the handler and his dog improved. Although the dog still had a tendency to cut her flanks, the handler was happier because he now knew what he needed to do too solve the problem.

CHAPTER 14
REDIRECTING YOUR DOG

The shepherd's dog not only needs to be able to use his initiative to work sheep, he also has to be willing to take command and be redirected when required. There are three main redirection commands: the *out* command, the *in* command and the *look back*.

The *out* and *in* commands are used to add versatility to the flank, outrun and drive manoeuvres that the dog has already learnt. For example, the dog may need to move *out* during his outrun to gather a dispersed flock or else hold some sheep in a settled state while the shepherd counts them. Alternatively, the same command may be used to ask the dog to move away to release pressure on the stock for example when a sheep has a young lamb. In contrast, the *in* or *here* command may be required when the shepherd wants only a few nearby sheep gathered. The *in* command may also be needed to encourage the dog to flank inside the handler when the dog is learning to drive properly. In addition, both the *out* and *in* commands are also used when shedding sheep or at the pen. The final redirect command, the *look back*, is used when the shepherd needs his dog to leave the sheep he is currently focused on and return up the field to gather another group.

My Natural Way training method is built on the dog's willingness to please rather than making him feel coerced to obey like a mindless machine. When teaching the three redirect commands it is therefore important that the dog considers that these are <u>requests</u> rather than reprimands. Many novice handlers find it difficult to adjust their body language to give just the right amount of pressure. Inappropriate pressure could make your dog either ignore you or else make him worry that he has done something wrong.

Be patient, do not expect perfection straight away: give your dog the opportunity to understand what is required and let him develop gradually. If you are impatient and push him when he is trying to figure out what you want, you will only give him mixed messages and confuse him as to what is required. Remember, each dog is different and you need to pay close attention to how your dog responds to your body language to determine when you need to apply pressure and when you need to release it. **Your dog needs time to learn**.

The *out* and *in* command

As I discussed before, when you start using voice and whistle commands you need to concentrate on the way you use them (see page 34 and Fact Box on page 96). When you want to encourage a long flank, draw out the commands (e.g. *cooome byee*) and at the same time use sufficient pressure to push the dog out and further around on his flank. In contrast, when you want a small flank, give the command in a short, quiet fashion (e.g. *c'me bye*) and only allow your dog to move a small distance. These subtle tonal differences will give you finer control of your dog's movements. However, there are times when these will not be sufficient and the *out* and *in* commands are useful additional tools to have.

The *out* command

Start teaching the *out* command when your dog is close at hand. Block to stop him because this will make him focus on your next command. Ask him to give to pressure by pointing towards his head. He should respond to this by turning his head away and then he should move further away from you. As your dog moves outward, give the command *out* in a quiet voice. When he gives, release pressure by lowering your hand to indicate that he has made the correct choice. As you are teaching him at this stage, you need to give him time to think about what the correct response should be. Therefore, if he does not immediately respond, do not go straight to a 'tell' or an 'insist'. Instead repeat your 'ask'. You may find that he initially gives only slightly to you by moving one or two steps outwards. Do not worry, but over time, gradually build on this by asking him to give more distance even though you have still exerted the same amount of pressure.

> *Julie's Tip. Do not expect an immediate improvement. Look for a response from your dog to start with, then gradually build on this. Even if he is giving sufficient room on his flanks or outrun, still practice stopping him and asking him to run wider with the out command.*

When learning the *out* command, your dog needs to understand that you are asking him to run further <u>off</u> the sheep, not just to flank around them. Remember, you are looking for him to try to respond as you want. If he does not try to move out, you should move back to a block position which is a neutral gesture that asks him to listen. Once he has again stopped, you should repeat your request for him to move out.

Make sure that you train him to go out on both flanks so that he associates the *out* with moving outwards rather than with just going either clockwise or anti-clockwise. Whilst I do this, I combine lengthened flank commands with the redirect command so that it sounds something like *cooome byee out* or *awaaaay out*. Some other trainers use different commands for each flank (for example *out* for clockwise and *keep* for anti-clockwise). As long as you are consistent with your commands and give them in an appropriate manner, it does not matter which words you choose to use.

As your dog reaches the intermediate stage of training, he should be willing to take the *out* command whenever you require it, for example, during his outrun or else to redirect his focus onto a second group of sheep that may be further away. If necessary, reinforce your voice command by moving forward and exerting some pressure towards his head in a similar fashion as you did when he was working close at hand. Even if your dog gives sufficient room on his flanks and outrun, you can still practice the *out* command by stopping him and then asking him to run wider still.

The *out* command
A Teach the *out* command on the flank when the dog is close at hand. I direct my stick at Ban's head to put pressure on him and ask him to give to this. As my pressure is directed towards his head, this turns his head out and he begins to move in this direction. **B** As Ban moves I say the command *out*.
C Over time, although I lessen the pressure intensity, I expect the dog to move out further.
D Gradually extend the distance your dog moves out as shown by the blue, purple and yellow arrows.

Using the *out* command
As the dog becomes more experienced, he should willing take an *out* command when required.
A How his direction should change during an outrun.
B The *out* command can be used to redirect his focus to another group of sheep.

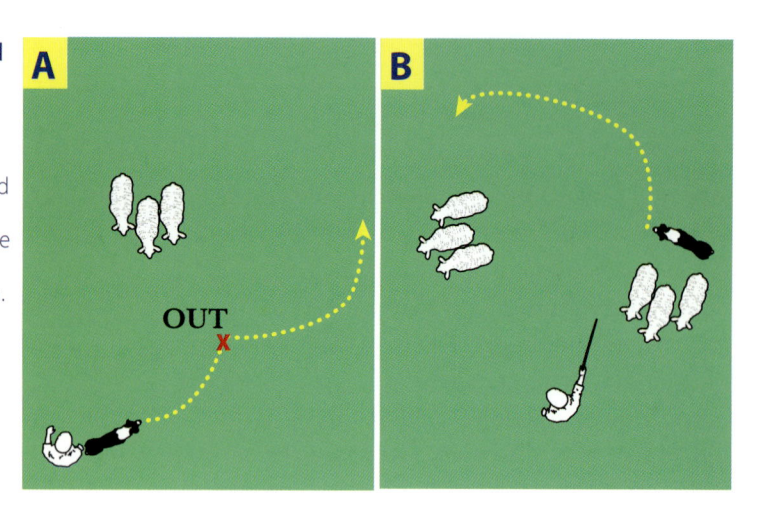

OUT

Julie's Tip. Use an assertive tone to give an out command if your dog is balancing flighty sheep that are trying to escape. This will tell him to move outwards in any direction necessary and so will sharpen his response as it encourages him to use his instinct to tuck the escapee back in. Furthermore, the tone of your command will remind him not to get overexcited.

As he gains in experience you should test his understanding. For example, you can test his response on sheep that are spread out over the field. Alternatively you could work him on difficult terrain where he cannot always see all the stock. If your own training setup does not allow for either of these, then intentionally send him on a tight flank and check that he responds appropriately to the *out* command. Be patient and increase the complexity of the tasks you give him in small stages. Remember, all dogs need to time to understand what is required and if you extend the difficulty of the tasks too quickly, it is inevitable that he will fail.

The *in* command

There is more than one way to bring your dog inwards. It depends on the situation and which sheep your dog are focused on as to which method you should choose to use.

The first method is the *here* command. Use this when you want to draw the dog towards you, for example to shed sheep or to teach your dog how to take the inside flank. As you give the *here* command, you should invite your dog into your space by turning your body and eyes slightly to the side, lowering your shoulder, and putting your hand down towards your thigh. You may also click your fingers of this hand as this will direct his attention towards it.

Julie's Tip. Practice using the here command while teaching the inside flank, this will help your dog when you introduce him to shedding sheep.

However, there are other occasions when this is not appropriate. If your dog is working at a distance and you want him to move closer to the sheep he is focusing on, then a *get up* or *walk-on* command will ask him to draw towards his stock. Once he has moved inward the desired amount give him the next directional flank.

In contrast, if your dog is eyeing a group of sheep and you want him to refocus on a different group that is closer to you, then a *that'll do* command will pull your dog away from the first bunch. Redirect him with a flank command once he has reached a position where you feel he will respond appropriately.

Calling the dog *in*
I invite Ban into my space by turning my body and eyes slightly to my side. Notice how my hand is down by my side.

The *look back* command

The *look back* is an extension of the *look* command that you have already taught your dog when you first introduced him to sheep (see page 73). In addition, he should be accustomed to scan the field for stock if you use this command before sending him on his outrun (see page 93). However, the *look back* is still a difficult manoeuvre for a dog to learn, so I recommend that you initially work close at hand and keep things simple. You will then be able to help your dog understand what is required.

At the basic stage work with a large group of sheep. Shed a few off (see page 142). After doing this it is important that you let your dog wear this group for a short while before you start attempting a *look back*. If you do not do this, but instead ask your dog to *look back* immediately after he has shed some stock then your dog may think he should always *look back* every time he sheds sheep. This is something you definitely do not want!

Once your dog has balanced the sheep for a short while, manipulate the situation so that the dog is positioned between the two groups of sheep with you on the other side of the stock he has just been working. Ask your dog to stop. Your dog's temperament will dictate how you initially encourage him to *look back*. If he is very sensitive to pressure then just walk through the sheep past your dog and ask him to walk with you. As he turns to join you, ask him to *look back*. If necessary, point at the second group of sheep and ask him to *look*. If your dog is fixated on the first group, you may need to break his concentration by putting some pressure on him by pointing at his head as you walk through the sheep.

Once he has turned, allow him to fetch the sheep to you straight away. Do not worry which direction he flanks in – let him decide. This will help him gain confidence and you will establish a good foundation for the *look back*.

Once your dog is able to do the basic stage of the *look back*, you should gradually increase the distance between the two groups of sheep. However, at this point you should also ask him to stop immediately after he has looked back (but before he has flanked to gather the stock). Introducing this stop will give him the opportunity to pause, think and look for sheep. Once he has looked for his sheep, you can choose the direction and give him the appropriate flank to gather the stock. If you do not include this stop at this point of his training, your dog may develop the habit of rushing off too soon and he may run in the wrong direction. As he becomes more experienced in taking the *look back* command, you will no longer need to include this additional stop.

The basic stage of the *look back*

A After splitting the sheep into 2 groups, your dog wears one group towards you. You should then move through the sheep and encourage him to look behind at the 2nd set which he should then gather to you. **B** I ask Ban to stop focusing on the group on the left and to pay attention to the two sheep on the right of the picture.

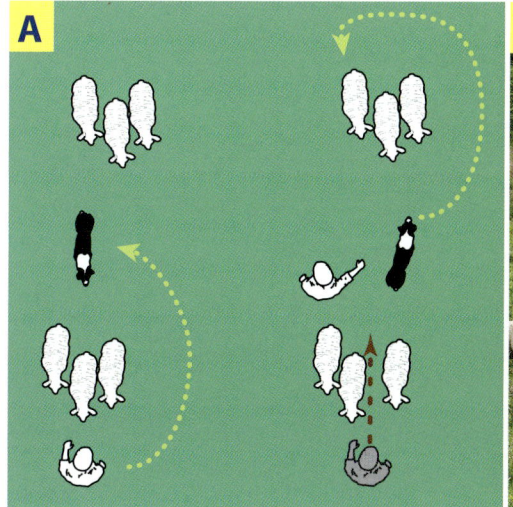

As your dog reaches the intermediate stage, you should stay on the far side of the group and as you give the *look back* command. To help your dog understand what is required, you should point at your dog to apply sufficient pressure for him to respond appropriately. With time, your dog should be willing to *look back* and take a redirect with just a voice or whistle command.

Obviously, as you increase the distance between the two groups of sheep, the position of the second one will not always be in the same place. You can make it easier for your dog to find them by stopping him so that the angle that his body makes relative to you and the balance point will indicate where this second group are. Again you can help your dog if you use similar position as that used to send him on different casts during his outrun (see page 94).

This technique is especially useful if you are working your dog on difficult terrain and you have to redirect him to *look back* and gather a second group of sheep that he cannot see.

You should also extend the complexity of the command by asking for the *look back* when he has only fetched the first group of sheep part of the way to you. This is something you may need if your dog gathers his flock and, after he starts to fetch them, you notice that he has missed some stragglers and he needs to return to collect them.

Take time to move through the stages of the *look back* and redirect commands and watch your dog gradually improve. Do not rush your dog through his training: it takes a lot of time and patience to perfect these.

Fact Box. The *look back* whistle

The *look back* whistle needs to be totally different to any other command whistle. If always you give an enforced flank (*out* command) before the *look back*, some dogs will start to think they need to *look back* every time they hear the *out* command. I recommend that your dog learns his *out* and *in* commands plus have both of them well established before you progress to teaching the *look back*.

The Intermediate stage of the *look back*
A After your dog has gathered the first group to you, stop him. Remain standing on the opposite side of the sheep and ask him to *look back* for his second group. **B** I ask Mac to *look back* and I lean forward with my stick slightly raised and pointing at him. This puts sufficient pressure for him to give as I say *look back*. **C** Mac gives to the pressure and turns around. **D** I give Mac an *away* and he flanks around the second group. **E** Mac gathers them to me.

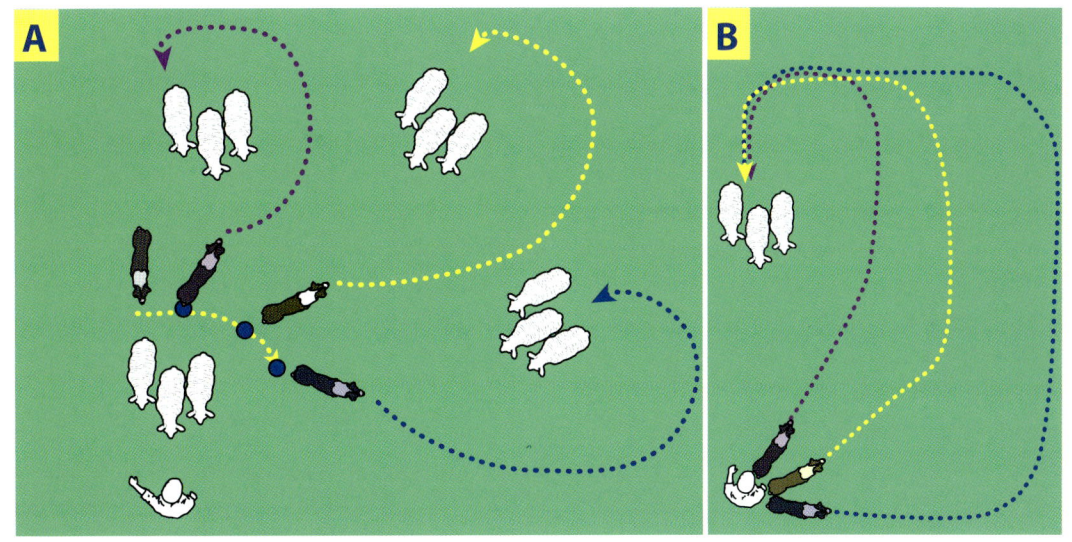

Help your dog find his sheep
During the *look back*, the second group of sheep will not always be in the same place.
A Flank your dog to the appropriate position where he can be asked to *look back* for the second group of sheep. The position that the dog is stopped prior to being asked to *look back* will create the same angle that the dog has learnt during his outrun training.
B Shows how you can angle your dog to set him on different outruns (also see pages 94 / 95).

Summary of the training stages required for redirecting your dog

The basic stage. The dog should:

• Work at hand.

• Respond to the handler's body language and be introduced to voice commands.

• Be given time to understand what the new redirection commands mean.

The intermediate stage. In addition to the basic stage, the dog should:

• Work at a greater distance.

• Respond to voice and whistle commands. However, the handler may still also need to use some hand signals.

The advanced stage. In addition to the basic and intermediate stages, the dog should:

• Be willing to flank in response to the *out* or *in* command.

• Be willing to alter his outrun response to the *out* or *in* command.

• Be able to *look back* and gather sheep over great distances at any angle and over any terrain.

• Be willing to take a redirection command even if he cannot see the stock he is being asked to gather.

Problems

As with all problems you need to stand back and consider what may be causing the trouble. Look at the issue from every angle and do not jump to an immediate conclusion until you have considered all the options.

The dog does not respond to the *out* command

There can be several different causes for this. You need to ask yourself several questions including 'Why is my dog not responding properly?' and 'What part of the request is he finding difficult?' Points to consider are:

• Does your dog really understand what you are asking for? If you have not taught him correctly, then go back to basics and gradually build up his response to your request.

• Are you asking with the correct body language and vocal tone? Perhaps you have not emphasised the command sufficiently?

• Look at your dog's body language, what is he telling you? If he is relaxed and trying, then you are communicating correctly with him. However, if you feel under pressure, then he is probably resisting you. You need to use the block position and exert more pressure on him to get him to pay attention to you. Work through the 'ask, tell, insist' scale and use the correct gestures and body language. Remember to release pressure when you see him trying to respond to you.

• Is your dog running wide because he is not paying attention? In these cases, he is avoiding the situation and indicating that he is feeling concerned. To deal with this, you need to relax, move to a block position and then gently ask him to move out again.

• Is your dog over-focused on his sheep? If so, you need to gain his attention by stepping into his space. You should then use sufficient pressure to get him to move back and stop focusing so intently on his stock.

In all cases make sure your dog is responding when you work close at hand and only gradually increase the distance that you stand from him when you ask for the *out* command. Remember to follow the stages in the outrun section for pushing a tight dog out (see page 98). Follow the same approach with the *out* on the flanks.

The dog does not respond to the *in* command

It will depend on your dog's natural inclination to run either wide or tight on his outrun that will determine how he responds to the *in* command. If he tends to run tight, then he will be more willing to come even further in towards his stock.

If you are having problems with the in command, then make sure that he understands what you are asking from him. I recommend that when you start teaching the command, start working close at hand. Do not initially ask him to respond from too great a distance. Although this is what you are aiming for, you cannot expect him to manage this straight away.

Some very sensitive dogs that have been pushed out during the outrun, will also sometimes worry about coming in when asked. If your dog is like this, you need to be especially patient. Work close at hand with

him and remember to reward any try that he gives you by immediately releasing pressure.

If a dog is having problems with the *in* command, I often find that it can help to teach it at the same time as the shed. After shedding some sheep and taking them away from the group, stop your dog. Let the shed sheep start to head back to the others, but then send your dog and use the in command so that he flanks between the two groups before they join up again. This is discussed in more detail in the chapter on shedding (see page 142).

The dog does not respond to the *look back* command

Again you need to analyse what the underlying problem is. Perhaps you have not taught your dog to respond properly or maybe he is so focused on the sheep in front of him that he ignores both you and the other stock.

If your dog does not understand what you are asking then make sure you go back through all the stages of teaching the *look back*. Only extend the complexity of the command when your feel that your dog has fully grasped what you require. Always train your dog at a pace he can manage and only progress when he is ready to move on.

Julie's Tip. Never ask a young dog to do an old dog's work.

If your dog is completely focused on the sheep in front of him, then he will not be able to listen to your commands and anything you ask of him will just be ignored. You need to use assertive, calm body language and physically move into his space to gain his attention before asking him again to take the *look back* command.

As you prepare for the advanced stage of training, your dog's nature, attitude and fitness become more important. Some dogs are just not able to cope with the pressure required to understand the advanced *look back* and redirect commands. Alternatively he may not be fit enough to manage the additional running required for this task.

The dog does not look for his sheep

Some dogs, when given the *look back* command, just turn around and run, but do not actually look for sheep. This is why I recommend that when you start teaching the *look back* command that you ask your dog to *stop* before he starts running back. This pause will make him start to pay attention to what you really require.

In addition, some dogs are better at spotting sheep than others. You will be much more successful with the *look back* command, if your dog can spot sheep at a distance. This is one of the reasons why I encourage my dogs to look for sheep from an early age (see page 73). If you train your dog correctly and build up his confidence in running out blind for sheep, then he will probably be willing to take guidance and directions commands from you as he runs. A dog like this will want to complete the task successfully, so he will tend to look harder for sheep the further he goes.

The dog comes back on the first group

If a dog is unsure or cannot see the second group of sheep, he may turn round and come back to the first group. To overcome this, make sure he is confident about looking back when working close at hand. Then only slowly build up the distance between the two groups.

Alternatively, a dog can become disorientated as he runs and end up back with the original group. You need to take time for your dog to gain in experience. The more times he succeeds in finding sheep, the more he will trust your directional commands.

The dog anticipates the *look back* command

Some dogs will anticipate the *look back*. If your dog is like this and you work to a set pattern, then he will learn to read the cues you give out. Yes, you need to use a set pattern when you teach the command, but you must watch how you give the signals that you use. For instance, if you tend to emphasise a flank command before giving the *look back*, your dog may learn to anticipate that this emphasised flank means you are about to redirect him immediately afterwards. This anticipation could become a problem if you need to emphasise your flank for another reason.

Some dogs will only anticipate the *look back* on certain occasions. These are usually knowledgeable workers who use their experience to predict when you are building up to a *look back*. If your dog reaches this stage, you will have the confidence to tackle any situation that arises both at work and on the trial field.

Moving On

Up to now you have been training your dog so that he can become a confident worker who can use his own initiative, yet still be willing to take commands, when he is working at a distance from you. In addition, there are times when the shepherd needs his dog to work close at hand. Shedding and penning are two such occasions. Each can present their own problems. However, if you have trained your dog The Natural Way and have also developed sheep-sense, then with practice, you will be well placed to succeed at both. In the next chapter I discuss shedding.

Anecdote. Clyde goes for a swim

Clyde, one of my young nursery dogs, seemed to be confused about what the *out* command really meant. I knew from experience that it is difficult for a dog to pull out when he is running downhill, so I stood on the top of the sea braes (where I used to shepherd) and sent Clyde on his outrun down towards the sea. He turned his head inwards and I knew he was about to start flanking tightly around the stock. So, in order to remind him that he needed to bend outwards towards the water's edge, I stopped him and then gave a whistle that he interpreted as an over-enforced *out* flank. To my horror, instead of continuing his outrun along the shore, he ran into the water and started swimming out to sea. I frantically gave him several recall whistles, but, unfortunately, these had the opposite effect as Clyde had now gone into avoidance mode. Standing on the top of the sea braes, the strong winds gusting off the North Sea muffled my sounds and stopped me making any further efforts to encourage my dog to come back. I stood there watching him get smaller and smaller as he swam further out. Eventually he realised that his effort to swim against the tide was fruitless. He turned and allowed the current to help bring him back to shore. Once on dry land, he shook the water out of his coat and collected his thoughts before carrying on to gather his sheep.

CHAPTER 15
SHEDDING

On a working farm, a shepherd and his dog will need to shed sheep on a daily basis. Often, the shepherd wants specific animals separated from rest. For example, one or more may require treatment or help lambing. Alternatively, stock can become mixed up when a boundary fence is damaged. Perhaps the heavier sheep have to be separated in order to be taken to market or tupping time has ended and you want to shed the rams off from the ewes. In order to perform these tasks, the shepherd and dog needs to work in close partnership while they encourage the stock to string out. In order to have a successful shed, the handler will first help manipulate the sheep so that a gap forms. He will then ask his dog to come through to shed and then wear the sheep away from the rest.

The command I use for shedding is *here this*. If you have followed my training method, you will have already taught the *here* command (see Julie's Tip on page 20). The *this* part of the command means 'Take control the group of sheep, I am looking at'. So, the *here this* command means that I am asking my dog to come towards me and then wear the shedded group of sheep away from the rest.

Similar to all aspects of sheepdog training, some dogs are naturally more talented at shedding than others. The predatory instinct in this type of dog enables him to draw out sheep with his eye. This encourages the ewe to separate from the others and helps create the gap that he can then come in through.

In addition, a good shedding dog needs to be sharp and have power. He also needs to be confident and I recommend that your dog has reached a certain level in his training before you start to teach him to shed. In my opinion, a dog should be able to:
• Work close at hand and not be anxious of either you or the stock.
• Work close to sheep without upsetting them.
• Hold stock without pushing them forward.
• Listen to your body language and respond promptly to your cues and vocal commands.
• Balance and wear sheep well.

Once you are satisfied that your dog has mastered these skills, you are ready to consider shedding. To get him further accustomed to moving through sheep, you could sometimes ask him to come through a large flock as you call him off his sheep. However, I recommend that you do not do this until you are absolutely certain that he will not disturb the stock.

You and your dog will find sheep much easier to manage if they are comfortable in your presence. So, you always need to consider whether either of you are putting undue pressure on them. Signs that sheep are becoming unsettled are tense bodies, raised heads, twitching ears and eyes wide with nostrils flaring. In contrast when they are relaxed, their ears will be soft, their head carriage will be more level, their eyes will be blinking and their bodies relaxed. As you or your dog move towards stock, look for stress signals. If you see any, move back so that the sheep can settle before gradually moving closer again.

Julie's Tip. Pressure from either you or your dog will cause most breeds of sheep to flock tighter together. This will make the shed more difficult. Instead, you both should move calmly and quietly so that neither of you stimulate the ewe's senses.

Positions for the handler and the dog for the shed

Both the handler and dog need to be on opposite sides of the gap with the handler facing the direction of the sheep that the dog is required shed off. **A** The dog is coming to the tails of the leading group. **B** The dog is asked to come to the heads of the facing sheep so that he blocks them before moving them away. The additional pressure on the dog from the sheep makes this harder for him to achieve. **C** The dog is in wrong position because as he moves forward, he will force the rear group to rejoin the front group. **D** Mac has balanced a group of sheep to me and is now lying down on the other side of the stock. I let the stock drift into 2 groups. If you use a large number of sheep it is easier to separate them into two groups that will happily stay apart. **E** I have let a large gap develop between the group and then turn to face the group that I want shed. Mac watches the same group and waits to be called in. **F** I call Mac in through the gap and start to work the shed group for a while.

When you teach the shed, try to ensure that he learns to follow a set pattern determined by you, so that he learns to wait for your cues before he comes in to shed. Make sure you are consistent, because otherwise, depending on his innate nature he may become confused or else try to take over. Initially, make the shed as simple as possible by using a large group of sheep. Let them drift into two groups. Then encourage them to separate out further so that there is a large gap between them. If the gap is too small, your dog may become confused and attempt to gather the sheep back together. After all, this is what you have imprinted onto him from the start of his training!

Julie's Tip. It is easier for a dog to shed sheep that are moving away from him rather than ones which are facing him.

When you feel the gap is large enough, make sure that your dog is in the correct position to come towards you and take the chosen sheep away. Ensure that you are not standing in the gap because your dog may not wish to come into your space. This will certainly be the case if your body language is signalling that you are blocking his forward movement. Instead, face the stock that you intend to shed because this will indicate to your dog which group you wish to shed off. Furthermore, as your body will be side-on to him, you should not be exerting undue pressure.

Lower your shoulder and tap your hand to your thigh while you give the *here* command. Move outwards, away from your dog and coincide this with his inward movement. This will let him feel more comfortable as he comes into the gap and give him further encouragement to move forward. If he does not respond to the *here* command, use the *that'll do* command to encourage him to come towards you.

As your dog comes through the gap, use the *this* command and start walking towards the sheep you want separated. Let your dog wear them away from the other group. He should be allowed to work them for a short while because this will help him appreciate that there is a reason why you want the sheep split. If you send him back to gather the other group as soon as he has come in to shed, he may start anticipating this every time you shed sheep. This could become an unfortunate habit such that he starts to automatically turn back before you are ready.

An additional problem that can happen if you do not let him work his sheep for a while after shedding is that he may stop trying to hold any sheep that bolt away from the group you want. If he believes that it is okay to let some sheep leave the group he is supposed to be wearing, he could become careless. In my opinion a dog like this can cause a lot of unnecessary work for the shepherd. In order to further ingrain that your dog needs to work the group he has shed ('the shed group'), it can sometimes help if you walk ahead of the sheep and let him balance them towards you. As he learnt to do this at the early stages of his training, this will feel much more natural for him. It will also make it easier for him to appreciate that wearing the shed group is an integral part of the task. In addition, if a sheep does try to escape back to the other group, if you have trained your dog The Natural Way, he will know to use his instinct to turn her back towards the shed group.

Intermediate stage of the shed 1
A As the dog gets more experienced, so you can decrease the gap and also call him to shed the group that are facing him. **B** I want a specific number so I ask Mac to wait for the appropriate moment before calling him through.

Continue at this basic stage of shedding until your dog appreciates what is required. You will know he understands this by the way he works during the shed: he will look at the correct group of sheep and run in to shed the ones you have chosen. He will then take control of them and wear them wherever you desire.

Once your dog has reached this level, you can gradually make the task more difficult. For example, he needs to learn to shed from smaller groups of sheep and also how to shed off sheep that are facing him. When he can manage both of these, add additional exercises to help develop his abilities.

The first exercise is to take the shed group further away from the other group. Once they are some distance away. Send your dog to head the shed group so that they turn back towards the other group. Stop your dog and wait until the shed sheep have started to move back towards the others. Then send him to gather the shed group before the two groups join up. Still use the *here this* shedding command to focus his attention on the running shed group, but only give this command once

he has past the shed group: the *here* will draw him inwards towards you and the sheep while the *thi*s will make him realise that you want those sheep held and fetched back. Make your dog turn them and balance them back towards you. While he is doing this, try to let him use his initiative to work out how to keep the two groups apart. Use plenty of words of encouragement and only the occasional correction when it is needed. As your dog gains in experience you can gradually let the shed sheep get closer to the other group before sending your dog to head them.

This exercise is useful for three reasons. Firstly, it teaches your dog to have patience and let sheep move away from him. Secondly, it helps him learn how to hold sheep towards me even if they want to escape. Finally, it prepares your dog for those occasions when you want him to fetch a few chosen sheep rather than gather the whole flock. You can further test his understanding of his commands by sometimes also using this exercise to practice the *out* command (see page 134). When you give this command, you will expect your dog to gather all the stock to you.

Intermediate stage of the shed 2
A Once the sheep have been shed, the dog is asked to turn the sheep back to the other group. **B** As the sheep start to move together, the dog is sent and called in(at the blue spot) to hold the first group before they join up. I use the command *here this*. **C** When sheep are running past, call the dog in to stop and shed the last few.

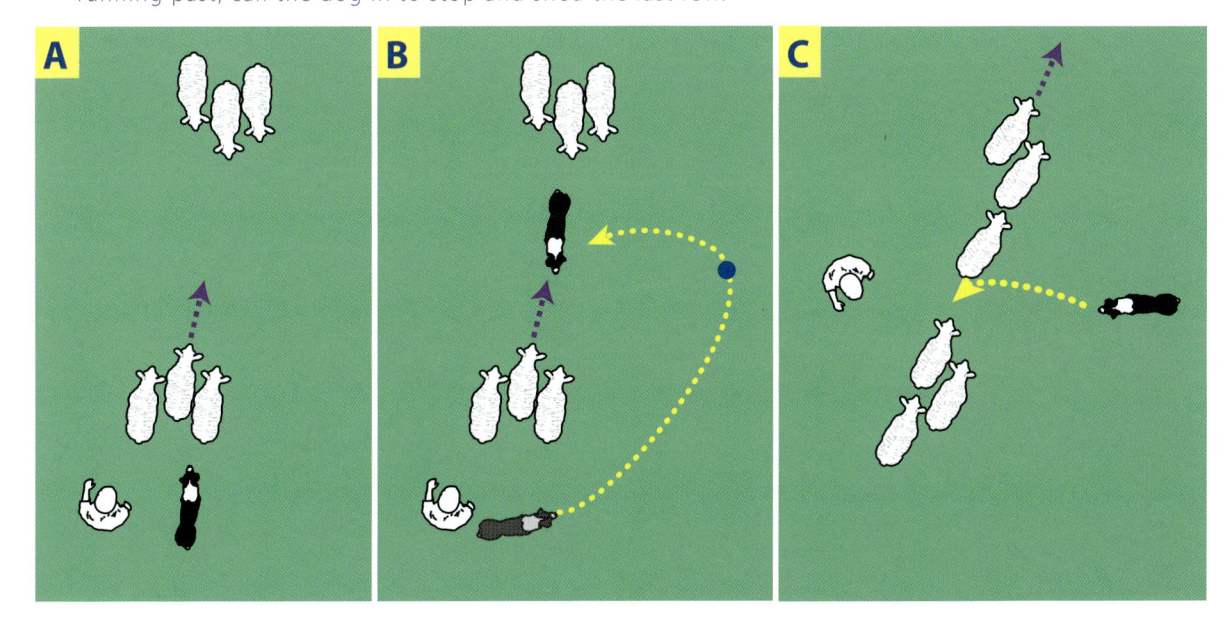

Stopping escaping ewes

A Sam has shed a small group away from the flock. **B** They try to rejoin the main group. I give him a flank behind gesture so that he turns to stop them from reaching their pals. **C** Once stopped, Sam turns the ewes and continues to drive them in the direction I originally intended.

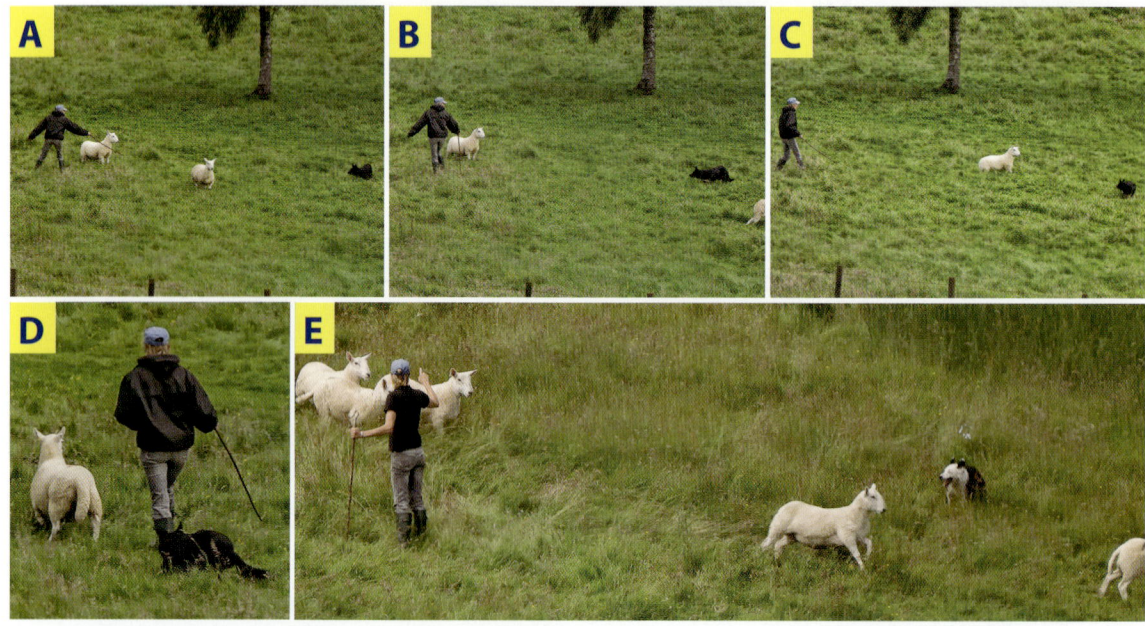

Advanced shedding

Mac and I are separating a single sheep away from another in order to drive her back to her heft. **A** Mac knows from body position that I require the rear sheep and so even though the front one is moving, Mac is focused on the one needed. **B** and **C** The single ewe tries to rejoin its pal even though Mac is putting pressure on it. He has to hold his ground and wear it correctly. **D** Mac and I drive the single ewe who is aware of us as her ears are pointing back. However, she is now more settled and willing to move in the direction we want. **E** Counting sheep in a flock. Ban and I are both focused on the main group. We let the ewes trickle between us as I count.

Another exercise that will prepare your dog for advanced shedding, is to ask him to let most of the sheep run past him but then come and hold the last few. Because it is a prey animal, a sheep's instinct to remain within the safety of a large group is very strong. So, holding the last few sheep can be very difficult for the dog. I have even seen ewes prepared to jump the dog in order to stay with their pals. It therefore helps when you start this exercise to ask your dog to hold a reasonable number back. As your dog's ability improves, gradually reduce the number that you stop until you ask your dog to hold a single sheep. This method of letting the unwanted sheep run, and holding back the ones you require is often used in a work situation.

Summary of the training stages required for shedding

The basic stage. The dog should:

• Come through a large gap made by the handler and take control of the group of sheep that the handler is facing.

The intermediate stage. In addition to the basic stage, the dog should:

• Shed with a smaller group of sheep.

• Being able to shed a certain number of sheep as required by the handler.

The advanced stage. In addition to the basic and intermittent stages, the dog should:

• Come into a shed while sheep are running.

• Shed any number of sheep required, down to a single sheep.

• Be sufficiently experienced to accomplish tasks that are needed in everyday work, for example at lambing time.

Problems

The dog will not come in and shed

One of the most common faults I have found while teaching in clinics is that the handlers take their eyes off the sheep while making the gap for the dog. As the handler moves forward to try to encourage his dog to come in, he does not realise that the split sheep have started moving around the back to join up again. If this happens to you, it is almost inevitable that your dog will not want to come in because either you are in the way, or your position relative to the sheep will be putting pressure on him to stay back and / or the sheep will have regathered behind you so there is no space for him to come through any more!

In addition to these common causes there are other options you need to consider:

• You may be giving the wrong body language and he may not want to come in especially if your stance is aggressive.

• You may be expecting too much too soon.

Do not push your dog to attempt to shed too early in his training. Similar to all aspects of sheepdog training, some dogs are naturally more talented at shedding than others. However, it is also down to you to teach the shed correctly. Your dog has to want to shed in order to be successful at it. Therefore, try to let him enjoy shedding. Once he has the desired sheep, let him work them away from the others for a while. Make sure you build up the complexity of the task slowly. Confidence plays a large part in a dog's ability to shed and for him there is a big difference between shedding a few sheep and stopping a single sheep at the head when she is running.

The dog anticipates the shed

It is better to have a dog that anticipates the shed than one who constantly needs to be called in. This type of dog is keen and eager to learn. These are both traits that will help him succeed. However, coming in too soon can create problems because the dog could shed sheep that you did not intend to separate out.

As always, you need to consider the reason why your dog is coming in prematurely before you attempt to address the issue.

Think carefully about his innate nature and temperament. Perhaps he is impatient or testing your authority. Some dogs make these impulsive moves because they are worried and concerned about the situation. Alternatively, the sheep or your movements could be making him too excited so that he does not wait for your command. Perhaps you are giving him the body language to shed before you are ready.

Try to make sure that your dog follows a set pattern determined by you, so that he waits for your signal before coming in. Be careful that you avoid giving mixed messages and that you are consistent with your body language.

If you do need to stop your dog from coming in too early, try not to put too much pressure on him, otherwise he may no longer want to shed. Be firm, but once you have asked him to come in and he has shed, reward him with encouragement. He will then understand that you are happy with him for being patient.

The dog grips as he comes in to shed

During his working life, a sheepdog will often be required to stop a runaway sheep or to take a firm stance in response to a challenge. The dog's innate temperament and confidence will determine how extremely he responds to this provocation and it is understandable if occasionally he uses his mouth.

Shedding is one of those situations where the tension can rise because of pressure emanating from either the sheep or from the handler's body language and gestures. The dog's character, and previous experience will determine how he perceives and responds to this. Furthermore, the level of predatory instinct within the dog will often dictate how difficult he is to manage and control during the shed.

If your dog grips during the shed, you need to consider the situation from his perspective. Some dogs grip because they are intimidated by the situation. Has your movement towards the stock forced them to push into him and has this pressurised him? Alternatively, have

you made an over-exaggerated gesture that has stimulated excitement in your dog?

Make sure during the early stages of training the shed, you do not ask him to come in through a gap that is too small. Asking him to come in through a small gap to wear an unpredictable sheep increases the pressure on him. Look at his body language and eyes. If his eyes are staring, then he is becoming too engrossed. Twitching ears indicate uneasiness while a stiff body signals that tension is building up inside. A raised tail shows you that he is excited by the situation. If you have trouble reading your dog's body language correctly, go back and review the chapters on canine communication and how to communicate with your dog (see page 6 and page 13).

Only progress to more difficult situations when your dog understands how to shed in a calm controlled manner and is sufficiently patient to wait for your signal.

I recommend that you wait until your dog has a good understanding of shedding sheep before you attempt to single. A solitary running ewe will stimulate his predatory instinct and your dog may become excited and start chasing her. Try to make the task simple and focus on keeping the sheep settled. Definitely do not rush in and chase her off because your dog will follow suit. The ewe will perceive his movements as those of a hunting predator. It is important that your dog is settled and is able to control his energy throughout the manoeuvre. Remember, you are managing a prey animal that will feel threatened by being separated from her pals. Try to let her run towards other sheep, even if they are in a different field as this will also help to decrease her stress levels. You will minimise the risk of a grip during the single, if you aim to keep the sheep, your dog and yourself as calm as possible.

Moving On

Shedding is a good example where you and your dog need to have a close partnership in order to be successful. Another task that also requires good teamwork between handler and dog is when penning sheep. This is discussed in the next chapter.

Watch your sheep when shedding

A client stands behind me as I show her how to position her dog to shed sheep.
A I set up the sheep so that they stand in two groups with a gap between them. **B** Both the client and I start calling the dog through the gap. **C** I realise the sheep are starting to regroup behind me. I therefore put my stick out to block the dog and stop him moving forward because I do not want him to fail in his attempt. However the client has not noticed the sheep and she continues to call the dog through even though it is inevitable that the dog would fail in completing the shed.

From the Clinic

Handler: My dog will not always shed and hold a single sheep. Sometimes he does it with enthusiasm, but on other occasions, he seems to sulk and refuses to come in and shed the single off.

I observed that the dog would only come into shed a single ewe that was not facing him. A sheep like this would be more willing to move away and so the dog's confidence remained high as he could wear her with little effort. However, when he was asked to shed a single sheep that was facing him, his response was very different. On these occasions, he came into the gap when commanded by his handler, but his body language indicated that he was unwilling and also very submissive. He clearly did not want to confront the ewe. Rather than attempt to turn and wear her away from the rest, he let her join back with the others.

My opinion: The dog lacked confidence and felt under pressure when the sheep challenged him. He could shed when the ewe was not facing him, but as soon as she started to defy him, his courage failed. In addition, the ewe had read these weak signals from the dog. She knew he did not want to confront her and so had the courage to regroup with her pals. Remember, it is not just dogs and their handlers that use body language to communicate with each other. Sheep and dogs use it too (see page 53).

My advice: The handler needed to build up his dog's confidence so that he felt capable to move sheep when they were facing and challenging him. To do this, I encouraged the handler to work close at hand with his dog to give him additional support. I then asked them to hold sheep against a fence. When the pressure from the sheep increased, the handler had to ask his dog to move the stock along the fence. This would demonstrate to the dog, that he could move sheep that were confronting him. With time, the ability to deal with this type of situation would build the dog's confidence and he would feel happier shedding a single ewe. In addition, I also suggested that until the dog's certainty had improved, that he should try not to let his dog work in a situation where he may be over-faced by a sheep.

When dealing with a dog like this, it was important that the handler did not growl at his attempts to shed, even though these were not always fully under control. A dog needs to have sufficient freedom to learn. To improve his dog's confidence further, I also advised that the handler should help him move the sheep away. Alternatively, he could work him alongside another more self-assured dog.

Anecdote. Moss decides the shed is just too easy

When Moss was a young dog, all I needed to do was point at a single sheep and he would run in like a bullet and shed her off. One day he decided that this was not sufficiently challenging and he stopped coming in quickly. Instead, he would hold the ewe I wanted in her tracks by subtly moving his head. He would wait and tease her, tempting her to run back to join up with the rest. To me, it seemed as if he was challenging her to see who was going to win. At the last second, he would make his move and successfully shed her with a victorious look on his face.

I knew Moss and was certain he was playing a game, but I was annoyed at him: it was costing us unnecessary points on the trial field. I'm sure that it seemed to the judges and other handlers that he had stopped shedding for me. Eventually even I started to wonder.

So, it was back to the drawing board. How could I convince Moss that he should come through and shed more quickly? I tried everything. I went back to basics and worked with a large flock. I attempted to use more stimulating tones to excite him. When these tactics did not work, I started to growl at him, insisting that he come in quickly. It started to feel as if there was nothing I could do to sort out the problem.

Eventually, I worked out what the issue was. His eye was causing him to wait. Moss was so focused on his sheep, that he was not listening to what I was saying. So simple, why hadn't I realised it sooner? He was not only using his eye to control the sheep, he was also using it to play his game. If I could overcome this, I would spoil his fun. From that day, I used to make Moss *lie-down* when I was preparing to shed. This stopped him leaning forward and using his head to hold the stock. Lying down also calmed the intensity of his stare, and because he was no longer provoking the ewe, she responded by relaxing. Both Moss and I were happy with this new arrangement: Moss, because he still found it challenging to complete a successful shed from a *lie-down* position, and me, because he was again responding promptly to my requests.

Fact Box. Counting sheep and performing an 'international shed'

These two jobs require the dog to use similar tactics. I have therefore chosen to described them in the same fact box.

Anyone, who has ever tried to count sheep in an open field, without a dog, will know that this is not always easy. Stock inevitably move around and it is often hard to know whether you have made an error and either missed one or else counted the same animal twice. A trained dog will make counting much easier. You should gather the sheep together and then allow them to trickle out between you and him. This way, only a few should move at any one time and they should be easier to count as they draw past you.

In order to be successful, you need your dog to lie at an appropriate distance from the stock. The actual position will depend on the character and fitness of your dog as well as the type of sheep you are working with. He needs to be sufficiently close to help you with your task while being far enough away so that he does not disturb the stock.

Use similar body language and gestures that you use during the shed and practice letting the sheep move between you and your dog. Keep his attention on those that are not yet running. This way, he will be focused on the correct group if any decide to brake away before you are ready to count them.

Sometimes let the sheep break through the gap, but on other occasions, call him in to stop a few sheep from running. This test will check his responses. It will also show him that different jobs require different disciplines.

An international shed is where five collared ewes are separated out of a small flock of twenty. This mimics a normal work-day task because you often have to hold back sheep that you require while letting those you do not need move away. In order to achieve this, you need stock sense and also be able to monitor the actions of several different sheep all at once.

During this task, your dog has to stay back to allow the unwanted stock draw away. Sheep want to be together and when one starts to flee, the others will probably wish to follow. If one of the collared ewes tries to escape, your dog needs to come forward to stop her. The better your ability to read sheep, the sooner you will be able to react and call your dog in to prevent this ewe from running. To be successful, use him in a similar manner as when counting sheep. Make sure he is in a position where he can stop sheep if required. If one of collared ewes attempts to run, he should come forward only a short distance to stop her. As soon as the escapee has been halted, your dog needs to double back so that the other flock members can leave.

Anecdote. Don't trust your watch during a trial *

It was the third day of trialling at the 2007 Scottish National Sheepdog trials which was being held in North East Scotland on a field that overlooked the Cromarty Firth in Ross-shire. The rain had poured down through many of the earlier runs, but fortunately, the sun started to break through the clouds just before mine started.

I was running my excellent bitch Tess, who the previous year had been reserve Supreme Champion. She was now nine years old and I knew that this would probably be the final year that she would compete on the trial field. Despite her age, she bounced on her toes like a youngster as we walked to the post: she knew exactly what was about to happen and seemed to relish the approaching challenge. However, once she spotted the sheep, she instantly settled and focused on the job in hand.

She ran fast and true on her left outrun, disappearing near the end into a little ditch before appearing at the perfect balance point to lift the sheep. The fetch and drive that followed were straight and we hardly lost any points as the Mule sheep (that had been so stroppy for others) calmly accepted Tess' authority over them. On to the first shed where we needed to separate two ewes without collars. Both I and Tess remained calm, while we waited for the sheep to settle. I angled my crook towards them to encourage them to part. A gap appeared in exactly the right place and Tess calmly came through it to shed off the final two. Then onto the pen. I opened the gate, and Tess brought the ewes to the mouth. She lay by the side of the pen looking at the stock as one ewe looked down as if to decide whether she could bully her. Tess remained cool and composed as she returned her gaze. The ewe decided not to challenge my dog and instead moved closer to the mouth of the pen. Tess flanked round to stand nearer to me and together we corralled the stock into the pen.

I looked down at my watch and suddenly was flustered to see that we only had a short time remaining to complete the final shed of the single collared ewe. Calling Tess to drive the sheep into shedding ring. I sprinted after her. Because I thought we had only seconds remaining, I pushed the shed and quickly called my dog to come through the gap. Over the years, Tess and I had worked together in some very tough environments. She knew me well and believed that when I spoke to her with such urgency that I needed the ewe stopped at any cost. She responded to my hasty tone and gripped the sheep. It was over. I'd let my dog down.

I felt gutted, even more so when I looked again at my watch and realised that I had misread the dial when I had previously quickly glanced at it. In fact I had plenty of time for that final shed. If only I had taken my time, it all could have been so very different.

*You can view this run on Horseandcountry.tv/episode/come-bye-2007-episode-9.
 My run starts at approximately 05.25 minutes

CHAPTER 16
PENNING

Stock will often need to be corralled into enclosures for a wide range of reasons. In order to pen sheep successfully, a shepherd and his dog have to work together as an integrated team. They both need to read the stock carefully and then precisely and calmly counterbalance each other's pressure as to block unwanted movement from the sheep and at the same time move so that the sheep do not become unduly stressed. The ewes will realise their options are limited and will eventually see the pen as safety. It will become apparent to her that it is better to walk into the pen rather than confront either the handler or his dog.

All sheep react differently when it comes to penning. Remember, they are prey animals who consider that you and your dog are predators. Sheep, especially the native breeds, have a strong survival instinct and will often try to fight or flee rather than risk being trapped inside a small space. Therefore, you and your dog need to concentrate and work together to encourage the stock that their best option is to walk into the pen. Your dog will have to use every skill he has learned combined with all the instincts that you have carefully nurtured by allowing him to work naturally throughout his training.

In addition, you will need to be able to read subtle signals given by the stock because the amount of pressure / release you and your dog have to use will vary depending on circumstances and the type of sheep you are trying to pen.

Julie's Tip. You need to monitor how your dog is coping with every element of his training. This includes how confident he is towards both the sheep and yourself. Make sure you do not over-face him. If at any point he shows worry or uncertainty you need to help him overcome his anxiety. The way you communicate with him will influence his perceptions about what is appropriate behaviour.

If the ewe has not already weighed up your dog during their previous encounters, she will certainly do so at the pen mouth. In order to remain in charge of the situation, your dog has to portray a calm confidence. He not only needs to stand back to settle sheep, but he must also be willing to stand his ground against a dominant ewe who may confront him. Remember, that as a prey animal, when placed in this situation, she will think that she is fighting for her survival.

One of the main aims of The Natural Way is to encourage your dog to be able to use his own initiative. You want him to be able to make the appropriate split second decision about where to move to stop the ewe escaping. If you have trained your dog to balance and wear sheep correctly, he should already have a good understanding of how to respond to stock. He needs to be allowed to make these judgement calls on his own, so that he can learn what works to control sheep and what does not.

To help your dog develop these skills, you should use the pressure / release technique to tell him whether he has acted appropriately or not. Before you start trying to pen sheep, there are several exercises that you can practice to help prepare your dog for the task.

Fact Box. Reasons to pen sheep		
A shepherd needs to pen sheep for a variety of reasons. These include:		
Sorting sheep	Giving mineral boluses	Shearing
Vaccination	Other medical treatments	Dagging
De-worming	Ear tagging	Lambing / twinning on
Hoof trimming and foot bathing	Loading onto trailers	Ultrasound scanning for pregnancy

The first exercise encourages your dog to use his instinct to hold sheep and turn in any ewes that attempt to escape. Take your sheep towards the fence. Ask your dog to hold them to you. He should keep control of the stock while not putting too much pressure on them. When doing this, use the *out* command to keep him back sufficiently. He should respond to this by flanking out in a manner that will stop the more determined ewe from running. He should then double back to stop the others from leaving. If he does this, then he has chosen properly and your body language has to be sufficiently relaxed towards him so that he understands that he has done the right thing. In contrast, if he flanks to turn in a sheep that is not escaping and by so doing lets the determined one escape, then you need to apply some pressure that nudges him to move to a position that stops the fleeing ewe (i.e. the one he should have originally turned).

In other words, you should control, but not command his direction. If any sheep escape, he should be allowed to work naturally to head the ewe back towards you. This exercise will help your dog learn how to react to sudden movements from the stock and this in turn will help him prepare for penning. Often a young dog will find his own distance and learn with experience. If he lacks confidence, do not push him out too far as he may develop a tendency to work off contact. If this happens, it can be extremely difficult to pen some types of sheep. With a dog like this, you can always put more pressure on him at a later stage to push him back out.

Every dog has a different reaction to this exercise. I recommend that initially you practice it for short periods. If he remains relaxed, you can consider practising it for longer lengths of time. Try to read how much pressure is building up in your dog. If he starts to feel too much pressure, he could dive into the sheep and scatter them. If you see that he is beginning to get worried, then before he rushes forward, release the pressure by walking along the fence line. Ask him to fetch and balance the stock towards you. Because he has done this from the start of his training, it should help release any tension inside him.

Preparing your dog to pen

A Initially working against the fence. The dog should be taught to hold and balance the sheep correctly and turn any ewe that is fleeing in an appropriate calm manner. **B** Sam holds sheep against the fence, he is focusing on all the stock. **C** His intense eye causes the ewes to bolt for freedom, Sam uses his natural instinct to flank out and turn back towards the fence. He gets excited by the sheep running and flicks his tail. If the dog's excitement is not checked then he may move into a 'chase' mode which can in turn cause him to grip. **D** Ban demonstrating how the dog correctly turns on his hocks to rebalance sheep.

If you feel your dog is not responding to sheep which are trying to flee, you will have to command him. At the same time use your body language to nudge him to respond to your vocal command. It is important that he moves rapidly to turn a sheep back to the rest of the group, so you need to respond promptly to the escape attempt, and give a quick command to alert him to the fact that he needs to react and move swiftly. If he does not, there is a good possibility that the sheep will escape. The further the ewe manages to get away, the harder it will be for an inexperienced dog to persuade her to return. In this event, it is likely she will run beyond the point of no return. You can further help your dog develop the skills to turn fleeing sheep by giving him quick commands for other tasks (e.g. flanking) and encouraging him to respond swiftly to them. If your dog does not respond promptly and willingly to your commands, back them up with appropriate body language and gestures.

The next set of exercises will help your dog to be careful and to think about what he is doing while he is also learning that he can control stock at different distances from them. Stand by the fence and stop your dog before he fetches the sheep completely up to you. Let the sheep settle. Then try the following:

• Stop your dog, watch the sheep and move them yourself so that you can practice the *out* command. Use a quiet tone to encourage him to flank correctly. You want him to move slowly and thoughtfully to hold the stock at the original position on the fence (this is the imaginary pen mouth).

• In a quiet voice ask him to *steady* and then *walk-on*. He should walk carefully up to the sheep. Gradually ask him to come closer to them until he is nearly touching them (if they will allow it). When he is at different distances from the stock ask him to take small flanks, again ask him to be *steady* while he does these.

When you do these exercises, keep a close eye on your dog and watch to see if there is any change in his attitude. If you see any evidence of excitement, for example staring eyes, then move into his space to remind him to keep a steady mindset. Then try the exercise again.

Once you have been successful with this preparatory work and your dog is responding well to your commands then try penning sheep in a square pen in a field with no help from a fence.

A dog that knows where to stop in order to balance his stock plus also understands when and where to exert the correct amount of pressure (and when to release it), will find penning sheep relatively straight forward. However, there is very little room for error.

Approaching the pen
A Ask your dog to bring the sheep so that you aim for the hinge of the gate. You should stand back. **B** Both you and your dog should block the escape routes as the sheep calmly look at the pen mouth.

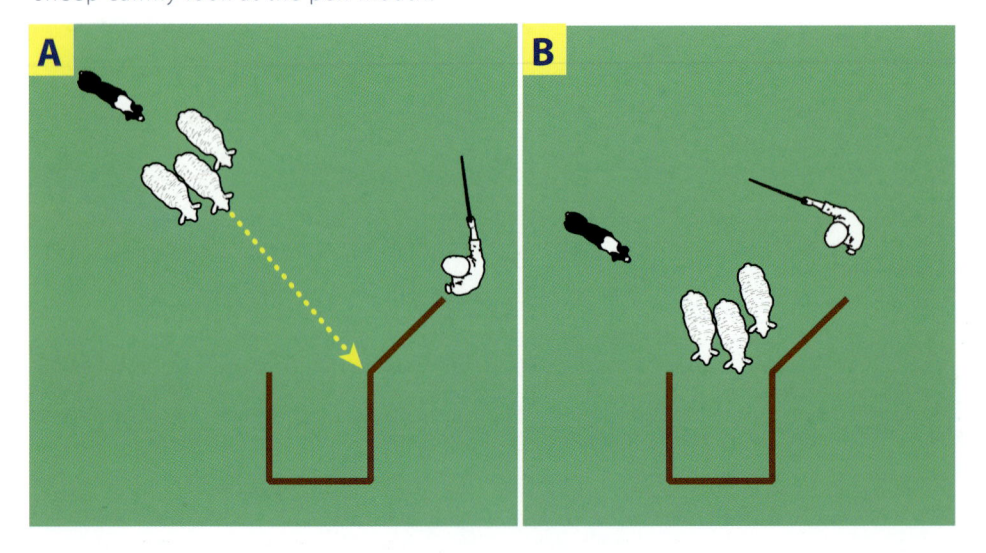

Penning sheep

Gyp and I are putting sheep into the round pen. **A** The sheep on the right is thinking about fleeing. **B** Gyp moves to cover and turn her back to the opening. **C** As we progress with the penning, Gyp is putting slightly too much pressure in the wrong place, causing the ewe to consider breaking away again. I realise the potential problem and am gently telling her to move back and out slightly to relieve some pressure. **D** This relaxes the sheep and we are able to pen.

Penning at an open trial

Penning Sheep at trials can be a challenge. The more you and your dog can read sheep, the easier it becomes. **A** Ban does a wide flank to stop an escaping ewe. **B** Once the ewes are relaxed and facing the pen, Ban and I put gentle pressure on them to encourage them to walk in.

If either you or your dog are even slightly off balance or are applying pressure incorrectly or have an inappropriate temperament, then you will probably have problems. If you find you are struggling to pen away from the fence, then make the move gradually. For example, you could start when the pen is near the edge of a field. Alternatively, you could ask your dog to balance the stock as you put them through field gates (remember to block your dog from chasing sheep as you let them into the neighbouring field).

Julie's Tip. The size and walls of the pen will affect how sheep respond to it. Sheep will see a larger pen which they can see through as less of a threat.

Open the gate and stand back from the pen mouth. The sheep will then be able see the gap as your dog brings them towards it. Try to keep the stock flowing steadily as they move towards the pen. Direct your dog so that they are aimed towards the hinge point. Try not to move forward too quickly as you will put pressure on the ewes who will probably respond by pushing back towards your dog. This will put pressure on him and make his job more difficult.

Encouraging the sheep into the mouth of the pen is a question of timing. You and the dog have to hold them while keeping them settled. Give them time to look for the opening into the pen. This stage is crucial and will decide whether the ewes are penned or not. Sheep, as prey animals, will look for a way to flee from the trap. Therefore, throughout the whole penning exercise (until the gate is closed), you need to keep alert in case any attempt to bolt. You need to have every escape route covered by yourself or your dog, so that the only option left for the sheep is to walk into the pen. This is where experience and the ability to read sheep can give a huge advantage for both you and your dog.

Read your sheep to determine when to put pressure on and when to release it. If any of the ewes have their heads up with ears twitching, they are unsettled and nervous. In this situation, you need to decrease the pressure so keep your dog back and ease back slightly yourself. If the sheep start to walk out towards your dog, then you need to release pressure while your dog increases his. Conversely, when the sheep push into your space, you and your dog need to do the opposite. If your response is too slow, then the stock can become cheeky and challenging. Finally, when the sheep are looking into the pen, you can gradually put the pressure back on again.

Do not expect perfection straight away. You and your dog need to keep calm, remain confident and both apply correctly timed pressure / release on the stock. With practice and experience, you will gradually improve your penning skills.

Using penning techniques on the farm
A Kim is holding sheep on a fence, whilst I use a leg cleek (crook) to catch the ewe I need to lamb. **B** Kim holds a Blackface ewe from escaping while I check its lamb. **C** Kim and I pen ewes and lambs on the farm. **D** On the farm I often sort groups of sheep by combining both the pen and shed.

A mule ewe confronts Mac at the pen
Although Mac remains lying down, his face says it all. He is warning her that if she does not back down, he will be provoked into retaliating.

Summary of the training stages required for penning

The basic stage. The dog should:

• Already have a good understanding of balance.

• Move in an arc as he flanks.

• Hold sheep to a fence and exert pressure and then release it as requested by his handler.

The intermediate stage. In addition to the basic stage, the dog should:

• Learn to improve his responses and movement.

• Respond to the *out* command and move to the correct balance point when only this command is given.

• Show instinctive reactions to the stock to stop them escaping.

• Watch his sheep and make the correct choice as to which ewe to turn in first.

• Be willing to come near to the sheep and to do this quietly and calmly.

The advanced stage. In addition to the basic and intermediate stages, the dog should:

• Be able to put into use all the preparation work you have practised with your dog to enable you to pen sheep in a small pen that is situated in an open space.

• Work in the pens and help you move sheep through handling systems.

Problems

Penning is a team effort and you need to work in close partnership with your dog to pen the sheep successfully. If the pressure from both of you is properly counterbalanced then the stock will be blocked from breaking away. However, if the pressure from one is too great while that from the other is too little, then the situation will be unbalanced and the ewes will try to break through the weak point. Once a sheep learns to escape, she will keep on trying. So, if possible try from the start to show your sheep that there is no escape route available.

As always, carefully assess the situation to determine the underlying cause of the problem. Remember, that your presence at the pen gate will effect how your dog behaves. This will, in turn, depend on your relationship with him as well as his innate character and temperament: some will lie back and others will want to come in close.

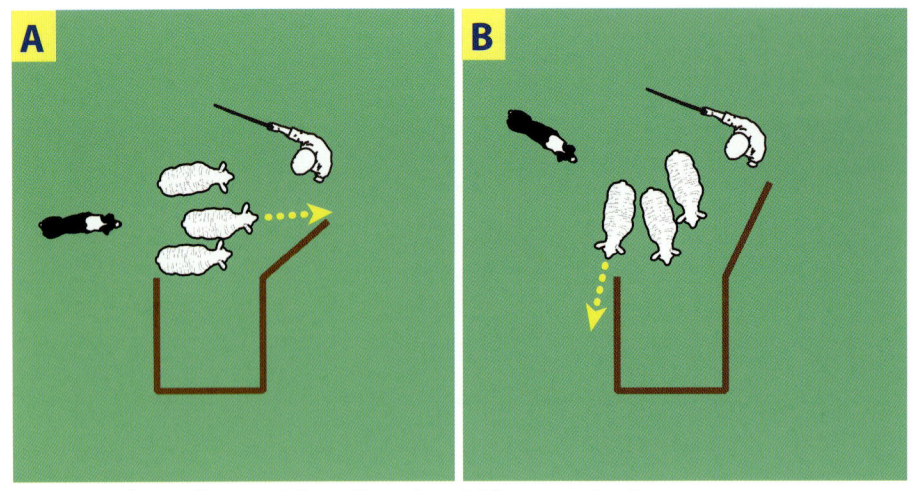

Pressure from dog and handler should be matched
A Dog putting pressure on sheep so that the sheep push past the handler.
B Handler pushing forward towards the sheep causing the ewe to go around pen rather than into it.

Too much handler and not enough dog

This can be caused for two reasons. Firstly, you attempt to do too much and do not use your dog properly. It is easy to do this unintentionally. So when you review the problem, make sure you consider this as an option. To solve the issue, try to let your dog bring the sheep into the mouth of the pen before you move too much. Then, consciously use your dog as well as moving yourself to encourage the sheep to walk into the pen. With practice, this will become second nature for both you and your dog.

The other reason why your dog may stay back is because you put too much pressure on him. This pressure could be applied either directly or indirectly. If you are applying too much pressure directly towards your dog, you need to think about what your body language and gestures are really saying to him. Alternatively, your pressure could be indirectly affecting him, because you are putting too much pressure on the sheep that in response push back towards your dog and as a consequence make his job much harder.

The dog lacks confidence

If your dog lacks confidence, then it is even more important that you do not push the sheep on to him. Furthermore, every time the stock stop, he has to put pressure on them to get them moving again. If this happens frequently, the ewes will begin to feel his apprehension and may start to challenge his authority. So, to bolster your dog's confidence try to keep the sheep moving right up to the pen mouth before you step in to help. If they suddenly feel threatened by you and your dog's attempt to corral them, then their first reaction will be to flee. Instead, you need to stand still and let the ewes see the opening before any movement from you distracts them or pushes them out past your dog.

Too much dog and not enough handler

When this happens, your dog is working and pushing too hard. As a result the sheep flee past you. Often the dog has a strong will and does not want to wait for you to make the decisions. In these situations, you need to take more control and make him respect the fact that there are two of you working together. Assert your authority and use body language and gestures to reinforce your *out* command in order to make him pull back. You may find that you need to insist that he listens to you. Many dogs need to practice being put back out and brought back in as required. So it is worthwhile spending time working on this until he willingly responds to your commands and does so in a manner that does not upset his stock.

Some dogs tend to unsettle sheep more than others. If your dog has an intense nature then his energy levels may be further stimulated when you attempt to pen sheep. You need to work on changing his attitude towards stock. It often helps to do this away from the pen. I have discuss a dog's attitude towards stock in detail in the balance chapter (see page 83).

The dog has no feel

The dog's innate talent will determine how much natural feel he has towards his sheep. Even if your dog struggles with this, in my experience most can be taught how much pressure they need to exert towards stock. They can also learn when to release this pressure. However, some dogs definitely need reminding more often to think about their actions and mindset around sheep.

Penning relies on teamwork between you and your dog. You need to help him understand what is required and if necessary prompt him to respond appropriately to the ewes' behaviour. The exact way you do this will depend on his temperament and natural ability. It is also why you need to continually reassess your dog's attitude towards both you and the stock as he progresses through his training.

The dog cuts his flanks

This is when your dog flanks tightly at the pen. As he does so, he cuts inwards and makes it hard to settle the sheep and therefore to pen them. This problem is discussed in detail on page 98. Penning sheep is a good opportunity to practise the *out* command in a real work situation. You are aiming to teach your dog that he needs to respond quickly to his flank commands, but that when he takes these he should turn on his hocks rather than coming forward on his front legs. Once you have this control on his movement, you will be ready to pen any type of sheep.

Moving On

Up to now I have focused on how you can train a single dog to work sheep. When I shepherd on the hill, I tend to use two or more dogs. In the next chapter, I will discuss how I train two dogs to work as a brace pair together.

From the Clinic

Handler: My dog runs tight on light sheep at the pen. This upsets them and when he flanks he will not stop before the sheep have run too far the other way.

I observed that the dog sometimes ran tight on the flank and immediately afterwards ran out wide on another flank. The dog also over-flanked the stock when he was turning them and this upset them even more. I asked the handler to use his dog to practice holding sheep up against a fence. When the dog did this, he was able to pull back and feel the stock properly.

My opinion: The dog was not used to working with light sheep and did not know how to adjust his responses to suit their more flighty temperament. He over-flanked because he did not know where the balance point was and so did not know where to stop. This dog did not feel sheep properly and so the handler needed to help him understand what is required.

My advice: This dog had not learnt how to balance his sheep correctly. This meant that he did not understand that both tight flanks and over-flanking were incorrect. Furthermore, the handler was exerting pressure at the wrong time and in the wrong place. He had been applying pressure towards his dog for not stopping fast enough. In fact, he should have applied pressure to tell him that the tight flank and over exaggerated flank were both incorrect. In order to address the underlying issue, the handler had to go back to basics and re-teach his dog how to balance and feel sheep properly (see page 83). The handler had to learn how to use the pressure / release technique correctly so that he could help his dog learn how to adjust his movements to suit what the sheep were telling him.

Fact Box. Working in pens

A shepherd often has to work in pens and a well trained dog can make the work much easier. For example when pushing sheep up a handling race to shed some off or for treatment or when coaxing them from one pen to another. To do this type of work, your dog has to be calm and confident so that the sheep remain settled even though he is confined in the same space as them. He also has to have the patience to lie and wait until you need him to calmly move the stock. Often you will need your dog to move between the fence and the sheep and the manner in which he squeezes through this small gap will affect the sheep's behaviour: any erratic movement or noise from either you or your dog will stress the ewe.

An inexperienced dog will often find the restricted space of a pen very intimidating. As a consequence, he may become anxious or overexcited. The whole situation can prompt some dogs to grip. This will obviously increase the sheep's stress levels further.

I recommend that you wait to introduce your dog to this aspect of work until you consider that he has developed sufficient confidence to work stock in a relaxed, calm fashion.

Anecdote. Scottish Blackies: a force to be reckoned with

Not long after moving to Scotland, I attended a sheepdog trial which was being run using Scottish Blackface ewes. This particular breed of sheep are renown for their hardiness and ability to survive outdoors on the Scottish mountains through the harsh winters when food is scare. They also have a well deserved reputation for being wild, independent, stroppy and extremely flighty! My dog and I were used to heavy domesticated stock, so trialling with these was a complete eye opener. Neither my dog nor I had experienced anything like it: both of us were left standing with gaping mouths as the Blackies kept outsmarting our every move.

I knew that if I were ever going to succeed on the trial field in Scotland, I had to learn how to outwit these temperamental ewes. Fortunately, my neighbour, Allan Gordon who was an experienced triallist agreed to give me a helping hand while I practised penning. Great, I thought enthusiastically, he'll show me exactly what moves to make. However, to my surprise the first thing he did was stand at the back of the pen.

Ignoring my complete look of astonishment, he encouraged me to start attempting to pen the stock. Then, every time my dog settled the sheep at the pen mouth, Allan would move suddenly and spook the ewes. The Blackies inevitably scattered and my dog would then have to gather them up and calm them down before we could try to corral them again.

Needless to say, Allan's disruptive tactics meant I never managed to pen sheep that evening. We left the field. Neither of us said a word to the other. Initially I could not understand why he had taken the approach he had. Suddenly it struck me, of course, he had helped me. The whole exercise had sharpened my dog's and my responses to these flighty sheep. His method had effectively and efficiently shown us how and why we both needed to apply pressure appropriately to control the Blackies' flight instinct. In addition, his unorthodox teaching style had silently developed our muscle memory. We now knew that we needed to release pressure if the sheep showed signs of flight, and also to allow them to settle before attempting to move them closer to the pen by asserting pressure quietly and calmly.

Chapter 17
Brace Training

A shepherd out on the hills and moors will often have more than one dog with him. This makes the work more efficient and gives him the flexibility to deal with unexpected events. For example, when gathering or driving a large flock, each dog can push at different areas to keep the sheep moving forward. Ewes and lambs can be a particular headache without a team of dogs, because some mothers will inevitably try to split from the group and move off in different directions as they try to lead their lambs to safety. A single dog will constantly have to reposition himself as he attempts to keep them together. Obviously, this type of work becomes much easier when there are several dogs to hold the stock in one place. Furthermore, during the long hot summer days, having several dogs enables the handler to let some rest while the others work.

However, a good brace team is infinitely more than 'just' working with two dogs that have been trained separately. My current brace dogs (Mac and Ban) and I are a closely knit, integrated team. Our partnership is built on mutual trust, respect and loyalty. I know they both have an excellent feel for sheep and that I can trust their judgement when they are working out of sight of me. In addition, they respect my decisions and will respond promptly to all my commands. The intuitive understanding and bonds that I have developed with Mac and Ban are truly exhilarating and go well beyond anything I previously believed possible.

If you intend to put together your own well-balanced brace team, then one of the most important things you need to ensure is that the natures of both dogs are similar. You may encounter problems if one of the dogs is strong willed but the other is a little sensitive. In this scenario, you would find that the pressure you exert on the stronger-willed dog may upset the sensitive one. This dog would then become very worried and the team would not be able to function as well as you would like.

Another consideration is the method that each dog employs when he works stock. As I have previously discussed (see page 45), every border collie has his own distinctive style of work. You, as the handler, need to harness all your experience and knowledge of canine and stock behaviour to make the best use of each

dog's attributes. If you can really understand the method that each employs during his work, then you will be able to capitalize on this as you nurture both dogs' individual innate talent. As I have discussed throughout this book, this is important when training a single dog to work. To my mind, it is even more crucial if you aiming to work with a brace pair.

The third key element to developing a successful partnership is that you must be prepared to spend a great deal of time working with both dogs together. This way (if both dogs have a suitable temperament), they will develop an understanding of each other's manner of work. Gradually, as they start to predict how the other dog will react to a situation, you will find that they subtly adapt their own actions such that they simultaneously balance stock to each other as well as to handler. The work will then appear to flow like a synchronized and carefully choreographed ballet.

When shepherding out on the hill, I work most of my dogs in twos or threes. However, not all dogs will be suitable to become part of a good brace partnership. Having had several highly successful teams, I know what I am looking for in a potential brace dog. I am also highly in tune with all my other dogs' temperaments and working styles. Therefore, from the very start of my youngsters training, I assess their particular characteristics to determine whether they may be suitable candidates.

I also carefully consider which other dog I can pair them up with. I do this because I like to have each dog on his or her own set of flank commands. It does not matter what words / whistles you use, as long as they are different and you train each dog to respond to his own distinctive set of commands. Personally, I tend to choose *come-bye* and *away* for one dog and *keep* and *go* for the other.

I keep the other commands (*lie-down*, *walk-on* and the redirection ones) the same. Originally, this was for my benefit, because when I started running brace pairs with Bess and Nell, I felt that if I used separate *lie-down* and *walk-on* commands, then by the time I had blown the additional whistles required to get both up, I would immediately be asking both to *lie-down* again! This would inevitably mean that the dogs would not flow smoothly as they worked stock. I think it is important that you should put yourself in your dog's shoes when choosing which commands to use. Keep things simple for his sake. In general, my command system for running a brace pair has

a lot of benefits. However, if I had chosen different words for all Mac and Ban's commands then Mac probably would not have jumped the fence at the 2012 international brace trial competition.

Apart from the decision about which commands to put my dog on, I still train them individually in exactly the same way as I have described throughout this book.

When I consider they are at a sufficient standard which is at least at the intermediary stage (see Fact Box page 70), then I start training them together. However I would not look for precision nor consider running them in brace competitive trials until they had were highly experienced and had reached the advanced stage.

Initially I work one dog while keeping the other lying beside me (if necessary with a lead on to start with). From here, I work close at hand, working one dog for a short while and then swapping over to the other. I flank each dogs individually while insisting that the other lies down until I give him his own commands.

Brace training

I spend hours with the two dogs, so that they learn to work together and flow together in synchrony. **A** I start by asking one dog to flank while the other remains lying down. **B** A good brace pair will balance to the handler and also to each other at the same time. **C** and **D** Walking with the dogs to teach them to match their pace on the drive. **C** I start close at hand and **D** then work at a distance. **E** To account for the different terrain, length of outrun and speed of both dogs means I have to judge and send each dog out at different times so that they both reach the lift point for the sheep at the same time. **F** Natural work on the farm with the 2 dogs on a daily basis bonds the team.

I then teach the dogs how to match their pace on the drive. I do this by walking with the two dogs asking them to get up together and then stop together. After I am satisfied that they are synchronised with each other, I introduce the dog's names. For example, a *Ban Ban* asks him to get up while Mac remains lying down. To stop just one of the dogs, I give his name assertively – *BAN!* While if I want one dog to *steady*, I put a slight growl in my voice as I say his name to remind him to watch his pace.

Once I feel that both dogs are responding, I start with small outruns, lifts and fetches. Different handlers have their own opinions on whether their dogs should cross at the top of the outrun or not. When I started running a brace pair, I believed that it was best for them to cross over because otherwise I thought they would start to pull up short on the outrun when each dog was being worked on his own. However, now I very rarely cross them at the top. In fact, I now consider that it is often counterproductive to ask a dog to run past sheep that could be pulling in his direction. Although there may be occasions when it would be appropriate. For example if a dog has a lot of eye which caused him to pull up short and you ran him in a brace pair, then I would advise crossing over at the top.

Overall, I think the final decision has to be based on the unique manner that each dog tends to complete his outrun and lift.

Both Mac and Ban have tremendous balance. When they work together as a pair, they naturally balance the sheep between each other but when they run as individuals, they instinctively balance the sheep on their own.

In addition, to deciding where to stop your dog at the top of his outrun, the other decision is when they should arrive at the lift. On most occasions, you want your dogs to arrive simultaneously. However, there are certain practical circumstances when you need one dog to arrive first. Perhaps you need the first dog to push the sheep towards a safer path. Alternatively, you may know that the ewes will pull towards one side. In these cases, it makes sense to ensure that the dog running towards the heavy side arrives first so that he can apply counter pressure against the sheep's draw. When the second dog arrives, the first should alter his position so that both continue to balance the stock towards you.

Gradually extend the outrun and driving distance and continue to practise keeping the flow of the two dogs together.

Finally, the best way to unite and bond us all together as an integrated team is to apply the training to plenty of natural work on the farm. For me, there is nothing better than working with two dogs who are in perfect harmony with each other and myself.

Anecdote. Mac is just too willing to take my *out* command whistle

I have worked with Mac and Ban together as a brace pair since they were young. However, the way the Scottish trialling calendar works means that back in 2012, the International Brace Sheepdog trial held near Cardiff in Wales was only the second time I had run them together in a brace competition. The course had an awkward layout on the left hand side because there was a second field that cut across the bottom of the trial field. As I watched the previous competitors run, I could tell that this was causing some issues and so I planned how I was going to send my dogs.

I walked out to the field and, as is now usually the case, my nerves settled as I reached the post. I sent Mac out to the left and waited. He ran out wide and once I thought he was well on his way, I sent Ban to the right. There was a small cluster of trees on this side and Ban started to come in tighter than I wanted.

I urgently needed to redirect him and so I focused all my attention on him and blew a forceful *out* command whistle. My timing for redirecting Ban was good. Unfortunately, it coincided exactly with the moment that Mac had just reached that part of the course where the second field abutted the trial one. On hearing my urgent whistle, Mac believed it was for him (both my dogs are on the same command) and he instantly thought I wanted him out of the field (he considers it completely natural to be asked to jump fences as he is required to do this as part of his everyday work). Mac therefore promptly took my command and jumped the fence. However, he knew where his sheep were, and in his mind he thought I had sent him on the most practical route to get to them, so he crossed the second field and then jumped straight back into the course field and by so doing cut the corner off his run.

It all happened so quickly, I never noticed what had happened: as far as I was concerned Mac had been in the course before I blew my whistle for Ban and when I looked at him again, he was back there running on the correct line. The first I knew that there had been a problem was when I got a tap on the shoulder from the course director asking me to retire due to my dog having left the course.

PART 3
Living
The Natural Way

It feels like it's been a long journey to get to where I am today. Sometimes it's been tough and I've had to make difficult choices. However, through it all, I've had my dogs. They have taught me so much and it is thanks to them that I have found deep contentment in my life at Carcant Farm.

Chapter 18
My Teachers

I feel privileged to have had some excellent dogs over the years. Each has had an unique character that has given me additional understanding into the on-going conversations that dogs have with each other, the stock and us. Although I started as a novice with little sheep sense, I quickly became competent both as a shepherd and on the trial field. In those early days, I believed that I had to use traditional 'obedience' methods to gain the upper hand and so I trained my dogs in this fashion. Although this was successful, I was not satisfied with what I was doing. Looking back, I realise that my dogs were also trying to tell me that there was another way that would achieve that elusive something I was looking for!

Over the years, I have trained and worked with hundreds of dogs, both for my own use and also to help clients with their dogs. No dog is perfect, but each has given me further insight and knowledge about the working border collie and dogs in general. In addition to the anecdotes I've told in earlier chapters, I hope that you also find the following 'warts and all' descriptions of my key dogs an useful insight into how and why I developed The Natural Way. The mutual respect, trust and loyalty that I now have with my dogs underpin our strong working partnership and am grateful to all the dogs I have known who have helped me see the light.

Meg

Meg was the first dog that I owned. She was a medium coated blue merle with an athletic build. She had a very laid back attitude away from stock and went everywhere with me: she was my work partner, my closest companion and my best friend. She was also the only dog that I have ever kept in the house, and she stayed in the porch at night. However, she also had an outside kennel and I found that she would try that little bit extra to please me, when she had been kennelled for a night.

Meg was a good all-round dog with a strong natural instinct, good work ethic and stylish manner. However, despite her nice nature, she was also strong willed and I sometimes found it hard to stop her as I did not understand how to gain her respect. Back then, I knew little about

sheep, but fortunately, Meg always seemed to know what I wanted from her and her willing nature gave me confidence to let her use her own initiative. She never needed much prompting, just a glance and a 'shush' would be sufficient and she would just get on with the job, whether it was catching sheep or keeping greedy ewes away from the troughs as I filled them. She was also fantastic working in the pens because she never gripped. If the sheep did not move up the race, she would either squeeze under them or go over the top of them in order to encourage them forward.

So as you can see, Meg was ideal for a beginner like me as she forgave many of my mistakes and did not take too much advantage of me. Not surprisingly, some of the local farmers wanted to buy her as she was able to work both cattle and sheep. However, there was no way I would ever let my best friend go. Sadly at the age of seven and after three operations to remove various cancers, l had to make the heartbreaking decision to put Meg to sleep. I held her in my arms, softly talking to her as she drifted off to sleep. I was devastated.

Cath

Cath was a small, compact tricolour dominant bitch with an excitable, keen, sharp, determined manner. I trained her from a pup, but I will be the first to admit that with the limited experience I had back then, I found this difficult. Her strong eye and keenness to work always drew her towards the sheep and it was

My first pack of dogs
Fly, Tot, Meg, Don and Cath.

hard to shift her focus away from them. I found it especially difficult to get her to flank on the drive and spent hours walking with her on a long line pulling her out and around on the flank.

Despite this difficulty, once she understood what I required, she would respond promptly to any command and she swiftly progressed through her training. In fact she started to compete in nursery trials at just ten months of age. I found running Cath in trials very frustrating: one day she would do an almost perfect run, but the next time, she would push on and not listen to my commands.

Looking back, I wonder whether her inconsistency was due to the pressure I put on her by training her at such a young age or whether it was her temperament. In reality it was probably a bit of both. She was certainly one of the first dogs to show me how important it is to gain your dog's respect because her stubborn nature made her determined to do everything her own way.

An experienced handler advised me to sell Cath because she was not suitable for competition. I ignored this because (then as now), I found it hard to sell a dog I had bonded with. I kept hoping she would improve as she aged. Unfortunately, she was still the same at ten years as she was at ten months.

Working with Cath taught me so much: how to calm a fiery nature, how fighting a dominant character only causes the dominant dog to push back. She also kept me alert and sharpened my response whilst handling her because I never could completely predict how she was going to respond. In addition, she showed me that a dog's temperament has a huge influence on the way they behave towards humans and stock and although you can help most of them, some are just not cut out for competition.

Tot

Tot was already three years old and fully trained when my first husband, Richard, bought her for me. She was a short coated, medium-built bitch, who was stylish, willing and easily managed. She never took advantage of my novice handling skills and her steady nature gently kept the sheep under control.

This gave me time to read the stock properly as well as the opportunity to learn how to time my commands appropriately. Overall she was a great teacher for me because she showed me that quiet handling of a dog can be a much more effective training method!

She managed most of the chores on the farm though sometimes she struggled to move heavy sheep even though she was giving me everything she had. Despite this, she was also the dog who I first ran in the local sheepdog trials and she gave me confidence to progress onto open trials where she had numerous placings.

Glen

Glen was a gorgeous looking, rough coated, black and white dog with tremendous style, balance and power. I bought him fully trained because, although Tot had been a good starter dog, I now wanted to test myself and handle a more 'pushy' type of dog in order to sharpen my own responses. Perhaps, not surprisingly, given my level of experience at that time, I found him difficult to handle because he would often try to take over. If I used pressure inappropriately, he would kickback at me and let me down at important moments. For example, despite the fact he usually would give a wide outrun when working on the farm, suddenly during a trial, he would decide to run straight up the middle of the field. As I had not raised him from a pup myself, I was uncertain how much of this was nature and how much was nurture.

Glen was not stupid and he felt I was treating him as if he were. A dog can only tell you through his actions what is bothering him. It is up to us, the human handlers, to understand these actions; acknowledge them and then respond appropriately: even if it means letting the dog have his head. Glen taught me that if I wanted to build a strong bond with him, then I should not always fight with him to prove who was the boss. Fight just creates fight. Would you listen to someone that dictated what you did, but at the same time did not have sufficient knowledge and instinct to respond quickly enough to the stock and the situation? I would not and so why should Glen? Instead of insisting he obeyed me, I needed to gain his respect and trust using pressure / release in a consistent appropriate fashion.

If dogs like Glen are not allowed to use their brains, they will not give you more than they have to.

Don

Don was a short coated, tricoloured dog who was powerful towards his sheep and very protective of me. When I originally bought him at less than 12 months old, he had just been started on sheep and showed a lot of instinct towards them. However at that early stage of his training, he tended to move into a 'chase / hunter' mode rather than remain in a 'working' frame of mind. We often seemed to have a clash of wills and I struggled to understand why he kept testing me. Looking back, I now understand that although he was obedient, Don did not consider me leadership material and so did not completely respect me. It felt like a yo-yo: he would take over and then I would wrench the leadership back. However, as soon as I relaxed, he would challenge again. I could not see the very subtle signals that he was sending as he tested my authority; so before I knew it, he had the upper hand and I was fighting for control again.

Don definitely showed me the importance of hierarchy within the pack and why I needed to gain Alpha status. Initially, I found it hard to portray dominance without showing anger. However, I persevered. Gradually, I learnt how to adapt my posture to take on a more authoritative stance and how to alter my tone of voice to influence his actions. As I perfected the subtleties of using body language properly, so I developed a clearer understanding of the cues he was sending me. These skills enabled both of us to communicate more effectively with each other.

Mirk, Gwen and Don

Gwen

Don became my main farm dog and nothing seemed to faze him. He had the heart of a lion and would stand his ground against any challenging ram; jump into a tidal river; leap large ditches and move any number of sheep, the heavier the better. I also won my first open trial with him. When we were in Cambridgeshire, I thought he could catch, shed and control any sheep in any situation. However, when we moved North to Scotland, I found that his intense energy disturbed the lighter hill sheep. I also realised that my lust for control and total obedience had stripped some of Don's innate talent away and he would wait for a command rather than instinctively stop a Blackface ewe that had split from the flock. Unfortunately, at that stage, I was not able to see or respond quickly enough to give Don an appropriately timed command to control these native sheep and so I came down to earth with a bump.

Don taught me so much. He showed me that leadership is much more than insisting on mere obedience. The position of the dominant Alpha in the pack should be based on mutual respect, loyalty and trust. This enables both handler and dog to work together as a harmonious team.

Gwen

Gwen was a small stocky tricoloured bitch who I bought as a twelve week old pup. She had a friendly mischievous nature and just loved everyone. She was the most talented dog I ever had and even from a young age, she could not get enough of sheep. Her ability to read stock meant that she instinctively knew how much pressure to use on her sheep and when she should release

pressure to settle them. Training Gwen was simple, I just showed her something and she did it. Take shedding as an example; she seemed to know exactly what I wanted. I would look at the sheep I required and she would come in and just take them off: simple as that. Because she was so natural, I initially did not have to redirect her on her outruns. However, once the complexity of the task increased, her very ability meant that I had not equipped her with a command that specifically asked her to move either in or out. This was an important point for me to learn. Ever since Gwen, I have made sure that all my dogs learn the basic redirection commands from an early stage of their training and that they build on this through experience.

Gwen had a natural pace with sheep. However, she did not willingly lie-down, instead she would just slow down to account for the sheep's attitude. I accepted that this was Gwen's way of working and so never enforced the *lie-down* except for the odd occasion when I needed an emergency stop. This approach worked well for both of us and we enjoyed a long and happy partnership together.

Trial achievements include
1989: Scottish National – 3rd place
1989: International Championship – winner qualifier round
1989: International Shepherd's Champion
1989: International Supreme – 8th overall
1990: BBC 'One Man and his Dog' – runner up
1991: Scottish National Champion
1991: National Farmer's Champion
1992: Champion of Champions – winner
1992: Grampian TV Sheepdog Trials – winner

Gwen, Bess and Nell
With trophies won at the Scottish National.

Bess

Bess was a seven month, pricked-eared, medium coated, young bitch that had just been started on sheep when I bought her. She was Don's full sister though out of a later litter and had a similar, intense nature around stock which tended to upset them. She was a good listener and very willing to learn, but compared to some of my other dogs, she was slower to do this. Furthermore, if she thought she was right about something, her way of telling me was to refuse my commands. Bess was excellent at driving and this came naturally to her. In contrast, she needed help with her outrun because she tended to drop in tightly at the top and so would upset the sheep as she lifted them. She also needed help with her flanks, especially going to her left. Most dogs have a favourite side, but Bess took this to new heights and tried to avoid flanking left at all costs. Perseverance paid off and she improved sufficiently to compete at trials. Bess developed into a very able worker who relished the day to day challenges on the farm and had the same work ethic as her brother, Don. Similar to him, she also seemed to intimidate sheep and Bess confirmed my thought about the predator instinct. It took a long time for her to learn to control her energy levels around sheep.

With experience she learned to calm sheep rather than alarm them and she went on to be very successful at competition, even when working tricky Blackface ewes. I also worked and trialled her in brace competitions with her daughter, Nell. They were my first brace pair and they showed me that working a team of dogs made shepherding jobs seem effortless. In addition, Bess was the first dog who made me realise that I could teach a dog how to alter its innate energy levels and she also taught me that patience whilst training dogs is definitely a virtue!

Trial achievements (with Nell) include
1991: Scottish National Brace Champions
1992: Scottish National Brace Champions
1992: International Brace – reserve champions

Nell

Nell was Bess' daughter. She was a tricoloured, medium-built bitch who was so shy of strangers that they probably thought she was timid. However she had no fear of stock and displayed a quiet, calm, gentle power that enabled her to move even heavy sheep. She was also very gentle with lambs and had a unique method of working them as she would put her nose under their belly to lift them off the ground and then carefully nudge them forward either towards me to catch or else back towards the ewe, whichever was required. She was the first dog that made me aware that dogs could intentionally lower their energy in a predator / prey situation as she would turn her head to the side whilst maintaining her body in a block position. This non-threatening stance would relax the sheep and stop them from panicking in her presence. However, if tups challenged her, she would

Nell and Bess
Holding sheep on the fence.

keep walking forward to push them back, while intermittently taking off the pressure by stopping and turning her head to the side. This pressure-on / pressure-off technique would give the tup the opportunity to back down and move away. If the tup ignored her gestures, but instead continued to challenge her, Nell would respond by nipping them on the nose and then as they turned would nip their backsides as if to reinforce that she meant it.

Unfortunately, Nell ate some rat poison, lost consciousness and was kept on a drip for three days. I slept with her on the sofa, monitoring her progress, praying that she would pull through. Although she survived this episode, it was soon apparent that she had forgotten all her training and so we had to start from scratch again. Despite all that she had been through, Nell recovered to be an excellent farm dog as well as being very successful in brace competitions with her mother, Bess.

Nell continued to have small strokes throughout her life. On Christmas day, aged just six years old, she had one final severe episode and I had to have her put down. It took me a long time to come to terms with losing her. Nell showed me that a dog could use gentle authority to remain in command of her stock and yet sufficiently understanding that she would release pressure to de-stress her sheep. She also taught me the importance of patience and how resilience and strength of character can bring you through the toughest of times.

Moss

Moss was Nell's full brother from a younger litter. He was a mottled tricoloured medium coated athletic dog. He was a very keen and sharp and at the early stages of his training proved to be quite a handful. He would occasionally grip and so I attempted to control the situation by not allowing him much freedom. In response, he started to object to my control by responding only grudgingly. I knew something had to change and so I let him work naturally throughout the winter with only minimal command. This is similar to what we used to do with the horses when they would be shown all summer and then the training would be relaxed during the winter and they were used for hunting to get some spirit back. This approach also worked with Moss and letting him work freely re-awakened the keenness inside him. I knew I had to find another way to train him and it took me time to realise that Moss was telling me to improve my communication skills with him. He showed me just how subtle the communication between dog and shepherd could be. I studied his actions and watched how the sheep responded. I realised that Moss could control his stock just by turning his head slightly. As I learnt to trust his judgement and listen to his body language, so I began to gain deeper insight into the silent on-going communication between dog and sheep.

Moss at the Supreme International held at Chatsworth in 1996
A An anxious moment as a mule ewe challenges. Moss stands his ground and displays his quiet authority that accomplished the winning run. **B** Just after our final run.

However, Moss' success was not completely down to his natural feel for stock: I also needed to show him what was acceptable. I remember one trial when he lifted the sheep too hard for my liking and I growled my disapproval. The following week, we were at another trial and he lifted so carefully, I thought he was never going to move the ewes. He obviously had remembered my reprimand from the week before and this showed me that dogs have good memories.

Gradually, I allowed Moss to gain experience both in competition and in his daily work. I adapted my approach to be more compromising; using consistent, quiet signals, I showed him what I wanted and importantly I gave him time to understand. This approach paid off and it let his natural ability and his tremendous balance develop to its full potential. Soon he could manage sheep that many other dogs found impossible to control.

He would calm the wildest stock and he had a rare trait of drawing sheep to him so that they would let him run almost with his nose at their tails, and yet they would still be settled all the way around the course. I remember one trial being run using wild Blackface sheep. One by one, each dog failed to manage the sheep and so were unable to complete their runs. When it was Moss' turn, he went out and the way he felt his sheep meant that they quickly trusted him. His natural talent and ability was mind-blowing. I just needed to let

him use it. He taught me how to work with a dog that has a sensitive nature and how to bring out the best in him. Crucially, Moss also showed me how important it was to listen to what my dog was telling me.

Trial achievements include
1996: Scottish National Driving Champion
1996: Supreme International Champion

Tess

Tess was a smooth coated tricoloured fine boned bitch with a whippet-like build. She was very fast and sharp, combined with a lot of natural talent with fantastic feel for sheep and good natural balance. In addition, she was very determined and no matter how tricky the situation, she would give me everything she had in order to please me. I remember when she was about 8 months of age, I decided to use her to help push some stubborn mule sheep forward through a race. The ewes thought they could just knock Tess out of the way. Before they (or I) knew what was happening, she was underneath them and then on top of them, all the while pushing them down the race. There was absolutely no ill intent in her behaviour, but she growled her annoyance if they turned to challenge her.

Despite this boldness, there was also a sensitive aspect to her nature and, during her early training, she needed both patience and, at times, reassurance. If I pushed her too hard over something, she would signal her concern. So in response, I had to learn how

Tess
A The ewe's laid-back ears, high-held head and general stance all indicate indicates that she may easily be pushed into flight. Tess keeps her settled by approaching with a quiet, calm authority.
B Tess shows her tremendous balance and focus as she singles the collared ewe away from the group.

to build her confidence. I did this by allowing her to make minor mistakes; encouraging and guiding her with situations she was struggling with as well as giving her more freedom and the opportunity to work things out for herself.

Tess was a great trial and work dog who seemed to make all shepherding chores stress-free, so much so, that even the hardest tasks were performed with ease. When she was a little older, she became my main dog and we faced a wide variety of gruelling tasks together: from heavy lowland flocks to the flighty sheep on the rough hills of Braegrudie. Tess stuck with me through thick and thin. She never quit, doing whatever I asked no matter what the weather was throwing at us at the time. Nothing bothered her, whether it was catching ewes and lambs or turning tups that were challenging her.

She usually had a nice, kind way with sheep and they responded well to her. However, there was one occasion during lambing time, when I asked Tess to move a few ewes while I went to check a lamb some distance away. As I looked up from my task to see that everything was going smoothly, I noticed another ewe charging towards Tess. My dog was focused on her work and was unaware of the impending onslaught. Before I could warn her to watch out, the ewe slammed into Tess knocking her flat. My instant gut reaction was 'Oh no, Tess has been killed', I rushed to her side and knelt down to put her head in my lap. Tess started to move and slowly came to her feet. She looked

around and spotted the culprit. Instantly, she sprang like a deranged animal towards her attacker and firmly told the ewe in no uncertain terms, that she would not tolerate that kind of behaviour from a sheep. As Tess returned to my side, she seemed to have a satisfied grin on her face as if to say 'That ewe'll not try that again.'

Tess gave me her heart and I loved her to bits. She taught me that if I could build confidence in a dog, then it would feel capable of doing anything. In later life, Tess had a well-earned retired with my good friend, Rosie, in nearby Innerleithen. Rosie gave Tess a wonderful retirement and Tess clearly loved Rosie in return. As Rosie is also a member of the Somerville family who own Carcant, Tess would regularly come back to visit and, in my mind's eye, I can still see her trotting down the path to greet me and the rest of the pack. She would curl up next to me and put her head on my thigh as if to say 'We made it through some tough times, you and I, but through it all, we had each other'. If ever a dog could be your soul-mate, then Tess was mine.

Trial Achievements include:
2002: World Trial -placed 7th
2005: Scottish National Brace Champion (with Fly)
2006: Scottish National—reserve champion
2006: International—winner of qualifier
2006: Supreme International—reserve champion
2006: International Farmer's Champion

Fly, Tess and Gail
A Fly and Tess balance to each other as they effortlessly drive the Blackface ewes.
B Gail lying patiently on the beach.

Fly

Fly was a smooth coated tricoloured bitch that was bred out of Tess. She had a slightly edgy temperament and was sensitive away from sheep. However, she could be determined and stubborn when she was working stock. She partnered Tess both at work and also in brace competitions. Along with Molly, Tess and Fly were my three main dogs whilst I shepherded at Braegrudie. However, as a young dog, she tended to lean inwards as she flanked and this would cause the sheep to flee, so she needed to be reminded about taking her flanks properly. Fortunately, she was tough enough to stand the pressure of training. Like many dogs who are learning their trade, she went through a phase of testing me and one way she would do this was by refusing to stop completely. One day, after not listening to me, she pushed sheep across a burn faster than I thought appropriate. I promptly sped up on the quad bike with the intent of heading her off.

She was shocked by the speed that the bike arrived next to her and instead of realising that I was using the bike to reprimand her inappropriate action, she took a distinct dislike to the noise of the quad, to such an extent that she would not work in the same field if the bike was there. It took months of gentle coaxing to change her mindset.

Initially, I put her on a long line and sat with her near it. Once she accepted this, I started the engine and over time, still with her on a line, she gradually settled sufficiently to run alongside the bike. Eventually, she was no longer concerned with the bike and was happy to work when I was riding it.

Just goes to show, a quick action on the handler's part in an attempt to sort out one issue may create another problem that takes months of patience to fix. Fly definitely taught me more about using pressure / release appropriately to get the best out of a dog.

Trial Achievements include
2005: Scottish National Brace Champion (with Tess)

Gail

Gail was a medium coated tricoloured bitch. Her previous owner had trained her to nursery standard, but their temperaments had clashed so I bought her because I needed a dog of that standard to run in that year's nursery trials. Initially she had boundless energy and was difficult to stop because she did not understand why she needed to be careful around stock. When I started working with her, I quickly realised the more pressure I put on, the more she fought it. I therefore decided to take the complete opposite approach as long as she did not unduly stress the stock. I therefore released all pressure, let her work naturally and did not ask her for precision. I could see that she wondered what had happened.

Once she had relaxed and was enjoying her work more, I gradually reintroduced slight pressure as I went into a block position to stop her. As soon as she gave any sign of giving to my wishes, I released the pressure. I could see that she was starting to trust me and understand that there was a reason behind my request to stop.

This encouraged her to work with me rather than fight against me. I worked with her in this fashion all through the winter and we developed a bond built on mutual trust and respect.

With time, she became one of my main work and trial dogs. Gail taught me the importance of building a sound relationship based on trust, respect and loyalty.

Molly

Molly was a friendly, smooth coated tricoloured bitch with pricked ears. She had immense stamina that enabled her to just keep going when other dogs would start to flag. I bought her as a young dog that had been trained to command but still lacked work experience. As I worked with her, I found that although she would instantly obey any command, she did not really seem to understand why she was being asked to do it. As you will have gathered by now, when I train my dogs I encourage them to use their instinct and to develop their natural feel for sheep. Unfortunately, Molly's lack of experience meant she did not have this. I remember one occasion when I was gathering the stock at Braegrudie and I sent Molly to gather some strays. I asked her to *steady* back as I could tell that one ewe was struggling to keep up on the soft boggy ground. Molly would not listen to me and kept pushing forward ignoring the signs that the sheep was giving her. Eventually, the ewe pulled away from the others and lay down. I was not very pleased with Molly and made her get back and *lie-down* out of the way. We had to wait about half an hour before I considered the ewe was ready to continue our journey as we still had several miles left to go. After we set off again, I repeatedly reminded Molly to be careful about the ewe.

It was experiences like this that taught Molly that she needed to be more aware and responsible for her own actions. Even then it took many months of work and everyday graft at Braegrudie before she really developed a good feel for sheep and could balance naturally.

Molly's strong work ethic and willingness meant that she became one of my main work dogs. She was also very in tune with her surroundings and was excellent at detecting sheep hidden in the undergrowth or lost in the snow. She would also stop for lambs that had fallen behind and I learnt to respect her judgement and to investigate anything that appeared to have distracted her from taking my commands.

Furthermore, even though she had learnt to be careful about stock most of the time, she seemed to understand that there were still circumstances when she needed to push them. An example of this happened when the height of the Bora river started to quickly rise after some torrential rain. Some sheep had become stuck on a small bit of higher ground that was soon going to flood. Molly swam out and then convinced the ewes that they needed to swim to safety through the raging water before the patch of ground was engulfed. Her determination and guts saved them from being swept away.

A good friend bought Molly. Her ability to work any type of sheep gave her the skills she required to work with range sheep in America. Her new owner is much more laid back than me and I could tell that Molly has relaxed more with her than she did when I handled her. Molly taught me to believe that a dog can change and that I should be prepared to give her time to learn what is required to do her job properly. When you work with a dog is important not to crush her natural spirit, but instead, get her to work with you, not against you. It is also clear that our own innate energy and mood influences our dogs. Molly's contentment with her new owner reinforces my belief that it is important to pair a dog with a person who has a compatible nature.

Molly ready for action

Kim

Kim is a daughter of Molly. She is a medium coated tricoloured bitch with plenty of power and a clean mouth. Although she likes to push forward, she has learnt to have a feel for sheep and will adapt her approach when the situation requires more sensitivity towards her stock. She is therefore excellent at working both light and heavy sheep. Overall, she has a tremendous nature and I know that even when the going gets tough, Kim will stick with me to the end. There are so many good things about her that it is not surprising that she has been one of my main dogs from a young age.

However, there is also definitely a stubborn side to Kim and she often requires assertive, authoritative handling to bring out the best from her. I believe that with a dog like her, if I insisted that everything were done exactly the way I would really like then I would either crush her spirit or else cause conflict between us. I certainly do not want to do either of these. Fortunately, my previous experience with her mother and some of my other dogs, has taught me how to adjust my approach. So I ensure that I 'give and take' with her. By this I mean there are aspects of behaviour which I expect all my dogs (including Kim) to adhere to, but there are other things that I will let her get away with. For example, she knows she has to feel her sheep and respond appropriately around them. Away from stock, I am a little more flexible and do not mind (much) if she does not have a prompt recall nor always walks to heel.

As my younger dogs have gained in experience, it has been possible to let Kim ease back from doing too much heavy work. Despite this, she does not believe that any other dog can work stock as well as she can and, given even the slightest opportunity, she will stick in and help out.

Kim has reinforced the importance of bonding properly with my dogs. Dogs like her need to want to please their handler in order to bring the best in them and this can only happen if the handler spends time creating the correct relationship.

Trial Achievements include
2008: Lanark, Lothian and Peebles Nursery League – winner
2010: Reserve for Scottish Team
2011: World Trial – represented Scotland

Mac

Mac is Tess' son. He is smooth coated black medium coated dog bred with natural ability, great balance and an excellent feel for sheep. He has a similar work ethic to his mother and over the last year has become my main dog as Kim takes more of a back seat. He is easy to handle because he is willing to please, a good listener at any distance and will respond promptly to my whistles. He trusts me completely and in return, I know that I can rely on him. All these traits makes him an exceptional hill dog and a pleasure to handle in competition. I know he will go out to find sheep anywhere on the hill even if he cannot see them from where I send him. He usually will bring them back exactly from where I sent him and if I have moved position, he will look round to find me. Moreover, when he is gathering sheep and he sees me move location, then he will bring the sheep back on a new route that brings them directly back to my new position. He will do all this without command and without stressing his sheep. Mac is intelligent and his desire to do the correct thing makes him appear sensitive.

Kim communicating with stock
Look how the ewe's right ear is directed towards Kim, while she uses her left one to monitor where her lamb is.

Ban and Mac working in sync together

He does not like being around people who are angry or shouting too much. He is also very shy of the sound of gun shot. As soon as I hear shooting, I will call Mac to me to reassure him with my touch. However, if a he hears gun fire when he is out being exercised by Bobby, Mac will forget everything and flee into the distance. Fortunately, he has always returned as soon as he hears me call for him.

Mac has reinforced to me why training The Natural Way is successful for all types of dogs. It has definitely allowed me to develop and nurture his working instincts.

Trial Achievements include
2010: Lanark, Lothian and Peebles Nursery League – winner
2010: Inter League Nursery Final – runner up
(2012-13 Brace achievements - see below)

Ban

Ban is a medium coated sturdy built dog that is home bred and brought up using The Natural Way. When he was a youngster, Ban definitely picked me. He would sit outside the porch door, leaning against the wood, softly blinking his eyelids at me. It was as if he was saying 'I know you can't resist me'. I was captivated and completely bowled over by his charm.

Although I am definitely his number one person, he is also very affectionate towards all humans and there are very few who can resist him. He is also very sensitive to human body language and energy. However this welcoming, empathic behaviour actually hides the devil inside. This other side to his nature becomes apparent around stock and when working Ban on sheep, I regularly need

to remind him to calm his energy and intent towards them. If a sheep challenges him, he can show his temper and insist they obey his wishes. However, even with this attitude, he shows tremendous natural balance and his innate talent means is he is very gentle with lambs.

Ban's sensitive understanding of human body language has taught me how subtle and wonderful the communication between dogs and people can be.

Trial Achievements include
2011: Lanark, Lothian and Peebles Nursery League – winner
(2012-13 Brace achievements - see below)

Mac and Ban as a team

I have worked Mac and Ban together since they were young. They make an interesting combination as Mac wants to keep everything sweet, while Ban wants to assert his authority. They know each other's working style and subtly gesture to one another as they figure out between themselves how to tackle each task. They complement each other perfectly and their 'good cop / bad cop' approach effortlessly gets any job done. I've known for a long time that running one dog that is in tune with me and the sheep is exhilarating. Now, I am completely awestruck to be part of this incredible team. Mac, Ban and I have an intuitive understanding and bond with each other. It is a truly inspiring and incredible experience that goes beyond anything I had ever previously believed possible.

Trial Achievements include
2012: Scottish National Brace Champions
2013: Scottish National Brace Champions
2013: International Brace Champions

CHAPTER 19
SNAPSHOTS ALONG THE ROAD TO CARCANT

I was born and spent a happy, safe and secure childhood in Scunthorpe (a town in North Lincolnshire), with my parents and older sister, Bev. My parents were excellent role models as each were hard-working and had strong beliefs about what was right and wrong. Although both parents freely gave both of us kids plenty of love and affection, my father, where necessary, could also readily control any unruly behaviour using a quiet, calm dominant manner that quickly brought me back in line. Despite setting rules and boundaries that were not to be crossed, my parents also gave me sufficient freedom to allow my character to develop. So, when not in school, I seem to remember spending a lot of my childhood outside climbing trees, playing football and other general rough and tumble games with the other kids in the neighbourhood.

Even as a young child, I absolutely adored animals. However, my parents, for very practical reasons, would never allow me to have more than a guinea pig at home. As I was desperate to be with larger, more companionable, animals, I would offer to walk the neighbours' dogs. My mother also has old photos of me as a young child sitting on a donkey at the beach and also on a pony at my great-grandmother's farm, so my parents must have indulged my 'whim', but I have to admit that looking back now I do not really remember either event clearly.

We did not visit my great-grandmother often, partly because she thought that only boys were worth considering and partially because she had disapproved when her son, my grandfather, had left the farm to work in a steel foundry in order to support his young family. Unfortunately, they were never reconciled because my grandfather died in an accident at work soon after moving away from the farm. As you may be able to gather from this description, my great-grandmother was a 'tough old boot' and difficult to be around, but I sometimes wonder whether my passion and subconscious need to work in agriculture stems from her.

You can imagine my delight when, at the age of ten, my parents reconciled themselves to having an animal-mad daughter and arranged for me to have my first riding lesson. Needless

to say, I was hooked and after that I would save all my pocket money to pay for further lessons. I was so determined to indulge this new passion that whenever possible I would cycle five miles to and from the stables just to be able to devote that single precious hour riding a pony. By the time I was twelve, I managed to convince the stable to let me help in the yard, and from then on, I spent every weekend and all my school holidays working there in exchange for the opportunity of riding the ponies.

The head lad was Terry Harrison. He was a highly capable horseman as well as a tough, but fair, boss. Along with my parents, he was one of the main influences who instilled in me the strong work ethic that has stood me in good stead all my life. My time at the yard was not all hard work and I had plenty of fun with the other youngsters who helped out there. Once our chores were finished, we would goad and encourage each other to determine who could manage the hardest jumps and fastest turns. I remember one occasion when I was riding a fast little pony and tried to jump a fence. Unfortunately, the pony had a different idea and she ran to the side as I carried on flying out of the saddle into the jump wing that held up the post. When I finally managed to pick myself off the ground, I found all my friends standing nearby and laughing at my sudden ungainly dismount.

My early years
A My mother and sister with Dad and me at the beach. **B** Jen, my faithful companion.
C The first pony I owned, Briarwood Lady Killer.

During my time at the stables, I also became attached to a Jack Russell bitch called Jen. She was very independent and often caused trouble. One day, she chased some pheasants and was then banned from going outside on her own. However, I wanted Jen with me, so I found a long line and attached it to her. This meant that she had to trail everywhere with me including when I had to ride a horse from the field to the stables. Looking back, it is amazing that she did not get completely tangled in the line. I always kept Jen with me whenever I was at the stables, until one weekend, I arrived to discover that she had vanished during the previous week. She never re-appeared and no-one knew what had happened though it was suspected that she may have got stuck down a burrow when out rabbit hunting. This was my first experience of losing something very dear to me and I was completely devastated.

My move to Cambridgeshire

I left school at sixteen and went to work in a local factory This meant I could continue to live at home which pleased my mother and it also paid a wage, but I hated the place and felt completely trapped. I longed for the weekends when I would go to do some unpaid work and also gain further equine experience at a famous show jumping yard near Doncaster.

When I was seventeen, the opportunity to work at a stud farm in Cambridgeshire arose and I jumped at the chance, even though it was completely daunting to leave everyone I knew and move one hundred miles away from home. The farm had 3 main stallions plus mares coming in for stud, show ponies, a

dealer's yard and a riding school. All together it meant there was always a full stable with over sixty horses. It was definitely a full-time job for the other two girls and me as all the horses that were stabled in the yard had to be mucked out, fed and watered by breakfast time. The rest of the day was then filled with other chores which ranged from grooming, riding and breaking young horses to teaching at the riding school. Like all animals, the horses obviously need caring for every day and so I was employed to work six days a week. However, I usually chose to work the whole seven day week in order to save up my free time. This allowed me to go home to Scunthorpe for a few days every month and catch up with my family and friends.

The horses on the farm taught me a great deal. You have to remember that this was before the 'horse whisperer' method became a popular training option and so I had to unravel the puzzle of how to interact effectively with them myself. My teachers were the horses themselves and they were tough taskmasters. Gradually I learnt to listen to them and to fully appreciate why they acted as they did. In return, I gained their respect and so together we developed willing partnerships with each other.

There are a few incidents that particularly stick in my memory. On one occasion, a stallion lunged at me with his teeth directed straight at my face. Usually he was calm and quiet and I was completely unaware that anything had changed in the yard to provoke this marked alteration in his behaviour. My lack of sensibility to the horse's viewpoint had put me in a dangerous situation and left me ill-equipped to deal with the half-tonne of

Scunthorpe
My family relaxing in the back garden with Meg and her litter mate.

Cambridge
Tot and I relaxing at the farm

testosterone-fueled power that was facing me. Needless to say, I quickly got out of the way.

Another time, I was 'long-reining' a young pony when he was spooked into flight. He spun around in panic and managed to wrap the reins around his neck. As I now had no control of his head, I was dragged face-down in the mud.

These hard lessons taught me that I had to stop being a soft-hearted teenager. Instead I had to become more confident and assertive whilst remaining empathic to the horses' needs. I gradually learnt how to read the situation sooner, respond quicker and react more appropriately so that potential problems were stopped before they could escalate.

Breaking young horses was also an education as I began to appreciate how to deal with their different natures and personalities: some would need coaxing and encouraging whilst the more stubborn and dominant characters required more authority and assertiveness. All needed praise when they tried to please me. As I grew in confidence, I began to alter my body stance to fit my requirements. For example, I would stand tall and use a stern direct gaze to be assertive and push the horse back out of my space. Alternatively, I dropped my eyes and turned to the side to become less threatening and encourage the animal to come towards me. I did not understand at the time that I was actually learning to use their own language. Now, looking back, I realise that it was during those teenage years that I started to develop my skills in animal communication.

My Introduction to shepherding

Although I was now working with horses, I still had not managed to fulfil my dream of possessing my own dog. This changed in 1982 when I acquired Meg, a farm-bred blue merle border collie pup, who quickly became my most cherished companion. She was mainly a pet but I was intrigued by her natural instinct and her desire to herd everything from geese to horses and so I started to use her to help with shepherding chores around the farm. Meg's natural ability taught me a great deal about the practicalities of moving sheep. I remember one night discovering that a flock of sheep had escaped out of the barn and only the occasional distant bleat indicated where they might be. I could not see a thing and so in sheer desperation I sent Meg into the darkness to look for them. A few minutes later the flock were back in the shed with Meg panting proudly at my side. Episodes like this taught me the importance of letting a dog use its own brain and I now appreciate how fortunate I was to have Meg introduce me to the wonderful world of the working sheepdog.

Over the next couple of years, Meg and I successfully shepherded a flock that was kept along a riverbank. As my interest grew, I decided I needed to improve my knowledge about sheepdog training. Therefore, in 1984 I signed up for a couple of agricultural training board courses taught by Norman Seamark who was President of the International Sheepdog Society (ISDS) at the time. Norman's keen interest in sheepdog trials inspired me to want to compete for myself and I joined the East Anglia Sheepdog Society the same year. I made a number of good friends there including Sarah Jenkins who has remained one of my closest confidantes ever since.

There were a number of other individuals at the East Anglia Sheepdog Society who were also learning how to trial. As we all started from a similar standard, we had the confidence to learn from our mistakes; the only pressure I received was from my own self determination and drive to succeed. As my passion for sheepdogs grew, so too did the number of dogs I possessed. My first husband, Richard Deptford, bought me an older trained bitch called Tot. She was one of the best teachers I could wish for as she knew her job, was easy to handle and very willing to please. Working with Tot significantly improved my confidence to handle sheepdogs and also to train young dogs from scratch.

During the day I worked full-time as a shepherd managing a flock of up to nine hundred Cheviot Mules. I carried out all the hard, heavy manual tasks such as shearing and dipping sheep alongside the men and my strong work ethic ensured that I did not quit no matter how painfully my muscles ached. On top of this, I also helped with the arable side of the farm by working in the fields or driving the tractors and other heavy machinery when required.

Every evening and weekend after finishing my work, instead of resting or socialising, I would train sheepdogs that either I would keep or sell on. I was determined to succeed and my experience with horses, especially with stallions, had taught me how to assert my authority over strong-willed animals. Richard would say 'If you do not criticise yourself and your stock then you will never improve'. Gradually, I started to understand and predict how sheep would react to my dog when

he gave a fast or wide flank, or when he did not cover or balance his sheep properly. I also noted that certain movements from my dog relaxed the sheep's alertness and calmed their behaviour.

I realised that not only did the dog make mistakes, but that I, often unwittingly, caused my dog to make these errors by accidentally encouraging inappropriate movement or by allowing him to move when I did not intend him to. I came to appreciate that those 'unexpected' responses from the sheep happened because I and my dog had created them. My mind felt like a sponge soaking up all this information and I spent nights awake scrutinising every last detail of my day's work and training. I analysed why things could have gone awry and worked out methods that might rectify my mistakes if the situation reoccurred.

As well as training sheepdogs for work, I also started running Tot in open trials and in October 1985 managed to be awarded the prize for highest pointed member of the East Anglia Sheepdog Society. The following year I picked up a few placings with both Tot and some of my other dogs.

It was around this time that I was introduced to Bill James, a traffic warden from Merthyr Tydfil in Wales who trained dogs in his spare time. He quickly became a close friend and one of my chief mentors and I often would phone him to discuss my dogs and ask his advice. Bill told me I needed more respect from my dogs if I wanted to improve. At the time I did not comprehend what he meant; my dogs took commands well and I was able to compete with some of them to a good standard. It was not until I starting working with Cath that I started to understand the significance of his comments. This new insight helped me get my first win in an open trial with Don in 1988.

Best Friends
Sarah Jenkins and I meeting at the International trial.

My move to Scotland

The opportunity arose for us to move up to Scotland near Elgin. However the farmhouse, land and fences had been neglected for several years prior to our arrival, so in November 1988, I went ahead of Richard to make the farmhouse at Glenlatterach habitable.

The land was very different from the flat fenland of Cambridgeshire and it must have been a shock for the horses and seven hundred Welsh mules we had brought up from the lush southern grass and milder climate. It took both the animals and us time to acclimatise and I certainly missed my family and friends desperately. Despite this, the natural beauty of Scotland worked its magic and I began to relish living and working in my new surroundings. I also enjoyed meeting like-minded individuals in the sheep dog world. One such person was my neighbour Allan Gordon. He was a retired shepherd and one of the top sheepdog handlers in the North of Scotland. It was Allan's enthusiasm at sheepdog trials that encouraged and supported me at the local competitions. His knowledge and contacts also made it possible for me to practice at a wide range of locations so that I could prepare my dogs for the Scottish National.

Allan also helped me learn how to work with flighty, yet stubborn Scottish Blackface (Blackie) sheep, though he sometimes had an unorthodox training method. I remember one evening while I was practising penning Blackie ewes he stood in the pen and every time my dog and I corralled the sheep towards the mouth of the pen, he would scare them away. Not surprisingly, I never managed to pen them with Allan blocking the entrance, but his approach certainly sharpened up both my dog and my reactions which helped me in the future.

In 1989, less than a year after we had moved to Scotland, I came third in the Scottish National with Gwen and therefore became a member of the Scottish team at that year's International trial. Here, we managed to win the qualifying trials and so earned our place to compete on the final day's Supreme Championship. Gwen had a unique, mischievous character; she also liked her food. On the morning of the Supreme, Gwen somehow managed to squeeze past the dog guard and into the car's back seat where she had promptly raided the sandwich tin. About three hours before we were due to run, I came back to the vehicle to find Gwen with an enormous belly that seemed to almost touch the ground. There was no way she could compete around the strenuous course with all that food inside her but fortunately I found a vet who gave her soda crystals that persuaded her to vomit. Even though this must have made her feel very queasy, we still managed a good enough run to gain eighth place in the championship.

Developing The Natural Way

Working wilder stock in Scotland, quickly made me appreciate two things. Firstly that Don was too intense around his sheep and the energy and intent from his stare would intimidate sheep. Secondly that I had put too much command on him. For example if a sheep broke from the flock, Don would wait for my command to move, rather than reacting instinctively to deal with the problem. I realised that I needed to change my training method. I still needed my dogs to take commands when I gave them, but they also had to understand that they could use their own initiative when required. I also wanted my dogs to feel their sheep better and to adjust their energy levels to suit the situation. Somehow they had to be gentle around a panicking lamb and steady their pace when working with light sheep yet still also be able to stand up to a defiant tup when the circumstances demanded it.

I knew I wanted to find a way that allowed my dogs and me to work in harmony together, but how was I going to achieve it? I thought long and hard about how I was training them. I had always been encouraged to be tough and master my dogs by enforcing my will on them. Yes, my dogs were obedient, perhaps even too obedient as demonstrated by the fact that Don would hesitate to turn a fleeing ewe unless commanded. Nonetheless, I still felt that I was always fighting with my dogs to keep on top of them. I came to understand that I was really striving to gain their respect and so I reviewed every single thing I did and everything I knew about dogs.

Nell, Bess and Gwen
At Glenatterach farm.

I watched my dogs communicate with each other in the pack: the way they looked at each other, how they held their bodies and the subtle gestures they made towards one another. I also analysed how my dogs interacted with sheep. I realised that different dogs caused distinct reactions from the sheep: some dogs could get close to sheep without stressing them, whilst others would upset sheep almost as soon as they saw them. I started to understand the subtle cues that the sheep were picking up from the different dogs. I used all this knowledge to change my training technique and gradually, through trial and error, I learnt how to communicate with my dogs in a consistent fashion that they completely understood.

The pressure / release method I developed enabled me to work with my dogs' innate instincts and I was able to show them, in a manner they completely understood, what energy levels were acceptable around sheep and which were not. My approach allowed my dogs to use their own initiative and in return, they responded by accepting and acknowledging me as the Alpha in the hierarchy and so were willing to take my commands.

In addition, because I could now communicate in a language they understood; all types of dog, from dominant to submissive, and sensitive to tough were happy to work with me. I admit it was not an easy path to take and often it was highly frustrating, but slowly and surely, over several years, my dogs and I developed the close, trusting, mutual partnerships I yearned for. Because my training method is derived from the dog's own language, I have called it 'The Natural Way' and its basis is fully described in the earlier chapters of this book.

Trials and other tales

Meanwhile, my trialling success continued and, in 1991, I won both the single and brace Scottish National Championship. The former was with Gwen whilst the brace was with Bess and her daughter Nell. I felt I was flying especially as this was the first year I had competed in a brace competition. Sadly, later that same day, I received the news that Don, who I had lent to a friend in Wales, had been gathering stray sheep in a quarry and had not returned. His body was never found.

Despite this upsetting news, I was proud of my dogs but most particularly of Nell who had a stroke after eating rat poison when she was two years old. It was a terrible episode. She had fallen unconscious and been connected to a drip for three days. If it had not been for the exceptional care that my vet Donald gave her, she would not have survived. When Nell recovered, it quickly became evident that she had forgotten all her training and I had to go back to basics with her and start from scratch. I still remember the sense of immense relief and joy when Nell was able to work again; the trials she won were just an added bonus. Nell and Bess went on to win the 1992 Scottish National Brace Championship title.

1991 Scottish team members
This was the year I won both the single and brace championship
with my dogs Nell, Bess and Gwen.

Overall, they also represented Scotland three times in the International Brace competition and in 1992 were runner up in this event. Unfortunately, over the next few years, Nell continued to have small stokes caused by internal bleeding, and after each episode, I felt I lost a little more of the Nell I knew. Eventually, at the age of six, she had one final severe attack and she had to be put down. I was heartbroken.

I've jumped ahead of myself to tell Nell's story, but to resume my main tale, after winning the 1991 Scottish National Championship, Gwen and I were invited both to compete at the Champion of Champions competition which was organised by the International Sheep Dog Society. I remember coming back to the hotel the night before my run at this competition and finding my father (who had come to see me compete) cuddling up in bed with Gwen. Prior to this, I had always thought that spoiling a dog often effects the way it behaved. However, the next day Gwen ran as well as ever and we won the competition, so obviously my 'spoiling' theory is only true for some dogs!

We also were invited to promote some farming related events. One of these was 'Food in Farming' that was being held in London's Hyde Park and I was asked to fly down from Aberdeen to promote it ahead of it opening. I remember standing at London Heathrow, one of the busiest airports in the world, waiting for Gwen to be brought through. As the minutes

ticked by I became increasingly anxious and eventually found someone to help me trace what had happened to my dog. Apparently she had been put on a flight bound to China, so you can imagine my relief when I had her back by my side. I then had to negotiate the London Underground system to get to the hotel and believe me, I think I'd almost rather face the worst Scottish weather than try to carry bags, crook and Gwen up station escalators again.

The promotional work started the next day. Gwen was in her element enjoying the friendly affection from all the schoolchildren who were also taking part. Our role must have sounded simple to the marketing executives behind the scheme. Gwen and I were to be photographed taking sheep out of a black London taxi cab. I'm not certain what the taxi driver thought, but it was obvious that the organisers had never considered working with stock and needless to say it was quite a palaver to get the sheep into the taxi. Luckily, the next bit was easy and the press cameras clicked as I opened the taxi door to let the sheep out.

Unfortunately, at around the same time, Richard and I grew apart. So, with a very heavy heart and just my dogs plus a few personal possessions in the back of my car, I drove away from the farm, the sheep and the horses. Kath, a friend I had met in Scotland through the horse world, let me lodge in her house and I managed to find an under-shepherding job with a company that ran two thousand sheep.

Throughout the winter of 1991-2, I helped feed the sheep and then I stayed on to help with lambing which gave me further experience of working with different breeds of sheep. Even though my personal circumstances were difficult at that time, I still managed to compete successfully at both single and brace trials, winning amongst other things the Champion of Champions competition, the Scottish Brace Championship and the Grampian TV trial. I also had my first opportunity to travel abroad when in 1992 I was invited to judge in Canada and also to teach sheepdog handling on courses in Norway and Sweden. I felt honoured and privileged to be asked and was somewhat surprised to discover that I thoroughly enjoyed teaching others how to handle dogs.

On my return to Scotland I became closer to George Simpson whom I later married. Initially we decided to go into business together and we both brought our individual skills and knowledge to the partnership. He taught me more about stock and I helped him with his dogs. We worked together to increase our own sheep numbers up to 500 by taking on further land. I also helped George with his contract work of dipping, shearing and dressing sheep. Furthermore, as we lived near the sea, the land rarely froze, so we would take extra sheep from other farms for winter grazing. In order to cater for this additional number we would rent land from diary farms and I remember calculating that we had to travel 100 mile radius a day just to check sheep. Overall, it was very hard gruelling work but on top of this, I still continued to train dogs for both my own use and also to sell.

I also became an Agricultural Training Board Instructor so I could pass on my knowledge to others. During this period Moss started to be highly successful at open trials. He was a very talented and stylish dog who could naturally steady even the wildest of sheep. He loved working on the farm and no job was ever too difficult. He especially enjoyed the challenges of lambing and was completely in his element as I required him to shed and hold sheep for me all day long.

I felt we were completely in tune with each other. He would sit on the back of the quad bike with his head resting on my shoulder following the direction of my stare. If I looked at a sheep, he also had his eye on it. I could feel his excited shivers through my back as he waited for his cue to jump off and balance the ewe towards me so that I could catch and then lamb her.

In 1996 after qualifying with Moss for the team at the Scottish National trial (where he also won the Driving Championship), I only managed a couple of practice sessions between it and the International trial that was due be held at Chatsworth House in Derbyshire a few weeks later. This was because we had a contract to dress five thousand gimmers and this needed to be fulfilled by a similar deadline. Catching a large number of sheep each day for days on end and then trimming their wool in order to present them for selling was backbreaking work and, after giving each sheep its beauty treatment, it became increasingly difficult to stand up. At the end of each day my muscles ached and stiffened and it was only sheer determination that drove me to get the job done on time. I also ensured that I regularly ran with Moss to keep him fit. When I saw the course at Chatsworth, I was pleased that I had managed to do this: it was huge and required a fit dog with stamina.

The International Supreme course had plenty of obstacles including trees and horse jumps. These combined with the terrain meant that the dogs could not be seen by the handlers when they came to lift the sheep. Fortunately, Moss had plenty of experience and a good feel for his stock. These combined with his natural balance meant that he could manage this crucial part smoothly and without command from me.

Moreover, the heavy mules used for the trial tended to challenge the dogs, but again Moss had sufficient power, confidence and ability to control them in a professional manner. His run had a nice flow throughout and his tremendous shedding ability and the fact that he could hold sheep back with just his head movement ensured that the international shed was successfully accomplished.

It was one of the proudest moments of my life when Moss and I were awarded the ISDS Supreme International Champion Blue Ribbon from the Duchess of Devonshire. I felt my success

Supreme International Champions 1996
Moss and I with the Duchess of Devonshire.

at becoming the first woman to win the title fully justified training my dogs The Natural Way.

During the next few years I continued working, training dogs and teaching new handlers. In addition I travelled a couple of times each year to Europe, Canada or America to visit friends, help with their dogs and also, when invited, to judge competitions or to give sheepdog handling training clinics.

It was also over this period that it became increasingly apparent that George and I wanted different things from life and our irreconcilable differences meant that I felt that I could no longer function properly whilst I was living with him. So for the second time in my life, my dogs and I needed to start afresh and find somewhere new.

Braegrudie

After staying with a friend for a while and helping him with his sheep, I was employed by the Scibbers Cross Sheepstock Club to be the sole shepherd for the Braegrudie Estate in North Scotland. It was an isolated place with a few farms dotted around the perimeter and the nearest village was five miles away.

The only house on the land itself was the neglected shepherd's cottage. As the cottage was run down, damp and cold, I decided I would continue living where I currently was and commute an hour each way to and from my work.

The estate covered 10,000 acres but the grass was sparse and the ground was very rough and uneven. Much of it was moss-covered bogs hidden beneath heather that was dangerous to walk on and impossible to traverse with a quad bike and so, whenever possible, I kept to the higher ground. As the overall quality of the land was poor, it could only sustain 1,000 Cheviot ewes and it took experience to know where to find them in what seemed to be a vast barren wilderness.

Fortunately, Robbie, the previous shepherd who had been forced to retire due to ill health, was very helpful and gave me valuable insights about the terrain, the weather and where the sheep grazed. He also pointed out the best routes to reach them safely. However, the area was very desolate and there were few obvious landmarks to use as navigation aids, so initially I stayed in sight of the river Bora and only gradually moved further afield as I learnt the lay of the land better.

When my five dogs and I started at Braegrudie in early summer 2004, I think we all believed we had boundless energy. However, we quickly learnt to pace ourselves so that we could cope with the long days. Even my younger dogs settled and lay down to sleep whenever I stopped, glad for a rest from the long hours of running alongside the bike or from gathering stock.

It was a steep learning curve for all of us and as time past my dogs' ability and skill in reading sheep improved. It made me realise how hill shepherds in the past could take young dogs out with them and how soon these amazing animals would gain knowledge far beyond their years.

Hill sheep have a strong deeply ingrained survival instinct and when my dogs and I were out gathering the flock there were always some ewes who would try to out-manoeuvre us by doubling back along cliff edges or by hiding in the outgrowth. A few just lay down and 'played dead'. In order not to be outwitted by their antics, I needed to think like a sheep! I also needed to heed my dogs' judgement when they stopped to investigate anything. In those long summer days, I thought that whatever happened it was manageable because we were a strongly bonded team that worked in harmony together.

Winter approached and the weather worsened as the days got shorter. Within minutes, a sunny sky could become angry and threatening as storm clouds gathered overhead. One day my dogs and I were caught out in a terrible storm on the open hill. Our only cover from the thunder and flashing lightening strikes was to squeeze down beside the quad bike (which in hindsight probably was not the safest place to be!). The sharp, bitterly cold rain battered into our faces as my dogs and I huddled together for warmth and safety until the worst had past.

As the temperature dropped, the snow and ice became additional problems. I needed to get around the estate every day to feed the sheep and to check that none had been buried alive in a drift. However, just getting into work was difficult. The narrow track into Braegrudie wound around the side of the hill, with the cliff face on one side and a shear drop on the other.

At that time, I drove a little 2-wheel drive Peugeot and on one occasion, as I reached the top of the hill, the car started rolling back in the ice. With no grip and unable to use my brakes, I was terrified that the car would topple over the edge with my dogs and I in it. I tried to steer the car towards the side and fortunately its descent was halted by a small drift. After that episode, I parked the car nearer the bottom of the hill and trudged the last mile through the snow to the old shepherd's cottage where the quad bike was stored, knowing full well that at the end of the day I would have to trek the same distance to get back to my car.

I think that many people would not consider the winter of 2004-5 to have had really bad weather, but the snow still came up to my knees and the wind blew the icy cold snow crystals into my face as I went about my work. The sheep remained out on the hill over winter, but they would tend to stay at specific locations where I would then feed them. Robbie, the previous shepherd, had made a sled that, if loaded with care, could carry about twelve small bales of hay. I would load the sled and then use the quad bike to pull it out to feed the sheep. However, if the bales were loaded even slightly unevenly then as I pulled the sled along the rutted ground, they would tip over and fall down the slope. Whenever this happened, I would have to slide down after them and manhandle them back uphill so that I could load up the sled again and head off to feed the sheep.

On one occasion, I was out on the hill checking tups on the quad bike with my dogs as usual running along beside me. I knew the area I was crossing was boggy with overlying heather, but because of the snow I could not see what the immediate underlying ground looked like. In an attempt to keep on secure ground, I was driving the bike along the bank slope. Suddenly there was a snap as the heather branch beneath the lower bike wheel snapped.

Before I knew it, the bike flipped over with me still holding onto the handlebars. Within a split second I was under the bike, pushing up against the handlebars as I tried to stop the full weight of the machine from falling on top of me. I could see petrol pouring out of the overflow pipe as I slipped and struggled to get a grip in the snow as I tried to save myself. In my fear, I suddenly felt my anger flare as the adrenaline surged through me. With this boost of energy I somehow found the extra strength to push the bike away from me and back onto its wheels. I was no longer trapped but the bike wheel was still stuck in the ditch and I no longer had the energy nor sufficient strength in my arms to pull it out.

Night was about to fall and I started to walk off the hill to find help to retrieve the bike. Amazingly, given the isolated area and weather conditions, I saw another walker in the distance and after a moment's hesitation, I waved and shouted at him.

He came over and together we managed to pull the quad bike out of the ditch. Fortunately, there was the sufficient petrol to get back and though my right arm felt sore and bruised for the rest of the winter, at the time I just considered myself lucky to have come through the incident relatively unscathed.

The harsh weather conditions meant that lambing did not routinely start until late April and so a couple of months before this, my dogs and I gathered the pregnant ewes for scanning. Hill sheep tend to have just a single lamb and I moved these to a 500 acre area to the east of the Bora river.

Although this area was still rocky and very steep with the river at the bottom, it did have slightly better quality grazing than the rest of the estate. I separated out the few ewes that were carrying twins so that they could have additional feed in the final weeks of pregnancy.

Lambing on the hill was very different from my previous experience of lambing in fields or in barns and I was grateful to have good dogs to help me. In general, hill sheep including Cheviots are considered 'easy lambers' as most give birth without problem or assistance. However, when one was in trouble, I would have to act quickly to catch and deliver the lamb before it died from lack of oxygen. This may sound simple, but the reality was very different.

During the evening, instinct drove the ewes to the top of the hill for safety. Usually, the imminent mother-to-be would separate herself away from the flock and remain on the higher ground for the rest of the day. In the early morning and then at regular intervals throughout the day, I would slowly drive along the top of the hill. My two best dogs, Tess and Molly would either sit behind me on the bike or else run quietly by my side.

We would look at all the ewes to see if any were showing signs of lambing or more particularly if any lambs had become stuck during the birthing process. I would ask my dogs to gently surround any ewe that needed our assistance. The dogs had to understand that at this point, they needed to hold the ewe but not put too much pressure on her as this could force her to flee. Using a leg cleek (crook) I then had a chance to hook her leg and catch her.

It was at this point that I realised that the arm injury I had sustained in the winter was worse than I originally thought. Often as I now attempted to hook the ewe's leg I would get an eye-watering sharp pain in my upper arm and would instantly lose all power in it.

The ewe was already stressed from the lambing process and I was fully aware that attempting to catch her would further increase the pressure. If I let go, I knew she would run through my dogs as if they were not there and then head off down the hill towards the river. So no matter what pain I was suffering, I had to do my best to hold on. Usually I was lucky: my dogs and I would hold the ewe and I could then turn her onto her side and deliver her lamb. However, occasionally the incredible strength of the small Cheviot ewe would pull me off my feet and drag me along the rocky bank as I hung on waiting for her to stop.

There were other times when the ewe would escape from me and hurtle off down the hill. If this happened Molly and Tess would keep running with the ewe, slipping on the wet ground, tripping over rocks, splashing through ditches as they ignored all distractions in their determination to do their duty and stop the escapee. When they had eventually managed to check the ewe, they would stand patiently with her, waiting for my arrival.

Throughout all my time at Braegrudie, but especially at lambing, my dogs gave me everything they had. I was regularly reminded about the value in owning a dog that can use its initiative and work alongside the other team members to achieve the overarching aim of caring for the stock.

Braegrudie
A and **B** My dogs take a well-earned rest as I spend a few moments to enjoy the beauty of my surrounds. **C** and **D** The beauty and perils of shepherding in the wilds of one of Scotland's toughest environments. **E** Lola and I pose on the footbridge to Braegrudie as her late husband, Jim, takes the shot. **F** Molly persuades a couple of sheep to cross the water to safety. **G** and **H** Lambing time at Braegrudie. Having a team of good dogs made lambing tasks less stressful.

Carcant

Early in 2005, I heard from a friend that the farm tenancy at the Carcant estate near Heriot in Midlothian Scotland would probably be coming available later in the year. Following a successful interview I was offered the vacancy and moved down with my dogs to take up this new challenge in November 2005.

The six hundred acre Carcant Estate is nestled in the Moorfoot Hills and has been owned by the Somerville family for over 100 years. The land is primarily hilly with rough moors and although it is only 25 miles south of Edinburgh, its tranquil natural beauty means that it feels a million miles away from the Scottish capital. I was quickly smitten with the place and was determined to run it as a productive working farm using traditional methods of 'dog and stick'. This approach to farming also ensures that the estate remains an attractive retreat for the Somerville extended family. In return, the family have always been very supportive of me, for which I am extremely grateful.

When I arrived, the farm cottage's interior needed refreshing so for the first few months I stayed in the Hayloft flat above the large family house. Every evening after working on the farm all day, I would walk down to the cottage to decorate it. My brother-in-law George built my kennels and other friends helped get me established.

One particularly helpful person was my new neighbour, Bobby Henderson. I had already known him for years as he was well respected on the sheepdog trial circuit and he too had previously won the International Supreme Championship. Bobby had extensive knowledge about hill shepherding in the local terrain and with his advice, I set about improving my new grazing stock.

On taking up the tenancy, I had also purchased the sheep that were already running at Carcant as these had been hefted to the hill. This means that the sheep should have known which area of the estate they belonged to. There were three hefts at Carcant and although two had kept to their proper grazing region, one had strayed onto the neighbours' land. At that time, I had little experience of the hefting system, so I followed Bobby's advice and for the first six months, I and my dogs would daily shepherd the thirty strays back onto their proper part of the hill until they learnt where their heft was.

The flock when I bought them were mainly Scottish Blackface with some Cheviot crosses. However, I decided from my experience at Braegrudie that I would prefer to keep pure Cheviots and I also wanted these to produce high quality lambs. I therefore initiated a selective breeding programme and reduced the sheep numbers to better suit the size and quality of the ground at Carcant. Gradually over the years, by managing the numbers and only keeping the better ewes combined with using good quality tups, my flock has prospered and now I feel fully justified to be proud of how healthy and well my stock look.

For the first few years I was at the farm, I was continually bothered by the arm injury that I had sustained in Braegrudie when my quad bike had tipped over onto me. Unfortunately, the sudden sharp pains and weakness seemed to get worse and the frustration at not being able to do my work gnawed away at me. Eventually, after lambing in 2009, over five years after that winter in Braegrudie, I could not stand it any longer and plucked up the courage to have an operation to repair the damage. After the surgery, it took months to get my mobility and strength back, but now my arm feels almost as good as new.

Looking back, I also remember that those first eighteen months at Carcant were especially hard graft. My own nature does not let me stop when there is work to be done and I pushed myself to get the farm and stock to the standard I wanted. On top of this, in order to help meet the costs of my new venture, for the first two springs, I also took on extra work as a night lamber for a nearby farm. I did this on top of managing my own farm during the day and the only sleep I managed was for a few hours in the early evening before I started my night shift. By the end of that period I was completely exhausted. Fortunately, shortly after those first two long lambings, Bobby moved in and joined me at Carcant. Our morning discussions to plan the day; the extra pair of experienced hands around the place and his on-going encouragement

Carcant
A Carcant sits in the beautiful Moorfoot Hills. **B** Even in winter, Carcant is stunning. **C** Looking up the valley to Carcant house and steading. **D** Heading for food. **E** The Lochan. **F** Springtime at Carcant **G** Neth hill rises up behind the farm. **H** Wedder lambs ready for sale.

to pace myself have all meant that I now no longer tend to burn the candle at both ends.

As well as his vast stock knowledge, another thing that Bobby has passed onto me is his love of wild birds. Since his arrival, we regularly feed the birds around the farm cottage. The pheasants' behaviour is particularly fascinating as their social interactions alter throughout the year. In winter, several males and females congregate outside the kitchen window as soon as they see someone moving around inside in anticipation of some food being thrown out to them.

Once the breeding season is about to start, the cock pheasants, each with their own distinctive markings, compete for the best territory. One takes charge outside the kitchen, another around the bird table in the garden and the rest compete for the different feed troughs in the fields. Each guards his area fiercely from competitors and use the food, along with cooing and strutting, to impress as many females as possible that he will be a good mate.

At this time of year, the cock pheasant will often stand straight up, puff out his chest and call as he flutters his wings to indicate his presence to both competitors and potential mates. When two males meet, they will display towards each other, bobbing their heads up and down and lowering their body to the ground as they suss each other out. Often the weaker of the two will back down without any further confrontation.

However, occasionally they will fight for the right to take control of the area. Whilst they do this, they seem completely oblivious to the sheep and will also ignore my dogs and me as long as we keep an appropriate distance from them. I feel privileged to be able to witness aspects of animal behaviour like this directly outside my front door and the close proximity of wildlife as I go around my daily chores is one of the things that make Carcant so special to me.

My father used to love coming to stay and he was especially fond of my dogs and would tend to spoil them in a similar manner as he had done all those years ago with Gwen. He always offered to look after the dogs and check the sheep so that Bobby and I could take short holidays away from the farm.

On one of these occasions, I rang up the evening before my return to check everything was okay. My father replied that all was well except he had just found a dead sheep on his morning rounds. I told him that I would deal with it on my return the next day. In the event, this was a sensible decision, because the sheep turned out not to be one of mine: my father had routinely been going through the wrong gate and so had been checking my neighbour's stock instead of mine!

Unfortunately, my father developed cancer and as his health deteriorated, he was unable to travel to Scotland to care for the dogs. He knew he was not going to get any better and towards the end of 2009, he decided to visit the farm one final time. As soon as Dad arrived, Ban rushed out to see him but rather than fawning over him, Ban just sat gently beside him and laid his head on his knee. It was as if Ban could sense my father's weakness. We all sat on the grass and cuddled each other. Ban put a smile back on Dad's face and that is how I want to remember him.

Dad, Ban and me
My Dad loved the farm and my dogs. His spirit lives on at Carcant.

Another major change that has also happened on Carcant Estate in the last few years has been the erection of three wind turbines. The work to install these occurred over the winter of 2009-2010. In addition to being the winter that my father died, the weather was some of the worst in living memory. Night-time temperatures fell below -20C, and some days, the temperature did not rise above -12C. Getting onto the hill to feed the sheep was a daily struggle because the snow was so deep.

Back then, I did not own a tractor, so we managed either by loading up a quad-bike trailer or just by hauling bags of hay on foot. The wind farm contractors tried to keep the farm lanes open so they could service the turbines, but there were occasions that even they could not get through.

One night, an additional 18 inches of snow fell on top of what was already lying and the following morning, it was much too deep to get food to the flock so I had to bring the sheep nearer to the farm. It was an exhausting exercise to trudge uphill through that unforgiving terrain.

Once my two dogs had rounded the flock up, we then needed to get them home. As sheep do not like moving through deep snow, my dogs and I had to encourage them to go one by one into the narrow track we had created on our way out. I was relieved once we had got the ewes through this tricky bit and as we headed down the hill, it felt like the older ewes knew they were going home.

That winter plus the one following were particularly hard, long and cold, so I was grateful that my traditional approach to shepherding means that I do not start tupping until relatively late compared to my neighbours.

As a consequence, lambing only begins in late April when the risk of any late snow has significantly decreased and the grass has usually started coming through. This is especially important as my ewes lamb outside

Even then, I still worry about the lambs when it is cold and wet outside so, during lambing, I'm always desperate to get out as soon as it is light enough to check the stock. That first check in the morning is always slightly tense in case any ewe has been struggling during the night. To try and minimise any issues during the day, my dogs and I also regularly check the stock to make sure that there are no problems that need to be dealt with.

It always amazes me just how robust the small Cheviot lambs are and how quickly most of them get to their feet and start suckling. On warm spring days, it is a joy to watch the lambs basking in the sun and most evenings they gang up with each other to race around the field before returning to their mother's side to settle down for the night.

As well as improving the lanes across the moor, the agreement between the wind farm and the Carcant Estate Trusties includes a range of measures to promote biodiversity. This is complemented by a couple of Scottish Rural Development grants that I have obtained. Combined together, the alterations in the estate in the last few years have been marked, with new fences, young hedges, bracken reduction, on-going water margin improvements, new barns.

Recently some of the mature conifer plantations have also being removed with the intent to replace them in the future with native trees. I have also altered my grazing management to further encourage habitat enrichment. Some of these changes have made it slightly harder to check the flock because tall grasses can hide the sheep and also parts of the moor have become more boggy because the drainage ditches have been intentionally blocked. On the other hand, these alterations are also gradually encouraging an even wider variety of wildlife to live in harmony with my flock.

Neth Hill Border Collies

In addition to the sheep and the land, there are, of course, Bobby's and my dogs. We both tend to have about six to eight dogs each at any one time. We work and train our own, but take turns to exercise all twelve to sixteen together. As our larger pack is stable and settled, I find that this number is easily manageable.

I personally do not like to have more than seven or eight dogs of my own at any one time. As long as I keep my own dogs down to this number, I find I can give each individual the attention, training, work and runs at sheepdog trials that he requires. I also want to consider my sheep and am keen that none of them, including the sheep we keep for training, are overworked. As Bobby has a similar number of dogs to me and I also have clients who bring their own dogs to train, it is important that my own kennel does not get too large.

However, sometimes one or the other of us has a few more dogs, or we have friends staying with their own packs. On these occasions, the number can rise to over twenty dogs and then the exercise field seems almost too full, especially if one of the visiting dogs has an excitable mindset.

I usually start two to three pups a year. As I have explained in earlier chapters, I prefer to raise my own dogs from pups using The Natural Way. I either breed these from my own dogs or else buy a pup from parents who possess the natural traits that I look for in a good working dog. I only occasionally buy young talented dogs that have been started by others.

Obviously, in order not to go over the maximum number I have set for myself, I also have to sell some of my dogs on. I always find it difficult to part with an animal that I have grown close to and I do my best to match the dog with the new owner, so that both will benefit from the partnership.

These dog sales help subsidise the farm, because similar to many others in the UK, the tenancy I hold is not financially viable on its own. When I moved to Carcant I wanted to choose a name for my business that reflected the area and decided on **Neth Hill Border Collies** because not only is The Neth is one of the hills (and sheep hefts) on the estate, but it also plays on my own surname.

In addition to dog sales, I also give sheepdog handling demonstrations and train sheepdog handlers either in private lessons or through training clinics that I hold both at home and away. Carcant has proved to be an excellent location for this aspect of my business. It is relatively close to Edinburgh and yet has all the necessary facilities to train a sheepdog: from round pens to small fields suitable for novice dogs and handlers right up to the open moor that can challenge even the most experienced dog and shepherd.

I have been fortunate to meet many wonderful people through the dog world and several have become close friends. In fact, certain clinics that I give in Norfolk, Holland and the USA have become an annual or biannual event, To me, one of the main joys of travelling to these, is the pleasure of catching up with old friends.

Despite this, as I sit writing in my small summerhouse, looking out over the fields with sheep grazing peacefully outside and a young pup sleeping quietly at my feet, I definitely think that home is best. My dogs have given me everything and I hope that this book helps you find similar contentment with your own canine companions.

Bobby, me and some of our current pack

GLOSSARY

Alpha. The leader of the pack.

Away. The command to move anticlockwise.

Balance. The natural ability of a working dog to position himself at the right location and distance from the sheep so that they are held or moved at a steady pace in the direction that the handler wants the sheep to be taken.

Balance point. The point where a dog needs to position himself so that he can balance the sheep to where they need to go. This is not always directly behind the sheep.

Balanced mind. A stable attitude.

Block. The block position helps to enforce the handler's request.

Brace. A pair of dogs that have been trained to work together.

Come-bye. The command to move clockwise.

Contact. The distance that each individual dog needs to be from the sheep in order to move them in an appropriate manner.

Cross drive. This is part of a sheepdog trial, when the dog needs to drive the sheep across the field in front of the handler.

Dagging. Removing the dirty wool from the rear end of a sheep.

Dogged sheep. These are sheep that are used to a dog. Because they are used to a dog's presence, they are usually calmer than sheep that have never seen a dog before. Well-dogged or over-dogged sheep that have been used extensively for training will often cling to the handler's legs.

Draw. The direction that sheep would pull towards if no dog is present to control them. This can be towards other sheep, a gate, food etc.

Drive. The dog takes sheep away from the handler.

Ewe. A female sheep.

Eye. This is the instinctive stare that border collies and other herding dogs have towards stock. It is this that makes a dog lower his head and front legs into the distinctive 'hunting' crouch as he works his sheep.

Fattening lamb. A lamb that is being raised to be sold for meat.

Feel. The understanding of what the animal is telling you from his body language and energy combined with the ability to act accordingly to manage the situation in a stress-free manner. A good handler will have a feel for both his dog and his stock. Similarly, a dog with natural ability will also have a good feel for his sheep.

Fight-or-Flight. This instinct is present in all mammals including dogs, sheep and humans. It happens when too much inappropriate pressure causes a large surge of the hormone adrenaline. The dog or sheep will react to the excessive pressure by either resisting (fighting) or else avoiding the situation (going into flight mode).

Flanking. The arc movement that a dog makes as he runs around sheep.

Flock. A group of sheep.

Follow up. When using The Natural Way, this is when the dog follows his leader. To follow up properly, the dog has to have the correct attitude and also accept the handler's Alpha status. He indicates this by showing respect and a willingness to please.

Gimmer. A young female sheep in her second year (just older than a hogg).

Give to pressure. Yield to pressure.

Grip. When a dog grabs at a sheep. There can be a variety of reasons why this happens. You need to assess the situation, the sheep and your dog to determine why he has gripped.

Heading. This is a dog 's instinct is to run towards the head of a sheep in order to stop and turn her back towards the handler.

Heavy sheep. These are domesticated breeds of sheep (e.g. Suffolk or Texel) that require more pressure from a dog in order to create movement.

Heavy side. The heavy side of sheep is the position where the dog needs to exert pressure to balance the stock so that they move in the direction required.

Heft. The region on an open moor or hill that sheep know they belong to. In general, if there is sufficient grazing in that area, sheep will not stray from the area they are hefted onto.

Here. The command to call the dog towards you.

Here this. The command to work with a particular group of sheep.

Hogg. A young sheep that has been fully weaned.

In contact. The distance that a dog needs to be from sheep in order to control their movement.

In lamb. A pregnant ewe.

ISDS. The International Sheep Dog Society. This charity aims to improve and promote the shepherd's dog. It maintains the ISDS studbook that registers working sheepdogs, records their parentage and their major trial successes. The majority of dogs added to the studbook each year are progeny of dogs already listed, but it is also possible to register a dog on merit. The ISDS also organise the four National as well as the International Sheepdog trials.

Into orbit. This happens when a dog is running very wide and is also not paying any attention to his sheep. He is out of contact with his sheep. He usually behaves in this fashion because he lacks confidence and is avoiding a situation.

Lamb. A young sheep in its first year.

Lie down. The command to stop and lie down.

Lift. The lift describes the first point of contact that the dog makes with his sheep.

Light sheep. These sheep (usually native breeds such as Scottish Blackface, Swaledale or Shetland) tend to have more instinct to run from a predator.

Look back. If the dog is focused on one group of sheep, this command asks him to leave those and look for others.

Loose-eyed. This is sometimes called a 'plain-eyed' dog. These dogs tend to flank more easily and are freer in their movements. Some loose-eyed dogs look less stylish because their eye does not draw their head down.

Man-made dog. This is a dog that lacks a natural ability to do one or more elements of his work. Instead, the handler has to teach him exactly how to perform these tasks. This requirement to teach a dog by "rote learning" is very different from training a dog with natural talent.

Mechanical dog. This is a dog that has been trained so that he will only act when his handler commands him to do so. A dog trained this way may stop using his own initiative even if the situation requires it.

Mindset. The attitude of a dog.

Natural ability. The innate talent in a dog to work sheep.

Natural drive. The dog balances sheep so that they are taken away from the handler. He does this with minimum command from the handler who may be walking behind or alongside.

Natural flank. The flank that takes the dog towards the balance point.

The Natural Way. My training method that uses pressure / release techniques to develop mutual trust, loyalty and respect between the handler and his dog.

Out. The command to move outwards. There is no direction to this command, you either intend the dog to use his instinct, or, alternatively, you should combine it with a directional flank.

Out of contact/off contact. When a dog works off or out of contact, he gives too much ground to the sheep, and lets them decide the direction they want to go. A dog behaving like this usually lacks confidence and is avoiding a situation.

Over-face. This is when a young, inexperienced or timid dog is confronted by a stroppy sheep and he does not have the experience or temperament to cope with the situation. You should support your dog in this situation so that he does not lose confidence.

Pen. An enclosure to hold livestock. Some penning systems are quite complex, containing multiple small enclosures that allow sheep to be shed (sorted) into different groups

Power. This is the ability of a dog to move any type of sheep in a quiet, calm, controlled manner without significant aggression.

Predator/Prey. This describes the relationship between dogs and sheep. The dog is a natural predator and will use his hunting instinct around the sheep (which are prey animals). You need to understand and control this relationship.

Pressure. The assertive energy that a dog detects from the handler, another dog, the sheep and the situation. In addition to the close proximity of the dog and the handler, sheep will also feel pressurized by certain situations (e.g. being corralled inside a pen or being on their own).

Pressure/Release. This is the system that I use to train The Natural Way. You need to apply appropriate pressure to inform your dog that he is acting incorrectly. Release pressure when your dog is acting appropriately (or is trying to act correctly).

Pull. The direction that sheep are drawn towards if no dog is present. In order for the dog to hold them on the required fetch or drive line, he needs to maintain a consistent pressure at the heavy point. If the stock need to be redirected, then the dog has to alter the amount of pressure he exerts. This alteration will depend on whether the new direction is towards or away from the line of pull.

Push onto. This is when the dog continues to over-exert pressure on the sheep.

Read sheep. The ability of a handler or a dog to interpret the sheep's body language and gestures correctly and then take the appropriate action so that the stock are controlled in a calm fashion.

Race. This is a narrow fenced area that only allows sheep to move in single file. It is used as part of a handling system to treat or shed sheep.

Ram. A male sheep.

Registered/Unregistered dog. A registered dog is recorded in the ISDS studbook. An unregistered dog is not.

Release of pressure. Pressure is removed when the dog has acted (or has tried to act) correctly. You remove pressure by stopping any forward movement and giving your dog more personal space. You should soften or lower your eyes and if necessary also turn to side. Removing pressure from a dog makes him feel more comfortable. This reward is sufficient to inform him that he has acted correctly.

Respect. This is a dog's proper mental attitude towards his handler.

Reward. When using The Natural Way, the only reward that a dog requires is release from pressure. Remember that at the end of a training session, you should also praise your dog in a calm fashion. You may also occasionally need to give a reassuring touch during a training session.

Sensitive. A sensitive dog has a deep intuitive understanding of human body language and so requires very little pressure from his handler to get an appropriate response. Some dogs are sensitive towards one specific thing such as gunshots or thunder. A sensitive dog is not the same as a timid dog.

Shedding. The act of separating off one or more sheep from the flock.

Sheepdog trial. A competitive sport which requires the handler to command his sheepdog to perform a variety of challenges that mimic various working tasks.

Single/singling. The act of separating off one sheep from the flock.

Square flank. This is an exaggerated flank.

Stand. The command for the dog to stop and stand.

Steady. The command for the dog to ease his pace.

Stick. A dog may stick when he has too much eye. He appears to become transfixed on the sheep and unable to move. This may make him pull up early on his outrun as he approaches the stock.

Sticky-eyed. A dog that has too much eye.

Store lamb. A lamb that is sold to another person (often a dealer) to fatten on.

Strong dog. This is a dog that is hard to hold back from sheep. This type of dog likes to get on with his work. The handler needs to be sufficiently dominant to handle this type of dog.

Style. The method a dog uses to work his stock.

That'll do. The command used to call the dog off stock at the end of a session.

This. The command to ask the dog to look at a particular group of sheep.

Tight flank. A flank that is too close to the sheep.

Timid. A timid dog is excessively wary of one or more situations. This may be caused by his innate temperament or from an unpleasant experience. Alternatively, if a dog has only limited exposure to different stimuli when he is young, he may become excessively timid to new things in later life.

Try. This is when your dog indicates that he is attempting to please you.

Tup. A ram / male sheep.

Unnatural flank. A flank where the dog has to move away from the balance point. The dog considers that this is not instinctive, so I call it 'unnatural'.

Walk-on. This command asks the dog to move towards the sheep at a steady pace and with the appropriate attitude.

Weakness. Any fault in the working ability of a dog.

Wear. To wear sheep means the dog balances the sheep using pressure / release correctly. The sheep are moved in the required direction using an appropriate manner.

Wedder (also known as Wether). A castrated male sheep.

Work Naturally. The dog controls his sheep with the correct attitude. He reads his sheep properly and responds appropriately to their actions and behaviour. This is done with minimal command from his handler.